DB2: The Complete Guide
to Implementation and Use
SECOND EDITION

Books and Training Products From QED

DATABASE

Data Analysis: The Key to Data Base Design
The Data Dictionary: Concepts and Uses
DB2: The Complete Guide to Implementation
and Use
Logical Data Base Design
DB2 Design Review Guidelines
DB2: Maximizing Performance of Online
Production Systems
Entity-Relationship Approach to Logical Data
Base Design
How to Use ORACLE SQL*PLUS
ORACLE: Building High Performance Online
Systems
Embedded SQL for DB2: Application Design
and Programming
SQL Spoken Here for DB2: A Tutorial
SQL for dBASE IV
Introduction to Data and Activity Analysis
ORACLE Design Review Guidelines
Managing Projects: Selecting and Using PC-
Based Project Management Systems
Using DB2 to Build Decision Support Systems
How to Use SQL for DB2

SYSTEMS DEVELOPMENT

Handbook of Screen Format Design
The Complete Guide to Software Testing
A User's Guide for Defining Software
Requirements
A Structured Approach to Systems Testing
Practical Applications of Expert Systems
Expert Systems Development: Building
PC-Based Applications
Storyboard Prototyping: A New Approach to
User Requirements Analysis
The Software Factory: Managing Software
Development and Maintenance
Data Architecture: The Information Paradigm
Advanced Topics in Information Engineering

MANAGEMENT

Strategic and Operational Planning for
Information Services
The State of the Art in Decision Support Systems
The Management Handbook for Information
Center and End-User Computing
Disaster Recovery: Contingency Planning and
Program Analysis

MANAGEMENT (cont'd)

Winning the Change Game
Information Systems Planning for Competitive
Advantage
Critical Issues in Information Processing
Management and Technology
Developing the World Class Information
Systems Organization
The Technical Instructor's Handbook: From
Techie to Teacher
Collision: Theory vs. Reality in Expert System
How to Automate Your Computer Center:
Achieving Unattended Operations
Ethical Conflicts in Information and Computer
Science, Technology, and Business

TECHNOLOGY

Data Communications: Concepts and Systems
Designing and Implementing Ethernet Networks
Network Concepts and Architectures
CASE: The Potential and the Pitfalls
Open Systems: The Guide to OSI and its
Implementation
VAX/VMS: Learning DCL Commands and
Utilities

PROGRAMMING

VSAM Techniques: Systems Concepts and
Programming Procedures
How to Use CICS to Create On-Line
Applications: Methods and Solutions
DOS/VSE/SP Guide for Systems Programming:
Concepts, Programs, Macros, Subroutines
Systems Programmer's Problem Solver
VSAM: Guide to Optimization and Design
MVS/TSO CLISTS
MVS/TSO: A Working Approach to Native
Mode and ISPF
VAX/VMS: Learning DCL Commands and
Utilities

SELF-PACED TRAINING

SQL as a Second Language
DB2: Building Online Production Systems for
Maximum Performance (Video)
Introduction to UNIX (CBT)
Building Production Applications with ORACLE
(Video)

For Additional Information or a Free Catalog contact

QED INFORMATION SCIENCES, INC. • P. O. Box 82-181 • Wellesley, MA 02181
Telephone: 800-343-4848 or 617-237-5656

SECOND EDITION

DB2:
The Complete Guide
to Implementation
and Use

Jeff D. Vowell, Jr.

QED Information Sciences, Inc.
Wellesley, Massachusetts

Library of Congress Catalog Card Number   89-8480
International Standard Book Number   0-89435-300-4

Printed in the United States of America

90 91 92 10 9 8 7 6 5 4 3 2 1

Library of Congress Cataloging-in-Publication Data

Vowell, Jeff D.
    DB2 : the complete guide to implementation and use / Jeff D.
  Vowell, Jr. — 2nd ed.
      p.   cm.
    Bibliography: p.
    ISBN 0-89435-300-4
    I. Data base management.   2. IBM Database 2 (Computer system)
  I. Title.   II. Title: DB two.
  QA76.9.D3V69   1989
  005.75′65—dc20

Contents

Preface

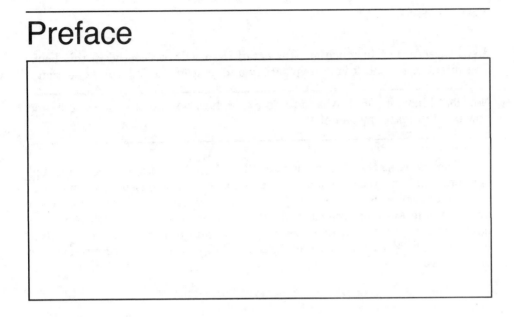

This DB2 guide is a document on the issues and topics that must be considered for the successful usage and implementation of the IBM Relational Database Management System known as Database2 (DB2) and its related products.

Database2 as a product is already changing dramatically the way data processing currently operates: the advent of referential integrity and distributed processing in DB2 will have an even greater impact. It must be implemented with caution, and you still MUST exercise control, though not the same kind of control as today. The end user is going to make the greatest impact. This is because he can now do so many things that he could not do before, and he no longer will have to wait for the applications groups to add his requests to their backlog. He also won't have to make do with extracted data for his personal computer to resolve many of the questions that the success of the business requires answers to. He can now, in many cases, use the ad hoc capability inherent in this product and its related products to answer those questions quickly and correctly.

This will not be a process that happens overnight. The people in data processing and the end user must work together to make sure that the end results are satisfactory, and, above all, meet the needs of the business. After all, if the business needs are not satisfied, there will be no business, and thus no data processing or end users.

This document contains many technical issues and details, all or most of which can be found in various IBM manuals. This document is designed to help IMPLEMENT DB2 and related software in such a way that both the future and present needs can be satisfied. Greater detail can be found in other manuals, and the intent is not to train anyone in writing application code or in the Structured Query Language (SQL). Many other classes and books address those issues in much greater detail than will be covered in this book. The intent of this book is to help satisfy and answer the following question:

Now that I have it (DB2), what do I do with it, how do I put it in and use it, and how do I maximize my use of it?

That is what this document is for. It is based upon my perceptions and opinions, and the recommendations and concerns are based upon my total experience of over 19 years in data processing at all levels, including application programming, systems programming, management of systems, vendor support, database administration, and quality control, and in particular, my involvement in the IBM DB2 Relational Database Software and related products for over two years.

Using this Guide

1

USING THIS GUIDE

Introduction

As defined in the preface, this guide is intended to be an overall assistance in the full implementation and usage of DB2 and its related products. It is intended to give an overview of DB2 itself and to point out the things to watch for in DB2. It tries to also add some insight and guidance into some of the areas that IBM misses or glosses over. The DB2 versions addressed in this edition include 1.2, 1.3, 2.1, and 2.2.

Additional features of this guide are the mingling together of information from many sources into a single source, and guidance to finding more specific information about various topics.

Intended Audience

This guide is intended to be used by all personnel who have some level of interest in DB2. This ranges from the person(s) in charge of the implementation of DB2, the person who wants to know what parts can help him, all the way to the system operator who wants to know how to issue a DB2 command. It is also intended to be used by various other people who would like to know more about DB2 than just Structured Query Language (SQL). These people would include the following:

- DB2 Systems Administrators
- DB2 Database Administrators
- Security Administrators
- Capacity Planners

- Performance Analysts
- Application personnel using DB2
- Managers of any of the above

End users will also find parts of the guide useful as well.

Another purpose of the guide is to provide recommendations for the following:

- Basic DB2 information
- DB2 implementation and planning
- DB2 policies and procedures
- DB2 standards

Above all, the guide is designed to help anyone interested in the implementation and usage of DB2 to get the job done.

Structure and Format

The guide is broken down into nine sections and 77 appendices as follows:

1. **Section 1—Using This Guide**

   Information on what this guide is all about and whom it is for.

2. **Section 2—Perspective**

   Perspective on the situation existing in data processing today.

3. **Section 3—Introduction to DB2**

   General introduction to DB2 and how it is structured. Also includes information on how it works and other systems it interfaces with.

4. **Section 4—Implementation of DB2**

   Contains information and guidelines on the implementation of DB2 and what to prepare for.

5. **Section 5—DB2 Policies and Procedures**

   Contains some guidelines for policies and procedures necessary for the implementation and usage of DB2.

6. **Section 6—DB2 Standards**

   Contains some recommended standards and 'rules of thumb' for using DB2 and related products. (Includes Application Development.)

7. **Section 7—DB2 and Related Products Usage Guide**

   Contains guidelines and information and the actual usage of DB2 and related products such as QMF, DB2I, SPUFI, DXT, etc.

8. **Section 8—Other DB2-Related Topics**

   Contains other DB2-related topics such as Capacity Planning, Performance Management, Application-Level Archiving, Dataset Migration Techniques, and others.

9. **Section 9—DB2 Futures and Interfaces**

Contains information on DB2 futures, interfaces with other IBM and non-IBM products, and other topics such as SAA and CASE.

10. **Appendices**

Contains copies of forms that can be used for the procedures described above, as well as containing diagrams of table relationships and DB2 Structural Relationships.

The table of contents contains more detail as to the subjects covered in each section.

Roadmap for Persons Responsible for DB2 Implementation

The following is a list by position of the sections of this book that would apply to these various levels of responsibility. All personnel interested in DB2 should take particular notice of the DB2 Personnel Education Requirements chapter in Section 3—Implementation of DB2.

Personnel responsible for the full implementation of DB2 and related products will find the entire manual helpful, but will be primarily interested in the following sections and chapters:

- Section 2—Perspective
- Section 3—Introduction to DB2
- Section 4—Implementation of DB2
- Section 5—DB2 Policies and Procedures
- Section 7—DB2 and Related Products Usage Guide
- Section 9—DB2 Futures and Interfaces

Remaining sections will be useful for a more technical understanding of DB2 in the areas of programming and usage.

DB2 system administrators. The System Administrator will need to know and understand all sections within this book. In addition, he will need knowledge of the following IBM products:

- MVS Operating System
- Time-Sharing Option (TSO)
- Interactive System Productivity Facility (ISPF)
- Customer Information Control System (CICS)—if used
- Information Management System (IMS)—if used
- Direct Access Storage Device (DASD) Management

The depth of additional knowledge will depend upon the size and complexity of the Data Centers involved, and the expertise of the personnel.

DB2 database administrators (DBAs). The DBAs need to take particular notice of the following sections and chapters:

- Section 3—Introduction to DB2
- DB2 Support Structure in Section 4
- Section 5—DB2 Policies and Procedures
- Section 6—DB2 Standards
- Section 7—DB2 and Related Products Usage Guide
- Section 8—Other DB2-Related Topics
- Section 9—DB2 Futures and Interfaces

Security administrators. The Security Administrators will need an overall understanding of DB2 and its structure, with a specific understanding of the security and authorization scheme within DB2. These are supplied in the following sections and chapters:

- Section 3—Introduction to DB2
- DB2 Support Structure in Section 4
- Security in Section 5
- DB2 Security in Section 6
- Query Management Facility (QMF) in Section 7

Capacity planners.

- Section 3—Introduction to DB2
- DB2 Support Structure in Section 4
- DB2 Design Review Process in Section 5
- Section 6—DB2 Standards
- Section 7—DB2 and Related Products Usage Guide
- DB2 Capacity Planning Chapter in Section 8
- DB2 Performance Management Chapter in Section 8

Performance analysts.

- Section 3—Introduction to DB2
- DB2 Support Structure in Section 4
- DB2 Design Review Process in Section 5
- Section 6—DB2 Standards
- Section 7—DB2 and Related-Products Usage Guide
- DB2 Capacity Planning in Section 8
- DB2 Performance Management in Section 8

Application personnel.

- Section 3—Introduction to DB2
- DB2 Support Structure in Section 4
- Section 5—DB2 Policies and Procedures
- Section 6—DB2 Standards
- Section 7—DB2 and Related-Products Usage Guide

System operators. System Operators need an overview of DB2 and what it is. While they will not be actually creating objects within DB2 or accessing the data, they need to know the support structure, whom to contact, and the stated policies and procedures for such things as production turnover and types of DB2 calls.

- Section 3—Introduction to DB2
- DB2 Support Structure in Section 4
- Production Turnover Procedures in Section 5
- DB2 Commands and How to Use Them in Section 8

Managers of any of the above. The managers of people involved in the usage and implementation of DB2 need to at least have an overview of the areas described for their personnel.

End users. The prospective users of DB2 need various levels of training and knowledge. They need to be aware of the structure of DB2, how to use the various DB2-related products, and definitely need to know some things about the Structured Query Language (SQL). Some of the information concerning these topics is in the following sections and chapters:

- Section 2—Perspective
- Section 3—Introduction to DB2
- SQL Creation Considerations in Section 6
- Query Management Facility (QMF) in Section 7

Disclaimer

The information provided in this guide is a composite of experiences by many different organizations that have or are implementing DB2 and the information supplied by IBM itself in various IBM manuals and seminars. As such, the information contained in this guide is intended to be just that—a guide. It is probable that this information will need to be tailored to fit a particular environment. It is also to be noted that many of these guidelines are dependent upon a particular release of the designated products and should be upgraded as the evolution of DB2 and related products continues.

IBM Software Levels

The information in this guide is based upon the following levels and releases of IBM software:

- DATABASE 2 (DB2) 1.2.0, 1.3.0, 2.1.0
- Query Management Facility (QMF) 2.1.0, 2.2.0, 2.3.0
- Data Extract (DXT) 2.1.0, 2.2.0, 2.3.0
- Database Edit Facility (DBEDIT) 1.1.2
- Database Migration Aid Utility (DBMAUI) 1.1.1
- DATABASE 2 Performance Monitor (DB2PM) 1.1.0

Review of the following new releases was also included (see Appendix 1 —New Release Analysis) as far as added functionality and features in comparison with the levels and releases listed above.

- DATABASE 2 (DB2) 1.3.0, 2.1.0, 2.2.0
- Query Management Facility (QMF) 2.2.0, 2.3.0
- Data Extract (DXT) 2.2.0, 2.3.0

Perspective 2

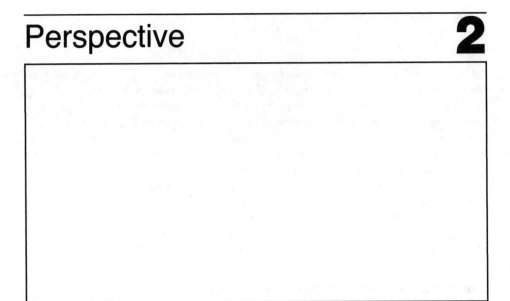

PERSPECTIVE

The New Data Processing Environment

During the past few years, data processing and its relationship and responsibilities to the businesses that it serves has undergone very great and dramatic changes. These changes have primarily centered on the dependency that these businesses have developed upon the various functions and facilities within data processing. Business must use these functions and facilities as much as possible to their greatest potential just to stay competitive and survive in this increasingly complex world. It is no longer possible to run any medium or large company without computers, and, in most cases, small companies cannot be run effectively because of the ever-increasing level of complexity of federal, state, and local reporting requirements, much less control billing, inventory, reordering, etc. But many problems that are caused, and in many cases nurtured, by many data processing functions are becoming an even greater threat to the competitiveness of almost every business in some way. The biggest of these problems are as follows:

- No centralized knowledge of corporate data
- Inability of end users to access actual data
- Lack of standardization
- Application backlog growth
- Lack of systems integration
- Lack of business acumen by data processing personnel

The immediate symptoms of these problems are shown in the ever-increasing number of requests for personal computers by the non-data processing community because the data processing group cannot respond to requests quickly enough, the ever-increasing requirements by those same people for access to data for their PCs, the increasing cost and time to develop applications, the inability of data processing to integrate applications, the repetition of the same data throughout a company to answer similar requests, the growing feeling of unease as to the reliability of data coming from multiple sources, and also the inability of the non-data processing people to do things on the mainframe as they can on their PCs, etc.

These problems, as they continue to grow or are ignored, are the direct cause of many of the massive foul-ups and mistakes that are seen in the news every day attributed to the almighty computer, and add to the already bad feelings that the general public has about the computer. How do these issues affect each company, and what can be done to reduce them?

Centralized Knowledge of Corporate Data

Centralized knowledge of corporate data is the key. A detailed knowledge of the data within the business, its description, location, relationships to other data and how it is used in the various processes is essential to get the control to provide the necessary access to respond to the needs of the business NOW, not next year, when your competitor has taken the lead. You must track and record and manage data just like any other corporate resource.

The idea of data as a corporate resource like any other resource is not new. The problem is that very few companies believe it, and most data processing organizations view the data as their own private property to do with as they see fit, which may explain why not many companies believe this concept. This is unfortunate in that without a full commitment from the top of a corporation concerning the effective management of the data resource, there will be little or no change, and the implementation of the software to assist in this will not be completely successful.

End Users to Access Mainframe Data

End users need to access the corporate data in a timely manner. They need current data that will give them accurate results upon which they can make decisions that affect the business. The use of shadow data, or data that has been recreated by them from listings, or the basic inability to get the data at all is not helping these people make the correct decisions. They need the real data NOW!

Need for Standardization

You must have standards. You cannot waste time trying to figure out where the data is, what it is called, how many versions of it are there, which version is right, etc. The lack of standardization probably accounts for between

15 and 30 percent of the time involved in development of applications and in maintenance because of all the necessary research that is required. Standards would save time, and time is money.

Application Backlog Growth

The issue of application backlog growth doesn't need any elaboration. The backlog continues to grow at a rate faster than the amount of applications that are put into service. And no one knows how big the 'hidden' backlog is, that is, that backlog of requests that just aren't made because of the time and cost involved. This gets more and more critical.

Lack of Systems Integration

Lack of systems integration is another issue that most are aware of but do not think about much. This is also where a lot of unnecessary time is spent in reproduction of function and duplication of data because of an inability or actual neglect of the ideas or needs of systems integration. If systems were designed up front with the concern for integration, and with a corporate data concept rather than an application concept, a lot of time and money could be saved during development and especially during the software maintenance phase.

Lack of Business Acumen by Data Processing Personnel

How many times have we heard about the system that went into production after many years of work, and went immediately into change mode because it did not provide the information and results that were expected? And why? Because the programmers and/or analysts missed the boat as far as what the business required. How to solve this? Get the business people into the process.

CONCLUSION

As has been implied, there needs to be a great deal of change in the way data processing is viewed within the business, and in which the business views data processing. The data processing function must become an integral and involved part of the business. To do this, the barriers between the two must be dissolved and the importance of the function must be realized by corporate management. Then, the standards and software need to be purchased and implemented to support and enforce the concepts. Also the non-data processing people, or end users, must be able to do more for themselves, and get involved in the process of using the data processing resources effectively. Without that, nothing will change.

Need for Data-Element-Driven Methodology

The most pressing requirement today is to change the thinking of data processing groups. They tend to think in terms of *applications* rather than *data*. Businesses today require access to *data* to solve business problems, not *applications*.

The continuing change of the business environment and the need to react requires that the business have *fast* and *reliable* access to data in a format that is easily accessible. Only a data-driven methodology will supply this, not an application or process-driven methodology.

Introduction to DB2

3

SOLUTION: RELATIONAL DATABASE

Given all that was talked about previously, the situation looks bleak, but, in reality, it is not. With the advent of commercially available Relational Database Management Systems (RDBMSs), notably IBM's Database 2 (DB2), the basic structure upon which to develop and implement the standards and processes needed to combat this situation are now beginning to appear. The reason why this particular structure known as a Relational Database is suited to this is that the relational structure is based upon a data element concept and the relationships that exist between data elements rather than a physical file structure. The relational database with its element or column-based structure allows the development and implementation of a true data-driven methodology. The IBM DB2 product also provides various interfaces and a Structured Query Language (SQL) which can reduce, and in some cases eliminate, the need for programmers, as well as providing the basis for effective data processing, rather than application processing.

This product, implemented with an idea towards the previously mentioned requirements, can go a long way toward resolving the issues listed above, but it will need some assistance. A product designed with the previously mentioned structure and philosophy built into it, in conjunction with DB2, can achieve the necessary goals and resolve many of the problems existing today.

WHAT IS DB2?

The IBM DATABASE 2 (DB2) software is a general purpose Database Management System (DBMS) that allows you to define, access, and recover data. Those services are available through a terminal operating under the Time-

Sharing Option (TSO) with added functionality through the use of the Interactive System Productivity Facility (ISPF) feature. Those services are also available through application programs initiated from:

- TSO foreground
- TSO background (batch)
- Information Management System/Virtual Storage (IMS/VS)
- Customer Information Control System/Operating System/Virtual Storage (CICS/OS/VS)

DB2 runs on any processor that supports IBM's Multiple Virtual Storage/ System Product (MVS/SP), either MVS/370 or MVS/Extended Architecture (MVS/XA).

The Relational Database Model

The Relational Database Model is a theoretical structure based upon a data structure that follows a set structure and rules. Its theoretical basis has been proven to be sound with strong mathematical properties. It has the ability to separate the logical data from the physical data with the resultant capability to reduce greatly development and maintenance costs.

The relational model itself is structured as follows:

Base table.

- A base table is a real or physical entity.
- All data are perceived as tables.
- Each of these tables consists of rows and columns.
- Order of the rows and columns is NOT important.
- A ROW is a set of column values.
- Data can be accessed by column.
- Physical organization of the data is NOT important.

View.

- A view is a virtual entity.
- A view produces a LOGICAL table.
- All data is stored in the base tables.
- Additional 'virtual' tables may be defined based on a subset of a base table or multiple tables.

Domain.

- A domain is a set of all possible values of a column.
- Each column is associated with a domain.

Primary key.

- A primary key identifies a column or set of columns used to identify rows within a table.
- A primary key identifies a UNIQUE set of column values.

Foreign keys.

- A foreign key identifies a column which identifies a primary key of a different table.
- A foreign key is used to identify ROWS in another table.
- A foreign key is used in JOINing tables.
- A foreign key is used in NORMALIZED logical design.
- A foreign key reduces redundancy.
- A foreign key allows extendability.

Relational Operators

A set of operations is part of the relational model. These are as follows:

Union. A union is the process involved in creating a set of data containing LIKE elements of two or more separate sets of data.

Intersection. An intersection is the process involved in creating a set of data containing all the data common between two or more sets of data.

Difference. A difference is the process involved in creating a set of data containing all the data NOT common between two or more sets of data. (Opposite of intersection)

Permutation. A permutation is the process involved in changing the order of the attributes or columns in a set of data.

Division. A division is the confirmation that all rows in a table satisfy a specific condition.

Selection. A selection is the process involved in creating a set of data containing all the data selected based upon some defined parameter set or predicate combination.

Projection. A projection is a subset of another set of values which contains only unique values. All duplicates are eliminated.

Join. A join is the process involved in creating a set of data containing UNLIKE elements of two or more separate sets of data.

Relational Rules

The relational model itself has the following relationship rules defined in it:

Entity integrity.   Entity integrity is defined as being the fact that any primary key in a base table CANNOT be a NULL value or be nonexistent. Every row in a table must have a value for the primary key.

Referential integrity.   Referential integrity is defined as being the fact that every foreign key defined in a base table MUST exist in its defined base table as a primary key or the value is NULL or nonexistent.

User-defined integrity.   User-defined integrity is defined as being enforceable integrity rules that are defined by the user.

DB2—A Relational Database

DB2 is a relational database even though it currently does not fulfill all the requirements for the relational model. Its structure is as follows (in comparison to the relational model):

- Base Tables   *YES*
- Views   *YES*
- Columns   *YES*
- Domains   *NO*
- Primary keys   *YES (Version 2.1 and later)*
- Foreign keys   *YES (Version 2.1 and later)*

DB2 supports the relational operator as follows:

- Union   *YES*
- Intersection   *YES*
- Difference   *YES*
- Permutation   *YES*
- Division   *YES*
- Select/Project   *YES*
- Join   *YES*
- Outer join/union   *NO*

The relational rules are suported as follows:

- Entity integrity *YES through the use of the UNIQUE index*
- Referential integrity *YES (Version 2.1 and later)*
- User-defined integrity *Partial through the definition by the user of FIELDPROCs and VALIDPROCs*

As is shown, some of the full support of the relational model is missing, but these features will be added to the product as time goes on, and many of the missing functions can be implemented through various controls, programming techniques, and design procedures.

DB2 Objects

DB2 is composed of objects. These objects are storage groups, databases, tablespaces, indexspaces, tables, indexes, columns, and synonyms. The primary objects are the ones involved with the DATA. These objects are the database, the tablespace, and the table. The database contains one or more tablespaces, and the tablespaces can contain one or more tables. The table is the object which actually contains all of the data. The table is composed of the data elements or columns and the rows of data. A row in a table contains one set of values of the columns defined for that table.

The tablespace can best be defined as the physical structure (in this case VSAM files) that contains the actual table or tables and index data. The storage group is a DB2 Definition for a set of physical Direct Access Storage Devices (DASD), or disk drives, that the tablespaces are allocated onto. The database is a logical definition which relates a set of tablespaces to each other, and also relates particular storage groups to tablespaces and indexspaces.

Indexspaces are the special types of data spaces that contain index data. An index is a combination of data fields which point to where particular rows are that contain specified values of the fields defined in the index. Indexes can be ascending or descending, clustered, and unique or non-unique. Indexes are used to enforce uniqueness in DB2 tables and can be critical for good performance for many types of access requests.

DB2 Structure

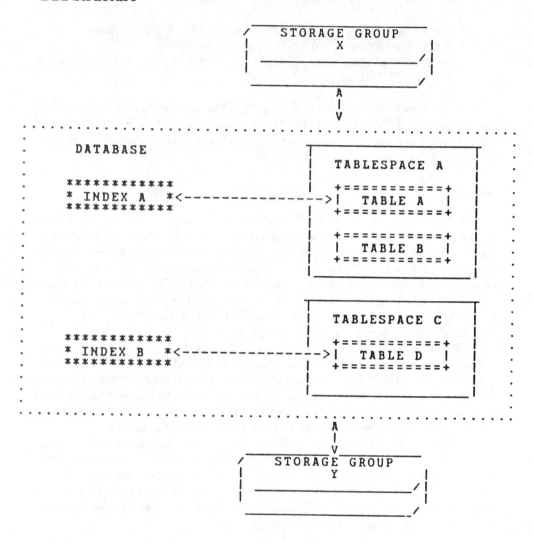

DB2 Referential Integrity

The biggest change to DB2 came about with the implementation of Referential Integrity within the DB2 structure itself with DB2 Version 2.1. This was essential to the progress of full Relational Model Implementation, but what was more important were the tremendous gains in PRODUCTIVITY and DATA INTEGRITY. The database itself will now take care of the Integrity of the data thus increasing productivity in the programming areas by reducing the amount of code to be written.

The other effect of this however is that a much closer adherence towards true Relationally-Designed (NORMALIZED?) Structures must be maintained to take the advantage of the internalized Referential Integrity support within DB2. This is because of the following rules:

1. Elements defined as PRIMARY KEYS MUST BE UNIQUE.
2. PRIMARY KEYS MUST EXIST.
3. PRIMARY KEY Values of FOREIGN KEYS MUST EXIST.
4. COMPOUND KEY Definitions can be defined as PRIMARY KEYS.
5. PRIMARY KEY Definitions MUST Have a DELETE RULE

   - SET NULL   If PRIMARY KEY Is Deleted, all FOREIGN KEY Values will be set to NULL
   - RESTRICT   If a Delete Attempt is made and FOREIGN KEY Values Remain, NO DELETE is allowed
   - CASCADE   If a Delete Attempt is made and FOREIGN KEY Values EXIST, ALL ROWS with the associated FOREIGN KEY Value will be DELETED

The physical implementation of Referential Integrity is accomplished as follows:

1. PRIMARY KEY defined as part of TABLE CREATE/ALTER.
2. Define DELETE Rule for PRIMARY KEY
3. Associated FOREIGN KEYS defined using TABLE CREATE/ALTER.
4. UNIQUE INDEX MUST BE DEFINED for PRIMARY KEY Definitions.
5. FOREIGN KEY Definition MUST be same as associated PRIMARY KEY.
6. PRIMARY KEY Definitions CANNOT BE NULL.
7. NULLs Permitted for FOREIGN KEYS.
8. Any Column in a COMPOUND FOREIGN KEY that is NULL, causes ENTIRE FOREIGN KEY to be NULL.

Steps to be followed in Referential Integrity Implementation:

1. Define PRIMARY KEY Definition

   - PRIMARY KEY Clause in TABLE Definition
     (either CREATE TABLE or ALTER TABLE for Existing Table)
   - Define SET NULL, RESTRICT, or CASCADE DELETE Rule in Definition (Default is RESTRICT)
   - Create UNIQUE INDEX for PRIMARY KEY Definition

2. Define FOREIGN KEY Definitions

   - FOREIGN KEY Clause in TABLE Definition (either CREATE TABLE or ALTER TABLE for Existing Table)

Migration from a system NOT using Referential Integrity to one that is using it is easily done using the ALTER Statement with the associated parameters.

DB2 Interfaces

DB2 has a central control concept. The other systems and users connect to DB2 through ATTACH facilities. Each system that needs access (TSO, IMS, and/or CICS) to DB2 uses this ATTACHMENT facility to pass to and receive from DB2 the information necessary to access the required data. If these AT-TACHMENT facilities are not up or are broken, no access to the data in the DB2 subsystem is possible. The creation of this access is called THREAD creation. This THREAD creation process must complete successfully for any transfer of data between DB2 and the requesting subsystem (TSO, IMS, and/or CICS). This includes the BACKUP and RECOVERY procedures that are used with DB2 as well. If the DB2 subsystem cannot become completely active, the BACKUP and RECOVERY procedures cannot be run (*except for certain unusual conditions which will be determined by systems and/or the DBA*).

DB2 Environment

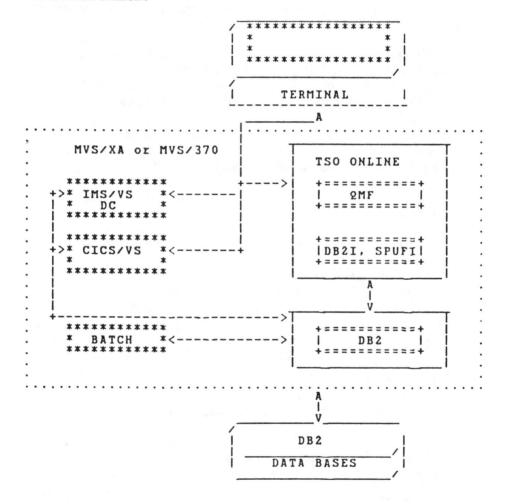

Types of Tables

DB2 has three types of tables within it. The first type is the DB2 DI-RECTORY. The directory contains all of the information that DB2 requires to be started. The second type is the SYSTEM TABLES. These tables contain all of the information that DB2 needs to operate itself, access tables, check access and authority levels, and to perform the RECOVER process. The third type of tables is the USER TABLE. User tables are the tables that contain the data that the users put in to be stored, accessed, and backed up and recovered if necessary. These tables contain the data that the company depends upon.

DB2 System Catalog

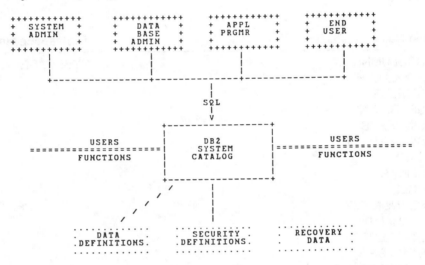

Directory tablespaces.   Directory tablespaces contain the tables that DB2 uses to initialize and operate itself.

Table Name	Tablespace Name
	DBD01
	SCT02
	SYSLGRNG
	SYSUTIL

System tables.   System tables are the tables that DB2 uses to control user-defined DB2 tables and related processes and authorization.

These tables also:

- Can be queried using SQL
- Are only modified by SQL DDL

- Contain physical storage statistics
- Contain DB2 object relationships
- Are used for
  - DB2 tuning
  - Application tuning
  - Disk management
  - Data administration functions
  - Security administration functions
  - Some data dictionary functions

The names of these tables and the tablespaces they are in are (as of DB2 V2.1):

Table Name	Tablespace Name
SYSCOLUMNS	SYSDBASE
SYSCOLAUTH	
SYSFIELDS	
SYSFOREIGNKEYS	
SYSINDEXES	
SYSINDEXPART	
SYSKEYS	
SYSLINKS	
SYSRELS	
SYSSYNONYMS	
SYSTABAUTH	
SYSTABLEPART	
SYSTABLES	
SYSTABLESPACE	
SYSCOPY	SYSCOPY
SYSDATABASE	SYSDBAUT
SYSDBAUTH	
SYSDBRM	SYSPLAN
SYSPLAN	
SYSPLANAUTH	
SYSPLANDEP	
SYSSTMT	
SYSRESAUTH	SYSGPAUT
SYSSTOGROUP	SYSGROUP
SYSUSERAUTH	SYSUSER
SYSVIEWDEP	SYSVIEWS
SYSVIEWS	
SYSVLTREE	
SYSVOLUMES	
SYSVTREE	

Description of system tables. Each system table that is defined within DB2 has a particular function within DB2 and can be accessed to find out certain details about the user objects defined. Following are descriptions of each of these tables and the type of information that can be extracted from each.

SYSIBM.SYSCOLUMNS. The SYSCOLUMNS table contains one row for every column defined in every table and view within the DB2 system. It contains such information as the name, character type, size, table/view it is defined in, the creator of that table/view, null option, and other information.

SYSTEM.SYSCOLAUTH. The SYSCOLAUTH table contains information on the update privileges that are held on individual columns by users.

SYSTEM.SYSCOPY. The SYSCOPY table contains the information needed for recovery of system and user tablespaces. The information in it is the name of the files used in image copies, the tablespace name and database name of the affected tablespace, and other recovery-related information.

SYSIBM.SYSDATABASE. The SYSDATABASE table contains one row for each database definition except for the directory database DSNDB01.

SYSIBM.SYSDBAUTH. The SYSDBAUTH table contains a record of all database-level authority held by users.

SYSIBM.SYSDBRM. The SYSDBRM table has one row for each DBRM defined within each application plan. This includes the actual partitioned data set name (PDS), the plan creator, and necessary time stamps.

SYSIBM.SYSFIELDS. The SYSFIELDS table contains one row for every column that has a field procedure (FIELDPROC) defined for it.

SYSIBM.SYSFOREIGNKEYS. The SYSFOREIGNKEYS table contains one row for each column that has a foreign key.

SYSIBM.SYSINDEXES. The SYSINDEXES table contains one row for every index that has been defined. The information in it is the name of the index, the creator of the index, the table the index is defined on, the index and table creator IDs, the database containing the index, and the rules concerning the creation of the index (uniqueness, clustering, buffer pool used, etc.).

SYSIBM.SYSINDEXPART. The SYSINDEXPART table contains one row for each unpartitioned index and each partition of a partitioned index.

SYSIBM.SYSKEYS. The SYSKEYS table contains one row for each column defined in a particular index.

SYSIBM.SYSLINKS. The SYSLINKS table contains one row for each link that is defined between tables. It defines the child/parent relationships and the insert rules.

SYSIBM.SYSPLAN. The SYSPLAN table contains one row of information for each application plan that has been created. This information includes the information about whether or not the plan is valid and/or operative and its creation information, such as validation time, isolation level, creator, and bind time.

SYSIBM.SYSPLANAUTH. The SYSPLANAUTH table contains the information about the privileges that are held by users over specific application plans.

SYSIBM.SYSPLANDEP. The SYSPLANDEP table contains the dependencies of any plan upon any tables and/or views, synonyms, tablespaces, and indexes. This will show the DB2 objects that compose a particular plan.

SYSIBM.SYSRELS. The SYSRELS table contains one row for each link that is defined between tables. It defines the delete rules and the parent/child relationships.

SYSIBM.SYSRESAUTH. The SYSRESAUTH table contains the information on the privileges held by users over buffer pools, storage groups, and tablespaces.

SYSIBM.SYSSTMT. The SYSSTMT table contains rows for all SQL statements in each DBRM.

SYSIBM.SYSSTOGROUP. The SYSSTOGROUP table contains one row for each defined storage group.

SYSIBM.SYSSYNONYMS. The SYSSYNONYMS table contains one row for each synonym that has been defined by the user.

SYSIBM.SYSTABAUTH. The SYSTABAUTH table records are table and view privileges that are held by users. This includes the grantor of the privilege, who has the privilege, the database name, the table/view name, the tablespace name, the appropriate creator, and the authorization level that was granted.

SYSIBM.SYSTABLEPART. The SYSTABLEPART table contains one row for each unpartitioned tablespace and each partition of a partitioned tablespace.

SYSIBM.SYSTABLES. The SYSTABLES table contains information about each table/view defined. This includes the creator, the database name, the tablespace name, and other information such as column count, validation procedure (VALIDPROC) name, edit procedure (EDITPROC) name, and others.

SYSIBM.SYSTABLESPACE. The SYSTABLESPACE table contains one row about each tablespace that is defined. In this row are the name, creator, database name, and creation rules such as buffer pool, lockrule, number of tables, close rule, and others.

SYSIBM.SYSUSERAUTH. The SYSUSERAUTH table contains the information on the system-level privileges held by the users.

SYSIBM.SYSVIEWDEP. The SYSVIEWDEP table contains the dependency information of views upon tables and other views.

SYSIBM.SYSVIEWS.   The SYSVIEWS table contains one row on each view that has been defined.

SYSIBM.SYSVLTREE.   The SYSVLTREE table contains additional parse-tree representation data that could not be included in the SYSVTREE table (if any).

SYSIBM.SYSVOLUMES.   The SYSVOLUMES table contains one row for each volume defined in every storage group.

SYSIBM.SYSVTREE.   The SYSVTREE table contains the parse tree of each view. Additional parse-tree data is placed in the SYSVLTREE table if the size of the parse tree exceeds 4,000 bytes.

DB2 Limitations

There are still some limitations within DB2 which are primarily in the areas of Lack of DOMAIN Support, and in the full implementation of the functions and processes that can be performed on the DB2 tables using the SQL Function. The major limitation in the function capability is the inability to do what is known as an 'OUTER JOIN'. An Outer Join is basically the process in determining what is NOT in a particular relationship defined in a JOIN request.

STRUCTURED QUERY LANGUAGE (SQL)

The usage and allocation of DB2 resources requires the knowledge and use of the Structured Query Language (SQL). SQL itself is composed of the following three components:

- Data Manipulation Language (DML)
- Data Definition Language (DDL)
- Data Control Language (DCL)

Each of these components contains the following:

Data Manipulation Language (DML)

The Data Manipulation Language (DML) portion of SQL is used to access and manipulate the actual data that is contained in DB2 tables. The four statements that compose DML are as follows:

SELECT statement.   The SELECT statement is used to acquire one or more rows of data from a desired table or table(s). The rows that are to be returned are determined by the search parameters that are defined within the SELECT statement itself.

INSERT statement. The INSERT statement is used to insert row(s) into an existing table within a DB2 database.

UPDATE statement. The UPDATE statement is used to update column values within existing rows in a table in a DB2 database.

DELETE statement. The DELETE statement is used to delete row(s) within an existing table in a DB2 database.

Data Control Language (DCL)

The Data Control Language (DCL) portion of SQL is to control the access, type of access, and functionality that is granted to users and programs to data within DB2.

GRANT statement. The GRANT statement is used to give authorization to other users on various DB2 objects and DB2 functions.

REVOKE statement. The REVOKE statement is used to remove authorization that has been previously granted. It should be noted that any authorization that is being revoked and that has granted authorization to other users will also be revoked. This is known as the 'cascading' effect.

Data Definition Language (DDL)

The Data Definition Language (DDL) statements of SQL provide the facility for creating and dropping tables and indexes, adding new columns to existing tables, adding comments to DB2 objects, and altering certain characteristics of certain DB2 objects.

Following is a list of the various DB2 objects that can be created, altered, dropped, and commented on.

CREATE statement.

- STOGROUP   ⟵ CREATE storage group
- DATABASE   ⟵ CREATE database
- TABLESPACE   ⟵ CREATE tablespace
- TABLE   ⟵ CREATE table
- INDEX   ⟵ CREATE index
- VIEW   ⟵ CREATE view
- SYNONYM   ⟵ CREATE synonym for table/view

ALTER statement.

- STOGROUP   ⟵ ALTER storage group
- TABLESPACE   ⟵ ALTER tablespace

- TABLE   ⟵ ALTER table
- INDEX   ⟵ ALTER index

DROP statement.   Any time a DROP is executed, any lower-level dependent DB2 objects are also DROPped, e.g., when a database is dropped, all table-spaces, tables, indexes, and related views are also dropped.

- STOGROUP   ⟵ DROP storage group
- DATABASE   ⟵ DROP database
- TABLESPACE   ⟵ DROP tablespace
- TABLE   ⟵ DROP table
- INDEX   ⟵ DROP index
- VIEW   ⟵ DROP view
- SYNONYM   ⟵ DROP synonym for table and view

COMMENT ON statement.

- TABLE   ⟵ Add COMMENT to SYSTABLES table
- VIEW   ⟵ Add COMMENT to SYSVIEWS table
- COLUMN   ⟵ Add COMMENT to SYSCOLUMNS table

Structured Query Language (SQL) Summary

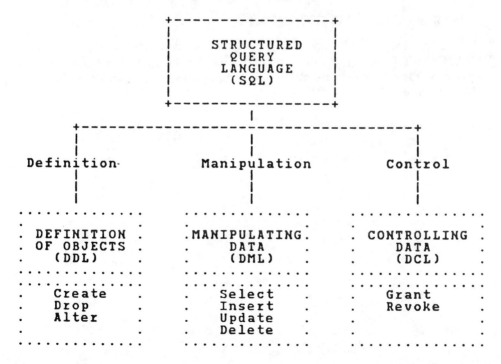

SQL and Data-Driven Methodology

A very important factor overlooked when the Structured Query Language is used is the fact that SQL is a column-based access method and complete and effective use of it requires that the underlying structure it is accessing needs to have a data-driven or 'normalized' basis or the complete use of it CANNOT be achieved. The biggest impact is shown in the usage of the SQL FUNCTIONS. These FUNCTIONS (AVG, COUNT, MAX, MIN, and SUM) are COLUMN-based. They process the values of specific columns. If you have denormalized by using such definitions as REPEATING FIELDS as an example, you are preventing the use of the SQL FUNCTIONS in order to perform the processes that these functions can do. You now have to write code to do these functions. This has an effect in two ways. It affects PRODUCTIVITY now by requiring extra program code to be written and tested, and affects MAINTENANCE by requiring the entire DATA-DRIVEN capability and ease-of-use and change within the relational environment to be severely undermined, thus causing even greater costs in the Maintenance Cycle.

Any deviation from a 'NORMALIZED' structure causes a loss of effectiveness in the use of SQL, especially in the PRODUCTIVITY and MAINTENANCE arenas. While it is true that sometimes it is unavoidable to 'DENORMALIZE', many times the full impact is not realized or understood.

The structure and use of SQL in the relational environment is another factor that must be taken into consideration when making design and implementation decisions.

DB2 OPERATING ENVIRONMENT

As described previously, users and programs access DB2 data through AT-TACHMENT facilities or interfaces. DB2 itself is composed of three address spaces or regions within the MVS operating system. These three regions are the following:

- DB2 Database Services
- DB2 System Services
- IRLM—Inter-Region Lock Manager

The environment is shown in the following diagram.

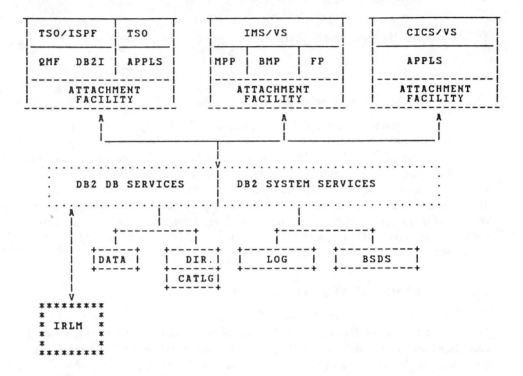

The functions of these regions are as follows:

DB2 Database Services

- Processes SQL commands
- Manages I/O buffers
- Contains following
    - DB2 code
    - EDM pool
    - Working storage
    - Buffer pools
    - VSAM control blocks

DB2 System Services

- Manages DB2 logging
- Manages and performs ATTACHMENTS
- Writes DB2 SMF statistics

- Manages DB2 storage
- Executes DB2 commands

IRLM—Inter-Region Lock Manager

- Manages DB2 LOCKING

DB2 Distributed Data Facility (Version 2.2)

The Distributed Data Facility is another address space to be added to the DB2 subsystem with the advent of DB2 version 2.2. Its purpose is to support the first phase of Distributed Data Support for DB2. This new structure will control the session management and conversations that will be ongoing when a distributed data request has been issued from one DB2 subsystem to another. It will be defined as part of the total network definition within an IBM network of host central processing units (CPUs) and applications defined within that network, such as TSO sessions, CICS regions, VTAM definitions, IMS/DC regions, etc.

PROGRAM PREPARATION UNDER DB2

Program preparation under DB2 is different in that it is composed of two parts. One part is the usual application code load module creation using the standard compilers and assemblers and linkage editor, and the other part is the process that creates the application plan, which tells DB2 how to get the data.

The program preparation process is shown in the diagram below.

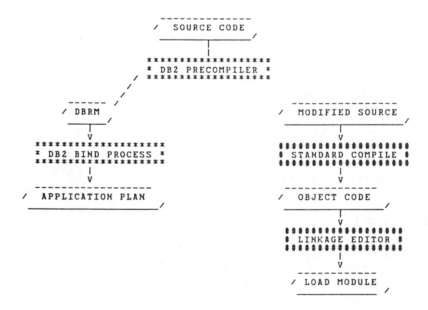

The process begins with the precompilation of the source code containing the SQL statements and from there splits into the Load Module Creation Step and the Application Plan Creation Step. The total process is as follows:

Precompiler

The DB2 Precompiler performs the following functions:

1. Preprocesses source code
2. Replaces SQL with CALLs
3. Checks SQL syntax
4. Constructs the database request module (DBRM)

Output from this process is the DBRM and the modified source code. The DBRM is input to the DB2 BIND process and the modified source code is input to the appropriate compiler.

DB2 Bind Process

The DB2 BIND procedure performs the following functions:

1. Checks authorization
2. Further validates SQL syntax
3. Selects the access path
4. Compiles the SQL
5. Creates the application plan

If all goes well, the load module associated with this application plan will be able to execute.

Compile and Link Process

The COMPILE and LINK process will be done using the modified source code created by the DB2 precompiler. The LINK procedure needs to have the DB2 load library with the Attachment Call Routines in it. If the COMPILE and LINK is successful and the BIND process was successful, the application program can now be executed by those with the appropriate level of authorization.

Implementation of DB2   **4**

OVERVIEW

DB2 is different from other database management systems (DBMSs), and, as such, needs to be thought of as being different in its implementation. It has the capability and power to overwhelm all existing resources—hardware, software, and personnel if you are not careful. With this in mind, examine the following list of concepts and topics that need to be considered for a successful implementation of the IBM Database2 (DB2) product and related software.

- Data-driven methodology
- Security requirements
- Control requirements
- Naming standards
- Support structure
- Numbers of DB2 subsystems
- Reliability
- Availability
- Serviceability
- Recoverability
- Ease and accuracy of migration
- Design considerations
- Referential integrity implementation
- Need for a data-driven methodology
- Data and program independence
- Performance considerations
- Installation considerations
- DASD contention considerations

By considering the above-mentioned topics and concepts at the beginning of implementation, rather than during or after, many problems and conflicts will be avoided.

Need for a Data-Driven Methodology

The real key to effective implementation of any relational data base is the implementation throughout the business enterprise of a data-driven methodology upon which to build the data structures the business will depend on and operate from. The data-driven methodology is simply this:

1. Every business process depends upon certain DATA ELEMENTS which are acted upon or used in some manner.
2. The business itself needs DATA not APPLICATIONS.
3. Each DATA ELEMENT is defined uniquely and has certain defined relationships to other data elements.

By taking these factors into consideration, and realizing that a relational data base is processed by INDIVIDUAL DATA ELEMENTS which have defined RELATIONSHIPS among them, a true DATA-DRIVEN environment can now be implemented using a DATA-DRIVEN METHODOLOGY. With NON-RELATIONAL data base management systems, a true data-driven environment was not achievable. Now it is. And as a corollary to this, A CORRECT IMPLEMENTATION OF A RELATIONAL DATA BASE IS NOT POSSIBLE WITHOUT A DATA-DRIVEN METHODOLOGY BEHIND IT.

In summary, if you are not willing to implement the relational data base environment in order to take advantage of the element-based architecture, stay in your current record and file environment. The limited gain from NON-DATA-DRIVEN implementation of a relational data base such as DB2 is greatly overshadowed by the problems caused by this type of DB2 implementation.

Security Requirements

DB2 has its own internal security. This security is implemented at various functions and levels within DB2. These functions include the following:

* DB2 system administration
* Database administration
* System operator functions
* Database control and maintenance functions
* Subset functions of the above

The levels of data security within DB2 break down into view, insert, update, and delete from the table level down to the column level in a particular table.

DB2 assumes that access is NOT ALLOWED until access is granted.

Because of these many levels of security, you can combine data into structures that could not exist before. However, you must be careful to make sure that neither too much nor too little authority is granted.

By thinking out a comprehensive security plan early on, many problems with data access and functionality can be avoided.

Control Requirements

- Formalize change-control procedures at all levels
- Develop formal process/forms for request of creation of certain DB2 objects
- Develop formal policies and procedures
- Coordinate table-structure changing
- Coordinate production migration
- Include special DB2 requirements in production turnover procedures

Naming Standards

Naming conventions must be developed for the following DB2 objects:

- Columns (data elements)
- Tables
- Tablespaces
- Databases
- Programs
- Application plans
- Storage groups
- Screen names
- Other files—fields
- Non-DB2 file names

Support Structure

A support structure with the following personnel needs to be developed:

- System Administrator
- Data Administrator
- Primary Database Administrator
- Secondary Database Administrators
- Capacity Planners
- DASD Administrators
- Security Administrators
- System Programmer
- System Operator

Numbers of DB2 Subsystems

The number of DB2 subsystems that are to be installed will depend upon installation preference. Within a single DB2, you can isolate test and development from production very effectively and with complete security using the internal authorization structure and an effective naming convention. You will probably need another DB2 subsystem defined for system maintenance testing. Most shops may end up with at least three subsystems, as follows:

- Production subsystem
- Test-and-development subsystem
- System maintenance subsystem

Whether or not the test subsystem should be on a separate machine from the production subsystem is a resource allocation issue for each installation. There will be overall resource contention if the two (or more) are together. The system maintenance susbsystem will only be running as it is needed to test maintenance and new releases and versions of DB2 and related software.

Reliability

The need for reliability within DB2 is much more pronounced than for other systems because of the ad hoc capability and the greater level of potential to do damage.

Availability

DB2 is designed for 24-hour operation, and any procedures or policies put in that prevent this should not be used. Also, system and application design that can cause concurrency problems should be analyzed for possible change. The page-level data-locking of DB2 should be used as much as possible.

Serviceability

Because of the need to maintain the DB2 operating software at as high a level as possible, the system maintenance procedures should include at least three levels of maintenance using the IBM System Maintenance Program (SMP). These should be an installation level, a maintenance upgrade level, and a production level. The production level needs to have the capability to have emergency fixes applied to it.

Recoverability

- Standard procedures must be developed using the internal DB2 backup/ recovery system in conjunction with standard, full-disk backups. Reliance on full volume DASD backup/restore procedures as the recovery vehicle is too complex to manage and has potentially catastrophic consequences.

- Develop DB2 imagecopy, mergecopy, and restore procedures for all tables going into production mode.
- Need procedures for all DB2 system catalog and directory tables.
- Determine need for test-and-development procedures.
- Use DUAL logging and DUAL BSDS.

Ease and Accuracy of Migration

Standards and procedures need to be developed to ensure a VALID and successful migration from test to production. This includes the following:

- Recreation of DB2 objects
- Unloading and reloading of data
- Granting of appropriate authorization

These procedures need to be developed no matter how many DB2 subsystems exist, and no matter how many CPUs DB2 resides on.

Referential Integrity Implementation

The Implementation of DB2 Referential Integrity within DB2 from a physical standpoint is relatively straightforward as defined by the Statement Syntax of DB2 (see DB2 Referential Integrity Section). The Key is the acceptance of the need for Referential Integrity with the corresponding requirement for the implementation of a true data-driven environment and associated methodology. As stated earlier, full Referential Integrity Implementation REQUIRES that a Data-Driven Methodology be implemented because of the very close relationship and correlation between the physical implementation of Referential Integrity and the Logical Model resulting from a Data-Driven Design Methodology.

The implementation of Referential Integrity within DB2 tables can be done either as the table is being created using the CREATE TABLE PRIMARY KEY and/or FOREIGN KEY options or after the table has been created using the ALTER TABLE with the same options.

Using the ALTER TABLE for FOREIGN KEY is the only way to implement Self-Referencing Relationships in a single table, otherwise relating a foreign key in a table to the primary key in the same table. You create the table first with the associated primary index and then ALTER the table to add the foreign key.

When using ALTER for the FOREIGN KEY definition, if any existing rows have relationships for that FOREIGN KEY which violate the FOREIGN KEY definition, the table is placed in a *check pending* status. Until this status is reset, the tablespace containing the table is unusable for *ANY* processing. The CHECK DATA option of the CHECK utility will examine the selected tablespace for referential integrity constraint violation and either list for delete the invalid rows (if any). If there are no invalid rows, or they are deleted, the tablespace will be reset. LOAD REPLACE and interrupting a LOAD job before the checking of the referential constraints will also place the tablespace and any other tablespaces containing dependent tables of the parent table as well.

Need for a Data-Driven Methodology

The complete successful implementation of ANY relational data base requires a full data-driven methodology from the design phase on through the programming phase. This includes the business analysis and user analysis phases as well. Process analysis as it is defined can also be developed in terms of data as well. You must be able to define the following for Data at the element level to effectively use the relational column-based data base structures:

1. Define characteristics about EVERY element.
2. Define Relationships between ELEMENTS.
3. Define WHO is responsible for each element.
4. Define WHERE each element and ALL of its versions are.
5. Define HOW each element is being used.
6. Define WHAT is being done to each element at any point in time.

This is not easy. But it results in the capability to change quickly and take advantage of the relational architecture and also shows up defects and errors that occur in the design process as it progresses.

Design Considerations

- Logical data design is necessary.
- Table design should be done by DBA.
- Use indexes.
- Consider denormalized structures in certain cases.
- Programmers and end users should use views of elements that are necessary for their needs, rather than tables.

Data and Program Independence

- Programmers and groups should not be too involved in table design and internal structure of DB2.
- Programmers and groups must be sold on the basic concept of why relational database is good: the concept of program and data independence and the idea of accessing at the data element level.

- Through the use of views, changes can be made to tables in many cases without changing programs, thus improving productivity and reducing maintenance time and costs.

Performance Considerations

- Consider system capacity. DB2 can use up your CPU.
- Poor table design can cause terrible performance.
- Evaluate SQL design.
- Use indexes (most of the time).

DASD Contention Considerations

- DB2 system Catalog and Directory Tables are highly used. Separate them from non-DB2 DASD.
- DB2 dual logs should be separated and not on DASD with DB2 system Catalog and Directory Tablespaces.
- DB2 dual BSDS should be separated and not on DASD with DB2 system Catalog and Directory Tablespaces.

Installation Considerations

During the installation phase of DB2, the following should be taken into account:

- Specify DUAL logging.
- Specify DUAL BSDS.
- Specify at least six DASD volumes for JCL creation.
- Create large enough EDMPOOL.
- APPLY all necessary maintenance BEFORE bringing up DB2.

A General Consideration

A very big concern is the actual leverage that exists in implementing a valid and strong Data and Database Administration (DBA) function. There seems to be a feeling that everyone can do as he or she pleases without regard for the possible consequences. The general feeling is that because DB2 has made many parts of the data processing function easier to understand and implement, many people have acquired all the knowledge that they need and need very little of the generic DBA-type support that has been painfully developed and implemented over the years. This is not true. The successful use of DB2 still requires most of the control and procedures that have existed with past DBMSs, and, with the potential for true data and program independence, in some ways requires even more control. If a DBA function does not exist currently it is needed. But to successfully implement this, support and a mandate must come from high enough in the organization to give the necessary clout to the processes and controls that will be developed. Without this clout, the whole concept will fail.

DB2 SUPPORT STRUCTURE

Basic Structure

The recommendation is to have a multi-tiered support structure, each tier with its own level of responsibilities and authorization. Other personnel also must be involved in the overall support of DB2 and its users.

The structure will be composed of Systems Programmers, a Systems Administrator, a Data Administrator, a Primary Database Administrator, various project DBAs, Project Leaders/Analysts, and a level of authorization for programmers and end users. The responsibilities and the authorization for each level are as follows:

Systems Programmer

Responsibilities	Authority Level
• Installs DB2 and related software • Resolves internal software problems • Applies necessary software maintenance	INSTALL-SYSADM

Systems Administrator

Responsibilities	Authority Level
• Assists in product installation • Creates backup/recovery procedures for system tables • Resolves system-wide performance problems • Monitors DB2 performance • Supports attachment facility access and other subsystem interface • Develops migration policies and procedures • Develops and maintains naming conventions • Evaluates and tests DB2-related software	SYSADM

Data Administrator

Responsibilities	Authority Level
• Assumes all logical data model responsibility • Develops logical design model and approved physical table structures • Maintains data dictionary/directory • Supports system integration and design projects	Select on system catalog tables

Primary Database Administrator

Responsibilities	Authority Level
• Assumes all production data responsibility • Creates databases for project DBAs • Grants DBADM authority to project DBAs for appropriate databases • Develops and maintains naming conventions • Grants BIND plan for each project plan to project DBAs • Reviews and approves requested table changes for production • Monitors performance • Creates backup/recovery procedures for production • Performs production system migration procedures	CREATE DBA BINDADD DBADM for all databases

Project Database Administrator

Responsibilities	Authority Level
• Grants BIND to programmers for plans they are working on • Creates tables/views as needed as they are approved • Defines synonym values for tables and views • Makes sure table/view definitions stay in synch	DBADM on assigned databases

Responsibilities	Authority Level
• Ensures naming convention compliance	
• Develops test backup/recovery procedures if deemed necessary	
• Presents table/view change requests to Primary DBA	
• Creates synonym value and DCLGEN from that synonym	
• If separate copies of tables are granted to individual programmers, only those tables which are needed will be created.	
• Eliminates unnecessary DB2 objects (tables, tablespaces, views, grant authorities, etc.) from project databases.	
• Creates table authority and other authorizations within the project databases to be granted by the project DBA to programmers as deemed necessary.	

Project Leaders/Analysts

Responsibilities	Authority Level
• Define plan/program names based on naming convention	BINDADD Select on system catalog
• Develop security/authorization requirements for production implementation	BIND, EXECUTE as needed
• Develop application migration plans (development—test integration—systems test—production)	
• BIND for assigned programs/plans	

Programmers

Responsibilities	Authority Level
• Create own needed synonyms	BINDADD Select on system catalog
• Ensure naming convention compliance	BIND, EXECUTE as needed
• BIND for assigned programs/plans	

Capacity Planning Personnel

Responsibilities	Authority Level
• Monitors DB2 resource utilization • Integrates DB2 utilization and GROWTH into capacity planning	Select on system catalog

DASD Management Personnel

Responsibilities	Authority Level
• Allocates needed DASD • Monitors and resolves DASD contention problems	Select on system catalog

Security Administration Personnel

Responsibilities	Authority Level
• Controls external access to DB2 (Top Secret, RACF, ACF2, etc.) • Ensures DB2 internal authorization is correct	Select on system catalog

System Operators

Responsibilities	Authority Level
• Monitors DB2 • Informs systems programmer and/or administrator of problems	SYSOPR

Production Control Personnel

Responsibilities	Authority Level
• Ensures successful completion of all DB2 backup jobstreams • Production job implementation	Select on system catalog

End User Personnel

Responsibilities	Authority Level
• Process and access data needed for performance of position	Execute for necessary plans Select, Insert, Delete, Update as required

DB2 PERSONNEL EDUCATION REQUIREMENTS

Training to some level is necessary for all support personnel and personnel using the DB2 environment. Following are minimum recommendations for DB2 training:

- System Administrator
  1. DB2 concepts and facilities
  2. Database Administration
  3. Systems Administration
  4. DB2 Capacity Planning and Performance Management
  5. DB2 Security Planning and Implementation

- Data Administrator
  1. DB2 concepts and facilities
  2. Database Administration

- Primary Database Administrator
  1. DB2 concepts and facilities
  2. DB2 applications workshop
  3. Database Administration
  4. Systems Administration

- Secondary Database Administrator
  1. DB2 concepts and facilities
  2. DB2 applications workshop
  3. Database Administration

- Capacity Planners
  1. DB2 concepts and facilities
  2. DB2 capacity planning and performance management

- DASD Administrator
  1. DB2 concepts and facilities

- Security Administrators
  1. DB2 concepts and facilities
  2. DB2 security planning and implementation

- System Programmer
  1. DB2 concepts and facilities

    2. Systems Administration
    3. DB2 capacity planning and performance management

- System Operator
  1. DB2 concepts and facilities
  2. Operator's class

- Application Programmer
  1. DB2 concepts and facilities
  2. DB2 applications workshop

- Project Leader
  1. DB2 concepts and facilities
  2. DB2 applications workshop
  3. Database Administration
  4. DB2/QMF/DXT Class

- End User
  1. DB2 concepts and facilities
  2. DB2/QMF/DXT

IMPLEMENTATION PRIORITY TASK LIST

The following tasks need to be completed by any installation that is attempting to implement DB2 and related products.

Administrative/Management Tasks

1. Implement DB2 support structure
2. Develop education requirements
3. Start necessary education
4. Implement logical data design procedures
5. Implement design review process
6. Implement data-driven methodology

Capacity Management Tasks

1. Evaluate performance/capacity requirements
2. Analyze overall computer system needs

Control and Standards Tasks

1. Standardize naming conventions
2. Develop migration procedures and forms
3. Integrate DB2 requirements into production turnover
4. Develop policies and procedures

5. Develop standards
6. Develop standard backup/recovery procedures
7. Implement data dictionary
8. Develop programmer productivity tools
9. Provide end-user access and tools

Implementation Task Issues

Most of these implementation tasks have been described previously, and recommendations were made for them. Particular issues to consider in the accomplishment of each of these tasks are as follows:

Implement DB2 support structure.   The process of implementing the DB2 support structure is critical and, in some cases, very political. The need for an effective support structure will make the difference between success and failure. The support structure provided in this document is designed to implement DB2 in such a manner that each particular group's needs are satisfied and yet the necessary control remains.

The DB2 Systems Administrator is the key to effective problem resolution. He or she needs to be knowledgeable about DB2, TSO, MVS, and just about everything involved in the MVS world, and also needs to understand the applications and their requirements. This person will be hard to find, but worth everything it takes to get and/or train him or her.

Develop education requirements.   Contrary to what IBM says, training is still necessary for this product and related products. Every person connected at all with the support and implementation of DB2 needs some training. In the cases of programmers it is not as high a requirement as before with systems such as IMS DB, IDMS, etc., but the requirement is still there.

Personnel should be required to finish their appropriate level of education before getting into DB2.

Start necessary education.   Plans for education are just a start. Getting it started is the prime need. The faster education is started and completed, the sooner effective use of DB2 can begin.

Evaluate performance/capacity requirements.   The particular task of evaluating performance/capacity requirements is not going to be easy to resolve. Normally, historical and known data is used. In the case of DB2, there is basically no historical data and very little known data. The only known data comes from IBM benchmarks, which are just weak possibilities run on stand-alone CPU environments. The other factors involved in this process are the needs and requirements of the end users, at this point, basically unknown. In every case to date, resultant end-user usage of DB2 has exceeded estimates by magnitudes of 10 or more. As a result, you can only guess by using the benchmarks and multiplying the user estimates, or create your own and hope that you stay close to reality. The main thing to do is to constantly track the usage from the beginning, and perform the estimates and projections often.

Analyze overall computer system needs.   The general consensus is that full implementation of DB2 and the use of it and its related products are going to cost MACHINES rather then just extra MIPS (millions of instructions per second). In addition, this product needs memory—the more the better. So plan accordingly. The product is the first to be designed to take advantage of the MVS/XA environment and to use the extended storage cabability so it can run well and will run well with enough resources and planning.

Standardize naming conventions.   As with everything else in data processing, naming conventions are needed. The actual degree and level of those conventions will be determined by existing standards, whether or not you are running multiple levels of applications under a single DB2 subsystem, and no matter how much control and access is desired. The appropriate naming conventions can be integrated into the system in such a way as to help make the management and control of the system easier or much harder.

Develop migration procedures and forms.   DB2 applications and usage of ad hoc queries will eventually need to be migrated from one level in a single DB2 subsystem to another level in the same system, or from one DB2 to another. The needs for control from a change-control standpoint and from a successful migration standpoint are greater than any other system. As such, the process needs to be well-defined, and appropriate forms and documentation need to be designed.

Integrate DB2 requirements into production turnover.   For the most part, current production turnover requirements are the same for DB2 as any other system. The differences are as follows:

- Added authorization levels
- Ad hoc requirements
- Authorization requirements for application plan

These differences need to be addressed and resolved. Recommendations are given later in this document.

Develop policies, procedures, and standards.   The policies and procedures need to be developed as soon as possible in order to assist in uniformity within the use of DB2 itself and to aid in the proper levels of control and understanding. The process of trying to change thinking and processes after the fact is always a difficult and time-consuming process. It is better to set everything up right before releasing the use of the product, and then to allow use of the product without any policies, procedures, and standards.

Develop standard backup/recovery procedures. The key to any DBMS is its backup and recovery capability. DB2 has a much greater level of integration of its backup and recovery system than other DBMSs. As such, its procedures need to be understood and documented before proceeding into a full production environment.

Develop logical data design procedures. In the past there have been many levels of discussion of logical data design procedures and the ideas of data modeling and corporate database. The problem has been that the other DBMSs have not provided an easy way to implement the logical data design because of their very rigid physical structure. DB2 and its element (column)-based architecture is very close to the actual structure of a logical data model. It is now possible to implement actual (or close to it) data structures that are logically based. This requires a different thinking on the part of designers, however. They must learn to design and implement data-driven designs rather than application-driven designs. By using and requiring logical data design and modeling techniques, this can be accomplished.

Implement design review process. The design review process is a part of quality assurance that needs to be implemented for the following:

- Capacity planning
- Performance management
- Effective database design
- Ergonomic considerations
- Effective resource utilization

The design review process recommended in this document expressly addresses DB2 issues. It should be integrated into a full-cycle quality assurance program.

Implement data dictionary. With DB2, the beginnings of the full-function data dictionary are already inherent. As time goes on, IBM will implement this further. For now, it is possible to add tables to enhance the current DB2 system catalog with additional tables and program code.

Develop programmer productivity tools. DB2 itself provides extra programmer productivity through the Structured Query Language (SQL) and the use of other products such as Query Management Facility (QMF), Database Edit Facility (DBEDIT), and others. Additional products that provide code generation and entire system generation facilities can also be acquired from IBM and others. With the backlog being what it is and continuing to rise, these tools are necessary.

Provide end-user access and tools. DB2 itself provides a high-level end-user access capability through the use of SQL and products such as DBEDIT.

Additional products that provide end-user support are the DB2 interfaces in Application System (AS), Focus, The Information Facility (TIF), APL2, and others.

With the true benefit of using DB2 being the end-user access to the data, the requirements for supporting this environment need to be analyzed early on. These include the need for additional CPU and DASD resources and for additional DB2 support personnel.

DB2 Policies and Procedures

5

OVERVIEW

One of the most important areas of the correct implementation of DB2 is the creation and implementation of policies and procedures. In these policies and procedures need to be the following subjects:

1. Administrative policies
2. Security
3. Usage
4. Design review process
5. Change control
6. Migration from test to production
7. New application development procedures
8. Backup and recovery
9. Production turnover

ADMINISTRATIVE POLICIES

Administrative policies for DB2 primarily center on defining the support structure and the responsibilities for each person and/or level in that structure. Also included in the administrative policies will be any other related policies such as statements of direction and interface requirements for other organizations and other policies.

SECURITY

As described earlier, DB2 has various levels and functions that can be defined within its internal security system. This security level controls access within

DB2. External security access to DB2 and its associated data sets have to be controlled through other methods external to DB2. Also, authorization for particularly powerful function-levels within DB2 needs to be controlled. These and other topics will be discussed in the following paragraphs.

External Security Requirements

DB2 subsystem access. Access to the various DB2 subsystems (if there are more than one) can be controlled by the use of various security system software packages such as IBM's RACF, or CAI's Top Secret or ACF2. These products have facilities to limit access by USERID to any subsystem.

DB2 data set access. Access to DB2 data sets must be limited to view-only by all personnel and systems except for the appropriate DB2 subsystems themselves, various DB2 utilities, and certain systems programming and systems administrator USERIDs. This can be controlled also through the use of the previously mentioned security software packages, or if they are not available, through the use of MVS data set PASSWORD security.

Internal DB2 Security Structure

DB2 has a very flexible internal security structure in that it can be turned off at installation, turned on and made very loose, or made very tight. Just about any system security requirements can be met. The commands that give and take away authorizations are as follows:

- GRANT
  Grants authorization functions and levels.
- REVOKE
  Revokes previously granted authorization functions and levels.

Specific descriptions of authorization levels and functions follow.

DB2 function levels. The defined DB2 functions, their capabilities, and recommended assignments are as follows:

SYSTEM-WIDE FUNCTIONS. System-wide functions that have system-wide authority no matter what specific level of authorization is granted are:

SYSADM: A user who has been granted SYSADM authority has TOTAL CONTROL over any DB2 resource and may grant and/or revoke from any other user the authority to access any resource (except for the actual creator of any object).

Because of the power of this authority, it should be limited only to personnel who have system-wide responsibilities, such as the overall DB2 System Administrator, Corporate Database Administrator, and the responsible System Programmer.

SYSOPR: The SYSOPR has the ability to issue certain DB2 commands and has no access to DB2 tables.

OTHERS: Other system-wide authorities are available that have subsets of the power of the SYSADM-level authority. These are the following:

- BINDADD
  Allows user to create new application plans using the BIND subcommand with the ADD option.
- BSDS
  Allows user to issue the -RECOVER BSDS command.
- CREATEDBA
  Allows user to create new databases and automatically gives DBADM authority over those databases.
- CREATEDBC
  Allows user to create new databases and automatically gives DBCTRL authority over those databases.
- CREATESG
  Allows user to create new storage groups.
- DISPLAY
  Allows user to display system information by issuing the -DISPLAY command (THREAD, DATABASE, etc.).
- RECOVER
  Allows user to issue the -RECOVER INDOUBT command.
- STOPALL
  Allows user to issue the -STOP DB2 command.
- STOSPACE
  Allows user to use the STOSPACE utility.
- TRACE
  Allows user to start and stop DB2 traces using the -START TRACE and -STOP TRACE commands.
- RLIMIT
  Allows start and stop of Resource Limit Facility (RLF) using the -START RLIMIT and -STOP RLIMIT Commands.

DATABASE-WIDE FUNCTIONS. Within DB2, creation of an object called a database is done. Within this database are all of the tablespaces and tables that are created within it. This logical creation allows a lower level of function to be supported with different authorization levels. These are database-level functions and are as follows:

DBADM: A person with DBADM authority has total control over those databases granted at this level of authority. This includes altering and creation of tables, creation of tablespaces, seeing and modifying data in all tables, and running appropriate utilities. He can grant lower levels of authority to the objects in his defined database if he has been given the GRANT option. He cannot grant any authorization to tables which have been created in his database by another user.

DBCTRL: The DBCTRL authority allows a person to run utilities and to create tables and tablespaces. He cannot, however, access data in tables that have been created by another user in that same tablespace without being granted specific access by the creator of that table or a SYSADM.

DBMAINT: The DBMAINT authority only allows a person to run utilities that do NOT update (COPY, RUNSTATS). He cannot use the LOAD utility, for example. He also does not have access to tables created by other users or the ability to DROP any tables other than his own or those that have been granted to him.

OTHERS: Other database-level authorities include the following:

- CREATETAB
  Allows user to create tables in any existing tablespace in this database.
- CREATETS
  Allows user to create tablespaces in this database.
- DISPLAYDB
  Allows user to check the database and tablespaces in this database through the execution of the -DISPLAY DATABASE command.
- DROP
  Allows user to DROP the database.
- IMAGCOPY
  Allows user to run the COPY and MERGECOPY utilities against tablespaces in this database.
- LOAD
  Allows user to run the LOAD utility to load tables in this database.
- RECOVERDB
  Allows user to run the RECOVER and MODIFY utilities against tablespaces in this database.
- REORG
  Allows user to run the REORG utility against tablespaces and indexes in this database.
- REPAIR
  Allows user to run the REPAIR utility against tablespaces and indexes in this database.
- STARTDB
  Allows the user to start this database by issuing the -START DATABASE command.
- STATS
  Allows user to run the RUNSTATS and CHECK utility against tablespaces and indexes in this database.
- STOPDB
  Allows the user to stop this database by issuing the -STOP DATABASE command.

GRANT ON DATABASE STATEMENT. Authorizations at the database-level are granted using the 'GRANT privileges ON DATABASE database' statement.

DB2 data access security levels (table level).   The following levels of access are granted at the table level within DB2. One thing to remember is that the creator of any table ALWAYS has full access to any tables that have been created by him. If the need for security is high, it is probable that you will NOT allow tables to be created with existing TSO USERIDs as high-level qualifiers (CREATOR-IDs) for any table CREATEs, especially in production.

SELECT.   SELECT access allows view-only access to data within a table or that data defined by a view.

UPDATE.   UPDATE access allows UPDATE capability to data within a table or data defined by a view.

DELETE.   DELETE access allows DELETE capability for rows within a table.

INSERT.   INSERT access allows the person to INSERT new rows within a table.

ALTER.   ALTER access allows the person to ALTER the table or view by adding additional columns.

UPDATE USING COLUMN-NAME(s).   UPDATE using Column-Name(s) allows the person to UPDATE ONLY those columns that have been defined in the GRANT statement.

ALL.   By granting ALL privileges, the person has all of the access authorities mentioned previously. This includes the ALTER capability. In many cases this is not desired, so a GRANT specifying SELECT, UPDATE, DELETE, and INSERT must be specifically defined to exclude the ALTER capability, yet give all necessary data manipulation capability.

GRANT ON TABLE STATEMENT.   Authorizations at the table level are granted using the GRANT privileges ON TABLE table/view statement.

DB2 application authorization (plan).   Application plans have two levels of authorization. A user can either BIND a plan and/or EXECUTE the plan.

BIND PLAN.   The persons with bind authority of a particular plan have the capability to create the plan through the use of the BIND command. For a bind to be successful, the person doing the bind must have the bind authority, and needs the access authority necessary to execute all of the SQL that composes the plan being bound. This includes the authority to access the data within the SQL. The exception to this is when the plan is to be bound with the actual bind taking place at execution time (as in the case of Dynamic SQL Plans). In this case, the person executing the plan at that time must have all necessary authorization or the execution will fail.

EXECUTE PLAN.   Any user granted EXECUTE capability for a plan has the authority to execute all SQL in that plan. He does not need specific authority for the data access defined in the SQL that composes the plan. The exception for this is as mentioned above. If the plan is a Dynamic SQL plan or if the bind authorization check was delayed until execution time, the user executing the plan must have the necessary authorization to execute all SQL defined plans, or the execution will fail.

GRANT PLAN STATEMENT.   Authorization is granted using the GRANT BIND, EXECUTE ON PLAN statement.

DB2 physical resource use authorization.   All DB2 resource usage must be specifically granted. This includes the use of the following DB2 objects:

- BUFFER POOL
- STOGROUP (storage group)
- TABLESPACE

If a user attempts to access a table that has been defined using a resource above that he has not been given authority to use, the access will fail. The only exception to this is a person with SYSADM-level authority.

GRANT USE OF STATEMENT.   Usage is granted using the GRANT USE OF statement.

WITH GRANT OPTION.   The WITH GRANT option can be added to any of the grant statements listed previously. This allows the person who has been given the grant option to grant levels of authorization up to and including the level he has been granted. For example, a user who has been granted DBADM over a database with grant option can grant CREATETS (create tablespace) to someone for that same database and grant DBADM to someone else for that database, but cannot grant DBADM for a database for which he is not a DBADM.

IF 'WITH GRANT OPTION' IS NOT DONE, NO GRANT CAPABILITY IS POSSIBLE FOR THAT USER.

Security of High-Level DB2 Functions

Because of the powerful capability of certain high-level DB2 functions (primarily the SYSADM), it may be necessary to add further protection to these functions.

Two types of SYSADM.   Within DB2, there are two types of system administration or SYSADM functions. One is the Installation SYSADM, and the second, any granted SYSADM authorities.

INSTALLATION SYSADM.   The Installation SYSADM differs from any granted SYSADMs in that the Installation SYSADM is the only one who can RECOVER certain DB2 system catalog and directory tablespaces. Another difference is that the Installation SYSADMs (up to two) do not go through any of the DB2 authorization checking, while granted SYSADMs must at least have their SYSADM level verified.

GRANTED SYSADM.   These SYSADMs are created by the grants issued by other SYSADMs.

Control of SYSADM.   It may be desired that the SYSADM IDs be used only sparingly to prevent possible accidents. This can be done by issuing two sets of TSO USERIDs for each person with SYSADM authority, only one of whom will have the SYSADM authority. It is also a good idea to have a SYSADM level of authority available for emergencies, preferably one of the Installation SYSADMs.

REVOKE 'cascade' potential.   The REVOKE SQL statement is used to revoke previously granted authority and access, as stated before. The issue to be aware of when using the REVOKE is the 'cascade' effect. This effect is caused when a user who has granted authority to other users has his authority revoked. DB2 checks all authority that has been granted by this person and determines that if that authority would NOT have been granted without the original GRANT, then he would also REVOKE those authorities as well. For example, User A grants User B DBADM WITH GRANT OPTION, and USER B grants User C SELECT access to Table A. User A then REVOKEs User B's DBADM authority. What will happen is that User B will lose his authority as DBADM and User C will lose his SELECT authority for Table A.

There are two options for solving the cascade effect:

1. Inactivate the appropriate TSO USERID (User B above).
2. Check catalog and/or use DBMAUI and recreate the GRANT statements.

DB2 Security Authorization—ID Implementation

With the advent of Version 2.1 of DB2, there are three levels of Authorization IDs available to users of DB2. These are as follows:

1. One Primary Authorization ID—this represents the USER of the session. Previous to DB2 V2.1 this was the only option. Individual authorization is established and accounted for under this ID.
2. One or more Secondary Authorization IDs—These are used to supplement the primary ID during authorization checking. The secondary ID can represent additional privileges for a user using the RACF Group authorization to which the user belongs. This can be used effectively to reduce the load on the security checking within DB2 and a USER can be easily removed from a group without impact upon DB2 by just DISCONNECTING the USERID from the RACF Group for which the authorization is defined. *RACF Implementation of the GROUP func-*

tion is required for this. RACF will pass the associated authorization IDs for the PRIMARY-ID to DB2 for processing by DB2's Security and Authorization processing.

3. One SQL Authorization ID—This ID is used for authorization checking when issuing DYNAMIC SQL statements, and can also be changed without terminating the THREAD connection. Very useful to create TABLES for use by other Secondary Authorization IDs, SYNONYMS for other people, etc.

Security EXIT Implementation

Previous to DB2 Version 2.1, the only way to reduce the security administration overhead within DB2 or to add a different level of control was to write an EXIT routine which intercepted the AUTHORIZATION-ID before it was processed by DB2 authorization checking. This routine would then convert that Authorization-ID to a different AUTHID and then pass it on to DB2. This worked, but the routine had to be written in assembler, and rewritten every time a change occurred. DB2 also had to be brought down and back up to implement the new version of the EXIT. DB2 Version 2.1 now provides this Grouping Capability and extra flexibility through the use of additional Authorization-IDs and the GROUP structure using RACF (as explained above).

DB2 DESIGN REVIEW PROCESS

Introduction

The first thing that must be understood when dealing with DB2 is that application design is different with it than has been done in the past with other products. This is because the ease of use of the product and the ability of DB2 to respond to change is so much greater than those of other products. As a result, some of the currently existing system development methodolgies and design techniques must be modified.

The key concept within DB2 is the understanding of its element-level (column) structure. This structure mandates the need to design tables and applications based on a DATA-DRIVEN methodology rather than an APPLI-CATION-DRIVEN methodology. The following design review process is based upon this concept, and the forms, processes, and other tools described are designed and created with this methodology in mind.

Design Review Objectives

The objectives of the design review process are as follows:

- Produce applications and systems that are:
  - Verifiable
  - Valid

 – Effective in use of resources
 – Functionally correct
* Ensure optimal and correct use of resources
* Ensure feasibility
* Ensure good man/machine interfaces
* Provide a forum for technical problem resolution
* Provide input to capacity-planning function
* Provide input for performance management
* Identify areas that need additional investigation
* Ensure data-driven design

Design Review Scope

The scope of the design review process is as follows:

* Logical database/table design
* Physical database/table design
* Data access and usage—transactions, queries, programs
* System environmental impact
* Human engineering
* Alternative analysis
* Effectiveness
* Meeting of corporate business goals
* Potential end-user/ad hoc usage
* System and program design
* Standards conformance
* Security requirements

Any other issues that are determined to affect the system and/or the corporation are also under the scope of this process.

Design Review Committee

The Design Review Committee is composed of different levels and types of people, both technical and nontechnical. There are permanent members of the committee, and other temporary members who are associated with a particular project that is being reviewed. Also, not all members of the committee are involved at each phase.

The committee itself should have at least a dotted-line, and preferably a direct-line, reporting relationship to the highest MIS officer in the organization.

Design review committee structure. The Design Review Committee is composed of the following personnel:

* Design Review Committee Chairman
* DB2 Systems Administrator

- DB2 Database Administrator
- Technical Services Representative
- Security Administrator
- Operations/Production Control Representative
- Quality Assurance Representative
- Application Project Manager
- Application Designer (as needed)
- Application Database Administrator (as needed)
- User Representative
- Information Center Representative (as needed)
- Application Programmer(s) (as needed)

These people will meet as defined later for each phase, and it will be the responsibility of the Application Project Manager to make sure all necessary documentation is received and that the required meetings are scheduled with the Design Review Committee Chairman.

Committee chairman qualifications.   As the moderator and, in many cases, the final decision-maker during the design review process, the committee chairman needs some level of expertise and knowledge in the following areas of data processing:

- Logical data design
- Data-driven design methodology
- Application development
- Systems programming
- Operations and production control
- End-user requirements
- DB2
- Overall data center needs
- Quality assurance

But most of all, the chairman must be aware of and know about the business and its needs. Any decision that is to be made sometimes must override the technical problems in order to resolve the CRITICAL BUSINESS NEEDS. To do this, the chairman must be cognizant and aware of what those business needs are.

Design Review Phases

The design review process is split into four phases that can be integrated into just about all system development methodologies and application review processes. At each phase, certain documentation requirements exist. Only those applying directly to DB2 and a data-driven methodology will be described. Other normal application review requirements and system design methodology requirements will be assumed to continue as they are in each company.

Conceptual design review (CDR).   In the Conceptual Design Review, the following subjects are reviewed:

- Overall system description
- Feasibility study
- Planned usage of DB2
- Initial capacity and usage analysis
- Logical data requirements

This phase requires the use of the following forms:

- DB2 Application Description, Part 1
- DB2 Application Description, Part 2
- DB2 Performance Impact Analysis (first attempt)
- DB2 Capacity Impact Analysis (first attempt)

Other necessary documentation includes the following:

- Overall system narrative
- Business and analysis
- Feasibility study
- Requirements analysis

Detailed design review (DDR).   In the Detailed Design Review (DDR), the following subjects are part of the review:

- Overall system description
- Detailed planned usage of DB2
- Logical database design
- Proposed physical database design
- Ad hoc query requirements

This phase requires the use of the following forms:

- Data-Element Description
- DB2 Table Narrative
- DB2 Performance Impact Analysis (second attempt)
- DB2 Capacity Impact Analysis (second attempt)
- DB2 QMF Procedure Processing
- DB2 QMF Query Processing

Other necessary documentation includes the following:

- Logical data flow diagram
- Detail design documents

Forms that will be used in the actual development process at this time but not part of the design review are the following:

- DB2 Initial Development Checklist
- DB2 Storage Group Creation Request
- DB2 Database Creation Request
- DB2 Tablespace Creation Request
- DB2 Table Change Request
- DB2 View Creation Request
- DB2 Plan Creation Request

SQL design review (SDR). During the SQL Design Review (SDR), the following subjects are reviewed:

- Proposed SQL Code for Static SQL
- Project Dynamic SQL
- EXPLAIN Results

This phase requires the use of the following forms:

- DB2 SQL Statement Processing
- QMF Procedure Processing
- QMF Query Processing
- DB2 Performance Impact Analysis (third attempt)
- DB2 Capacity Impact Analysis (third attempt)

Pre-installation review (PIR). During the Pre-Installation Review (PIR), the following subjects are reviewed:

- Test-to-production migration procedures
- Scheduled dates
- Security requirements
- Capacity and usage analysis
- Backup and recovery
- Special requirements

This phase requires the use of the following forms:

- DB2 Storage Group Creation Request (Production)
- DB2 Database Creation Request (Production)
- DB2 Tablespace Creation Request (Production)
- DB2 View Creation Request (Production)
- DB2 Plan Creation Request (Production)
- DB2 Security Authorization Request (Production)
- DB2 Migration Request (Batch, CICS, DBEDIT, and/or QMF)

- Production Control Migration Request for DB2 Applications
- DB2 Backup/Recovery Requirements
- DB2 Performance Impact Analysis (final attempt)
- DB2 Capacity Impact Analysis (final attempt)

Post-installation audit (PIA). At some point after the system has been successfully installed, a Post-Installation Audit (PIA) will be performed. In this audit, the following will be examined:

- User satisfaction
- Overall system performance
- Additional concerns
- Actual capacity and usage analysis
- New requirements

This phase requires the use of the following forms:

- All forms supplied for PIR

Systems Development Methodology/
Design Review Integration

The design review process defined above can be integrated into most systems development methodologies (SDMs) or system development life cycle processes relatively easily. One such integration follows:

Conceptual design. In the conceptual design phase, the Conceptual Design Review (CDR) will be held. Its placement in the SDM will be as follows:

- Intitial planning
- Requirements analysis
- Alternative evaluation and selection
- Cost/benefit analysis
- Preliminary design
- CONCEPTUAL DESIGN REVIEW
- Gaining approval

Detail design. In the detail design phase, the Detail Design Review (DDR) will be held. Its placement in the SDM will be as follows:

- Refine plan
- Reevaluate preliminary design
- Prepare detail design
- Implement action plan
- Reanalyze cost/benefits

- • DETAIL DESIGN REVIEW
- • Gain Approval

Programming.   In the programming phase, the SQL design review will occur. The purpose of this phase is to ensure that any invalid sets of SQL are identified and changed early. Because of the tremendous power of SQL, the review of the SQL Code itself is necessary. The actual review itself will be scheduled when the SQL has been designed. The timeframe for this is as follows:

- • Complete program design
- • Begin programming
- • Design SQL
- • SQL DESIGN REVIEW
- • Finish programming

Test and implementation.   The Pre-Installation Review will be scheduled as the system is being prepared for installation after testing has been completed. The time frame of the review is as follows:

- • Test written code and procedures
- • Prepare production implementation documentation
- • Provide training
- • Complete acceptance testing
- • PRE-INSTALLATION REVIEW
- • Gain approval
- • Install system

Post-installation audit.   At some designated period after the system has been installed and in use, the post-installation audit will occur. The prime purpose of the audit is to ensure that what was planned has indeed been done, and to try to recognize any outstanding or missed requirements.

CHANGE CONTROL

Need

Within DB2, the need for change control becomes more critical because of the many different subsystems that can attach to DB2 (CICS, TSO, etc.) and because of the higher level of internal complexity of DB2 as well. This results in the fact that arbitrary changes cannot be done within a CPU that might affect the DB2 systems. Also, the same type of changes to internal DB2 objects cannot be done without analyzing the consequences. Then, to make the situation even more complex, you can no longer just turn over the application code to production control for implementation and, figuratively, just go away.

You must now provide extra levels of security, you must involve the DB2 Systems Administrator, and also be aware of the tremendous ad hoc capability that now exists.

Additional Areas of Concern

In summary, additional integration and procedures need to be added to current procedures. The particular areas that need additional change control are as follows:

- Changes to system software effect on DB2
- Additional backup/recovery requirements
- 24-hour operation of DB2
- Access to DB2 from other subsystems
- Internal security levels
- Changes to DB2 objects
- DB2 system migration

Responsibilities

Additional involvement in change control is necessary by the following personnel:

Application project managers. Application personnel and especially their management must understand the implications of ineffective or nonexistent change control. They must also be involved from the aspect of changes to applications and changes and/or enhancements to DB2 and its family of products. DB2 is a relatively new product that is undergoing continual change and improvement.

DB2 system administrators. The DB2 System Administrator, as the overall controller and chief problem solver, has the most involvement in the areas of change control. He is the one who has to analyze any change that is proposed and its potential effect upon the overall DB2 subsystem, if any. Changes in applications, security levels, new queries, non-DB2 software changes, DB2 maintenance and upgrades—all of these must be analyzed by him for effect.

Production control personnel. Production control personnel needs to know the changes to production processing just as always—new systems, changes to existing systems, additions to the DB2 backups, etc.

Security administration personnel. Because of the potential damage that invalid authorization within DB2 can cause, security administration personnel need to know how the DB2 security authorization is set up, and what each function is capable of. They must be kept aware of any changes in the authorization levels that have been granted, and be aware of any impact that may be caused by personnel who leave.

Database administration (DBA) personnel. DBA personnel are involved in the change control over changes made to the physical tables within DB2. They also must manage changes that are made to see that minimal impact occurs within applications and personnel that are using the tables assigned to that DBA.

Systems programming personnel. The systems programming personnel, with the Systems Administrator, will analyze, track, and test any changes that are made to the DB2-related systems software. This includes preventative maintenance, system replacement and upgrades, and problem resolution maintenance.

Existing change control personnel. Personnel currently involved in the change control process will need to be made cognizant of the broader impact of changes in the DB2 environment. Changes to certain software that formerly, in many cases, were done in a vacuum without concern for other software now need to be analyzed on a far greater scope.

DB2 Change Control Forms

The following forms are all part of the change control process and are essential to the management of the tasks necessary to control and administer DB2. Some are also integral parts of other processes that occur in the systems development life cycle. A sample of each is in the appendix indicated.

1. Logical Design Forms

    – DB2 Application Description (Appendix 3, Appendix 4)
    – Data Element Definition (Appendix 11)
    – DB2 Table Narrative (Appendix 9)

2. Physical Design Forms

    – DB2 Initial Development Checklist (Appendix 14)
    – DB2 Storage Group Creation Request (Appendix 12)
    – DB2 Database Creation Request (Appendix 16)
    – DB2 Tablespace Creation Request (Appendix 17)
    – DB2 Table Change Request (Appendix 8)
    – DB2 View Creation Request (Appendix 10)
    – DB2 Index Creation Request (Appendix 15)
    – DB2 Plan Creation Request (Appendix 19)
    – DB2 Object Creation Request (Appendix 13)
    – DB2 QMF Query Processing (Appendix 31)
    – DB2 QMF Procedure Processing (Appendix 29)
    – DB2 SQL Statement Processing (Appendix 30)

3. DB2 Change Control Forms

   – DB2 Change Request Completion Notice (Appendix 5)
   – DB2 Change Request Checklist (Appendix 6)

4. DB2 Production Turnover Forms

   – Production Control Migration Request for DB2 Applications (Appendix 32)
   – Production Control Checklist for DB2 Applications (Appendix 33)

5. DB2 System Administrator—Migration Forms

   – DB2 Backup/Recovery Requirements (Appendix 18)
   – DB2 Migration Request—Batch (Appendix 20)
   – DB2 Migration Request—CICS (Appendix 21)
   – DB2 Migration Request—IMS/DC (Appendix 22)
   – DB2 Migration Request—QMF (Appendix 23)
   – DB2 Migration Request—DBEDIT (Appendix 34)
   – DB2 Migration Checklist (Appendix 25)
   – DB2 Utility/DXT Usage (Appendix 28)

6. DB2 End-User Request Forms

   – DB2 Report Request (Appendix 7)

7. DB2 Performance and Capacity Planning Forms

   – DB2 Performance Impact Analysis (Appendix 26)
   – DB2 Capacity Impact Analysis (Appendix 27)
   – DB2 SQL Statement Processing (Appendix 30)
   – QMF Procedure Processing (Appendix 29)

MIGRATION FROM TEST TO PRODUCTION

Need for Procedures

When starting to move applications and programs from test to production, there must be a set, documented procedure in order to make sure that all necessary tasks are accomplished. It is not enough to just move the related programs into production load libraries as is done in most production turnover standards. Within DB2, you must also make sure that appropriate DB2 object creation has been completed, and that all necessary authorizations have been granted. If this is not done, the system and/or programs will not work correctly.

Separating Different System Levels

How you separate different system levels (development, integration test, systems test, user test, production, etc.) depends upon how many subsystems you decide to run.

Multiple systems on a single DB2 subsystem. It is possible to run all levels of systems on a single DB2 subsystem by doing the following:

TABLE NAME HIGH-LEVEL QUALIFIER. You separate the different levels of tables from each other by making the high-level qualifier on each set of tables different (TEST.TABLE, PROD.TABLE, etc.). Then, by using synonyms at each level during the BIND process, and by NOT hard-coding the full table and/or view name in the code, there is no need to change the code as it moves from one level to another. You just have to BIND REPLACE.

UNIQUE PLANNAMES. You must remember that each planname must be UNIQUE within a single DB2 subsystem. In order to put multiple versions of the same plan in a single DB2 subsystem, the recommendation is to use the eighth character in the planname as an identifier as to what level it belongs to—D for development, S for systems test, P for production, etc.

Single system on a single DB2 subsystem. With a single system on a single DB2 subsystem, any naming convention will work, and, in fact, the names of table, view, and plans can be the same. You should use the naming convention listed above in any case because of the potential for multiple subcopies of data that may be required, and you should use synonyms in any case.

DB2 Migration Forms

The following forms are to be used in the migration process:

- DB2 Migration Request—BATCH (Appendix 20)
- DB2 Migration Request—CICS (Appendix 21)
- DB2 Migration Request—IMS/DC (Appendix 22)
- DB2 Migration Request—DBEDIT (Appendix 34)
- DB2 Migration Request—QMF (Appendix 23)
- DB2 Migration Checklist (Appendix 25)

See 'DB2 Forms Procedures' for instructions on filling out forms.

Recommended Procedures

See 'Production Turnover Procedures' for recommended procedures concerning the production turnover process. The following process will be the process necessary to FULLY migrate a DB2 application system from one DB2 subsystem to another.

1. Send Migration Forms to DB2 Systems Administrator (SysAdm)
2. DB2 SysAdm will do the following:
   a. CREATE new tables and views (if necessary)
   b. CREATE Synonym before BIND (if necessary)

    c. GRANT appropriate table authorization (Dynamic SQL only)
    d. BINDADD (or BIND REPLACE) application plans
    e. GRANT Plan Execute privileges
    f. Check authorization structure
    g. Complete checklist
    h. Notify production control (if production)
    i. Notify CICS systems programming (if CICS)
    j. Notify Application Manager

3. Systems programmer generates RCT entries (if CICS)
4. Check

NEW APPLICATION DEVELOPMENT PROCEDURES

Forms

The following forms will be used in the application development processes:

- DB2 Application Description (Appendix 3, Appendix 4)
- Data Element Definition (Appendix 11)
- DB2 Table Narrative (Appendix 9)
- DB2 Initial Development Checklist (Appendix 14)
- DB2 Storage Group Creation Request (Appendix 12)
- DB2 Database Creation Request (Appendix 16)
- DB2 Tablespace Creation Request (Appendix 17)
- DB2 Table Change Request (Appendix 8)
- DB2 View Creation Request (Appendix 10)
- DB2 Index Creation Request (Appendix 15)
- DB2 Plan Creation Request (Appendix 19)
- DB2 Object Creation Request (Appendix 13)

See 'DB2 Forms Procedures' for instructions on filling out forms.

Procedure

In the process of developing new applications, the following will occur after the forms mentioned above have been filled out and accepted by the DB2 Systems Administrator:

The DB2 Systems Administrator will do the following:
    1. CREATE storage group on test DB2
    2. CREATE application database on test DB2
    3. CREATE initial 'dummy' Bind for plans
    4. GRANT DBADM with grant to group DBA for database
    5. Complete checklist as required

Group DBADM will do following:

      a. CREATE tablespaces in group database
      b. CREATE tables in appropriate tablespaces
      c. CREATE views
      d. GRANT necessary authorization to programmers

Programmers will do following:

      a. CREATE synonyms for themselves
      b. Develop and test SQL
      c. Develop and test applications

Use of Program Preparation Panels Under DB2I

The use of program preparation panels is recommended for reasons of faster turnaround and in ease of problem isolation if problems in these processes occur.

Batch Program Preparation

Batch program preparation can be accomplished by executing the appropriate batch procedures listed in the appendices indicated for the following language compilers. The results of these procedures will be DB2 applications that are ready to be executed AFTER a successful BIND has been done.

Batch procedures.   Batch procedures for the following exist, and a sample of each is listed in the appendix indicated.

- DSNHCOB2—COBOL II (Appendix 69)
- DSNHCOB—VS/COBOL (Appendix 70)
- DSNHPLI—PLI (Appendix 71)
- DSNHASM—Assembler (Appendix 72)
- DSNHFOR—Fortran (Appendix 73)

Using DSNH in batch mode.   The TSO DB2 command DSNH is what is used by the DB2I program preparation panels in the execution of the program preparation process. This process can be submitted as a batch job through the DB2I program preparation process or through execution of the DSNH command under TSO or under batch TSO using the IKJEFT01 batch TSO program. This TSO command will do the complete PRECOMPILE, COMPILE, BIND, LINK, CICS PRECOMPILE, PLI MACRO EXPANSION, and RUN the program if so desired.

Creation of DSNH JCL and parameters can be done by selecting the EDITJCL option on the DB2I main program preparation screen and then executing the program preparation process based upon the parameters that you enter. A sample of this is included in Appendix 74.

BACKUP AND RECOVERY PROCEDURES

Effective and complete backup and recovery procedures must be in place before production implementation of DB2. A general overview of the process is defined below. Complete procedures are defined in the document 'DB2 Backup, Recovery, Reorganization and Migration Procedures' by this same author.

DB2 Logging

One of the very important parts of the DB2 backup and recovery procedures is the DB2 log. In DB2, all changes made to any table are written out to the DB2 log. DB2 has a dual logging process in which it writes out each change to two different log files. When either these active logs fills up or an I/O error occurs on either log, DB2 will send a request to the console to have tapes mounted for those active logs to be archived.

DB2 Logging Overview

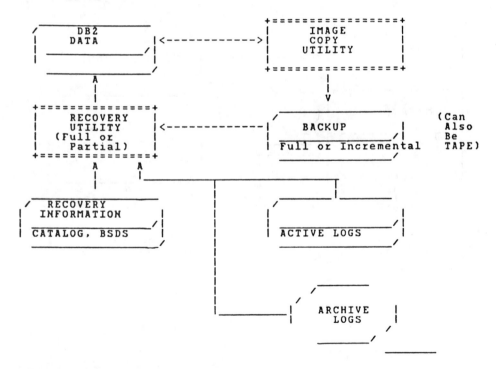

DB2 Backup and Recovery

To backup and recover a DB2 database, you must make periodic full image copies of each necessary tablespace by using the DB2 COPY utility. These can be supplemented with incremental image copies, which contain only the pages within each tablespace that have changed since the last full image copy was taken. Once these are available, you can recover the appropriate tables by just running the DB2 RECOVERY utility for those damaged tablespaces.

DB2 assists with BACKUP and RECOVERY by logging all changes that have been made to recoverable tablespaces, and by restoring any database to a consistent state after program or system abends. DB2 also records all of the information about any image copies that are taken. Thus, when a RECOVERY process is initiated, DB2 requests the most recent full image COPY, merges in all incremental image copies, rebuilds the tablespaces, reapplies any changes on the logs, and resets the catalog for DB2 to continue.

DB2 Backup and Recovery Overview

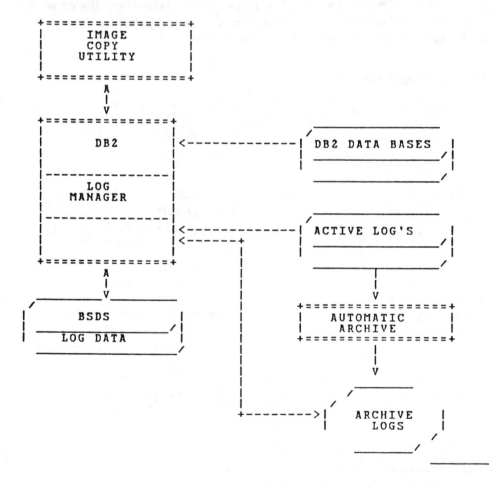

DB2 Backup Procedures

The backup process is a very critical part of the recovery process. Without the backups, it is possible that the only possible recovery that can be done is by using the full-volume backups. This will cause some degree of loss of data and possibly many problems related to synchronization of the data through the DB2 subsystem, depending upon the way in which the full-volume backups were done, and what type of restoration procedure was followed. With the implementation of a DB2 backup procedure and the use of the DB2 logging system, almost any recovery requirement can be met with very little to no loss of data by both system and user, and reduced downtime.

Types of DB2 BACKUP procedures include:

- Full image copy backups
- Incremental backups
- Merging backups
- Directory backups
- System table backups
- User table backups

Full image copy backups.   The full image copy backup is part of the DB2 COPY utility. It takes a copy of every DB2 page in a tablespace and places it into another file (either Tape, DASD, MSS, etc.).

Full image copy JCL is shown in Appendix 64.

Incremental backups.   The incremental backup differs from the full image copy in that it only copies those DB2 pages which have changed since the last image copy (either full or incremental). When tables get large and time for backups becomes limited, this process in conjunction with the MERGECOPY (which is described next) will become the BACKUP process.

Merging backups.   The MERGECOPY process creates a new full image copy backup by combining the last successful full image copy backup with all incremental copy backups that have occurred for the requested tablespaces.

Directory backups.   The DB2 directory backup is different from the rest of the backups throughout DB2 in that the COPY process must be a full image copy process, not incremental, and only a person defined with SYSADM authority or the installation defined SYSOPR can run the job. This is because the directory database (DSNDB01) is not defined in the DB2 system catalog, and thus authority to run the IMAGCOPY cannot be granted.

System catalog backups.   The system catalog backups are run as any other backup except that it must be remembered that parts of DB2 will be unavailable while it is running, and that this will cause some response problems. Only SYSADM personnel can run the job and those operations personnel granted the authority to run the production version of the backup job.

User table backups.   The user table backups are run as any other backup by the people who have been granted the authorization to run those backups:

in the production system, only people with SYSADM level authority and those personnel in production job control who have been granted the authority to run the production data backups.

DB2 Recovery Procedures

Determining what type of recovery is necessary. What type of error occurred will dictate what type of recovery must be done. The first thing to determine is what happened. The possible failures are the following:

- Hardware errors
- IRLM failure
- MVS failure
- CICS-related failures
- DB2 failure
- DB2 system resource failure
- DB2 database failures
- DB2 catalog or directory input/output errors
- Tablespace or indexspace input/output errors
- Out of space errors
- ICF catalog VSAM Volume Data Set (VVDS) failure
- Application program error
- 'Old Data' Restoration
  - Active log
  - Archive log
  - BSDS

Hardware errors. Failures in hardware per se will not be covered in this document because the recovery of a hardware error is dependent upon what part of the hardware crashed and what had to be done to recover that crash. The other part to consider is what, exactly, was done to recover from the crash, and you have to determine what part of the DB2 system was affected by the crash and recovery. What part was affected and the resultant error messages received will determine which of the following procedures will be used in the DB2 part of the recovery process.

DASD volume recovery. The one area to consider in checking out for initial recovery is: If it is determined that a volume indeed has been recovered, any DB2 data sets on those volumes will need to go through the appropriate recovery process. Determine which one to use by selecting the appropriate process from the following sections.

IRLM failure. Following are possible scenarios and the resulting operator action based upon the problem, associated symptoms, the system action, the operator response, and the DBA action.

PROBLEM: The IRLM fails in a wait, loop, or abend.

SYMPTOM: DB2 abends and the following message appears:
    DXR013E irlmname ABEND UNDER IRLM TCB/SRB

SYSTEM ACTION: If the IRLM abends, DB2 terminates. If the IRLM waits or loops, then terminate the IRLM, and DB2 will terminate automatically.

OPERATOR ACTION:
Cancel IRLM Address Space   'MODIFY IRLM,ABEND'
Start DB2 and IRLM   '-START DB2'
(This will also restart the IRLM)
Start CICS Attachment   'DSNC STRT'
If any of the restarts fail, operator must contact Systems or DBA.

SYSTEMS/DBA ACTION:
If DB2 comes up only partially, check JCL procedures and JES2 log for MVS and/or file-related messages. If DB2 goes into a wait state, probable error is region allocation and/or data set allocation problem. Check the JES2 log for problem.
If following occurs, refer to appropriate section:
CICS ATTACHMENT failure
    Check 'CICS Related Failures' section.

MVS failure.   Following are possible scenarios and the resulting operator action based upon the problem, associated symptoms, the system action, and the operator response.

PROBLEM: MVS or processor power fails.

SYMPTOM: No processing is occurring.

SYSTEM ACTION: None.

OPERATOR ACTION: IPL appropriate MVS system using standard procedures.
If DB2 fails to restart, operator must contact systems or DBA.

SYSTEMS/DBA ACTION: If DB2 comes up only partially, check JCL procedures and JES2 log for MVS and/or file-related messages. If DB2 goes into a wait state, probable error is region allocation and/or data set allocation problem. Check the JES2 log for problem.
If following occurs, refer to appropriate section:
CICS attachment failure
    Check 'CICS Related Failures' section.
Other Failures
    Refer to appropriate sections.

CICS-related failures.   Following are possible scenarios and the resulting operator action based upon the problem, associated symptoms, the system action, and the operator response.

CICS APPLICATION FAILURE.

PROBLEM: CICS application terminates abnormally.

SYMPTOM: The following message is sent to user's terminal.
DFH2206 TRAN tttt ABEND aaa BACKOUT SUCCESSFUL

SYSTEM ACTION: CICS and DB2 backout the failing task.

OPERATOR ACTION: If the abend code was AEY9, the CICS attachment was not up and must be started (DSNC STRT). For all others, refer to Systems and/or Development.

SYSTEMS/DBA ACTION: Check *IBM DATABASE 2 Diagnosis Guide* and/or *CICS/OS/VS Problem Determination Guide* for more diagnostic information.

CICS NOT OPERATIONAL.

PROBLEM: CICS region abends or is down.

SYMPTOM: CICS may be looping, in a wait state, or abending. Determine problem using standard CICS procedures and contact appropriate CICS support personnel.

SYSTEM ACTION: DB2 detects the abend and backs out in-flight work. DB2 also saves indoubt tasks to be resolved when CICS is reconnected.

OPERATOR ACTION: Contact Systems and/or Development to correct problem causing abend. Then do Emergency Restart of CICS. This is essential to put CICS and DB2 back into sync to prevent further problems. Then restart the CICS attachment. If this fails, contact Systems.

SYSTEMS/DBA ACTION: Using standard CICS procedures, resolve CICS problem and make sure operations does an Emergency Restart. If Emergency Restart is not successful, and it is determined that a Cold Start of CICS must be done, refer to 'CICS Cold Start' section for appropriate action.

CICS UNABLE TO CONNECT TO DB2.

PROBLEM: CICS region cannot attach to DB2.

SYMPTOM: CICS remains operative, but ATTACHMENT facility terminates abnormally. System will create dump and abend inflight threads. CICS issues message DFH2206.

SYSTEM ACTION: CICS backs out affected transaction.

OPERATOR ACTION: Contact Systems and/or Development to correct problem causing abend. Then restart CICS ATTACHMENT facility (-DSNC STRT). CICS will then resolve indoubt threads through information received from DB2.

SYSTEMS/DBA ACTION: Check system X'04E' dump for reason code on JES2 log or CICS job log. Check *DB2 Messages and Codes Manual* for definition and resolution of reason code that was issued. Make sure that the ATTACHMENT facility is restarted successfully. If ATTACHMENT facility fails to restart, check and resolve problem defined by the X'04E' dump and reason code.

CICS INDOUBT RESOLUTION FAILURE. Indoubt or abended threads that exist whenever CICS is started can fail to be resolved. The three cases of this problem are described below.

CICS COLD START

PROBLEM: CICS is cold-started and cannot resolve DB2 indoubt units of recovery.

SYMPTOM: The following message is sent to the terminal from which the -DSNC STRT command was entered:
DSNC001I CICS UR INDOUBT RESOLUTION IS INCOMPLETE FOR name

SYSTEM ACTION: The connection process continues as usual.

OPERATOR ACTION: Report problem to Systems/DBA.

SYSTEMS/DBA ACTION: Perform Emergency Restart of CICS if possible. If this is not possible, refer to *CICS Recovery and Restart Guide* in analyzing last CICS log and in determining what action to take. Also use the -DISPLAY THREAD INDOUBT command to find the current status of the DB2 indoubt units of recovery, and then issue the -RECOVER INDOUBT command to either commit or abort the threads that are indoubt. Most of the time you will probably want to abort the indoubt threads. MAKE SURE THAT YOU ARE CONNECTED TO CICS BEFORE ISSUING THE -RECOVER INDOUBT COMMAND!!!!!

DISAGREEMENT ABOUT COMMIT AND ABORT

PROBLEM: The final dispositions of CICS and DB2 are different.

SYMPTOM: The following message is sent to the terminal from which the -DSNC STRT command was entered:
DSNC036I INDOUBT RESOLUTION FOR name IS INCONSISTENT

SYSTEM ACTION: The connection process continues as usual.

OPERATOR ACTION: Report problem to Systems/DBA.

SYSTEMS/DBA ACTION: This situation occurs when a -RECOVER INDOUBT command was issued before CICS reconnects to DB2. DB2 will perform the final disposition which it contains, rather than CICS's. Either an ABORT or COMMIT from the DB2 side will be carried out. Use of the -RECOVER INDOUBT command will have no impact. Manual intervention in CICS and/or DB2 may be necessary to reach a consistent state. Watch for additional messages and respond appropriately.

DISAGREEMENT ABOUT WHICH UNITS ARE INDOUBT

PROBLEM: The CICS list of indoubt tasks does not match the corresponding DB2 indoubt list. This indicates an incorrect CICS restart.

SYMPTOM: One or both of the following messages are sent to the user's terminal.

DSNC034I INDOUBT RESOLUTION FOR name IS INCORRECT
DSNC034I INDOUBT RESOLUTION FOR name IS INCOMPLETE

SYSTEM ACTION: The connection process continues as usual.

OPERATOR ACTION: Report problem to Systems/DBA.

SYSTEMS/DBA ACTION: Refer to 'CICS Cold Start' section for action.

DB2 failure. Following are possible scenarios and the resulting operator action based upon the problem, associated symptoms, the system action, and the operator response.

PROBLEM: Subsystem termination has been initiated by DB2 or by an Operator CANCEL.

SYMPTOM: Subsystem termination occurs. Usually some specific is identified by DB2 messages and the following messages will appear:

DSNV086E—DB2 ABNORMAL TERMINATION REASON = xxxxxxxx
DSN3104I—DSN3EC00—TERMINATION COMPLETE
DSN3104I—DSN3EC00—SUBSYSTEM DB2 READY FOR -START COMMAND

SYSTEM ACTION: CICS will continue. In-process applications will receive SQL Return Code -923.

OPERATOR ACTION: Contact Systems/DBA.

SYSTEMS/DBA ACTION: Make sure that the SYS1.LOGREC gets printed, and collect other information to determine the reason for failure (console log, dump, and SYS1.LOGREC). Attempt to restart DB2 (-START DB2) and restart CICS ATTACHMENT facility (DSNC STRT).
If restart fails, check log for JCL and/or system resource failures. If other errors occur, refer to appropriate section.

DB2 system resource failure. Following are possible scenarios and the resulting operator action based upon the problem, associated symptoms, the system action, and the operator response for DB2 systems resource failures which are associated with the active log, the archive log, and the bootstrap data set (BSDS).

ACTIVE LOG. Four possible problems that are associated with the active log are defined below.

ACTIVE LOGS OUT OF SPACE

PROBLEM: Out of space in active logs. Caused by delays in off-loading. This condition should never occur.

SYMPTOM: The following message appears:
DSNJ111E—OUT OF SPACE IN ACTIVE LOG DATA SETS

SYSTEM ACTION: Normal shutdown not possible.

OPERATOR ACTION: If system is waiting for a tape mount, MOUNT THE TAPE. If you cannot mount a tape, report to Systems/DBA. Procedure should be to force DB2 down and restart DB2. Off-load will occur in start-up process, and work in progress will be recovered.

SYSTEMS/DBA ACTION: If tape mount fails, force down DB2 by using MVS CANCEL. To minimize archive mount requirements, define additional larger active log data sets. Restart DB2. The off-load will be initiated during start-up, and work in process when DB2 was forced down will be recovered.

DUAL LOGGING IS LOST

PROBLEM: Dual logging is lost.

SYMPTOM: The following message appears:
DSNJ004I—ACTIVE LOG COPYn INACTIVE, LOG IN SINGLE MODE, ENDRBA = ...

SYSTEM ACTION: Continue in single mode until off-loading completes. Then dual logging continues.

OPERATOR ACTION: Check that off-load is proceeding and not waiting for a tape mount. Report problem to Systems/DBA.

SYSTEMS/DBA ACTION: Make sure off-load of remaining log completes and that it is successful, and that dual logging gets restarted after the off-load is complete. Run PRINT LOG MAP utility (see Appendix 45 for JCL list and locations of Library and member name) to determine status of all data sets, and take appropriate action.

WRITE I/O ERROR ON AN ACTIVE LOG DATA SET

PROBLEM: Write I/O error on active log.

SYMPTOM: The following message appears:
DSNJ105I—module-name LOG WRITE ERROR DSNAME = ... ,
LOGRBA = . . . ,
ERROR STATUS = cccffss

SYSTEM ACTION: Continues processing and marks log as TRUNCATED and goes on to next log data set and sets up off-loading process.

OPERATOR ACTION: Report problem to Systems/DBA.

SYSTEMS/DBA ACTION: Make sure off-load of both logs occurs successfully. If errors continue on this file, DB2 needs to be taken down after the next off-load and to use Access Method Services and the CHANGE LOG INVENTORY utility (see Appendix 65 for JCL and procedure data set and member name) to add a replacement.

I/O ERRORS WHILE READING THE ACTIVE LOG

PROBLEM: I/O errors while reading the active log.

SYMPTOM: The following message appears:
    DSNJ105I—LOG READ ERROR DSNAME = . . . , LOGRBA = . . . ,
    ERROR STATUS = cccffss

SYSTEM ACTION: Continues processing and tries to use dual log copy.

OPERATOR ACTION: Report problem to Systems/DBA.

SYSTEMS/DBA ACTION: If second log has no error, processing will continue. When off-load occurs, the good log will be used for off-load. If both logs are bad, image copies of all affected tablespaces must be taken. (See Appendix 65 for JCL and procedure data set and member name). The log data set should be replaced as soon as possible if errors continue. (See previous section for details.)

ARCHIVE LOG. Three possible problems that are associated with the archive log are defined below.

ALLOCATION PROBLEMS

PROBLEM: Allocation problems.

SYMPTOM: The following message appears:
    DSNJ103E—LOG ALLOCATION ERROR DSNAME = dsname,
    ERROR STATUS = eeeeiiii
This message also may appear:
    DSNJ1115I—OFFLOAD FAILED, COULD NOT ALLOCATE AN AR-
    CHIVE DATA SET

SYSTEM ACTION: If RECOVERY is executing, the recovery will fail. If off-load is occurring, it will try again next time off-load is scheduled. Eventually, this must complete, or DB2 will stop.

OPERATOR ACTION: Check the allocation code and get problem resolved. Allocate necessary drives if needed, or else call Systems/DBA.

SYSTEMS/DBA ACTION: This will occur if the RECOVERY utility is executing. This recovery will fail. Ensure allocation problem has been resolved. Then check status of utilities by issuing the -DISPLAY UTILITY command. If utility is on hold, issue the -TERM UTILITY command and then resubmit the RECOVERY job.

WRITE I/O ERROR ON AN ARCHIVE LOG DURING OFF-LOAD

PROBLEM: Write I/O error on archive log.

SYMPTOM: No specific DB2 message. Following MVS error message may occur after a second attempt:
DSNJ114I—ERROR ON ARCHIVE DATA SET, OFF-LOAD CONTIN-UING WITH ONLY ONE ARCHIVE DATA SET BEING GENERATED

SYSTEM ACTION: Stops off-load and tries to start over.

OPERATOR ACTION: Ensure that there are no tape drive or tape problems.

SYSTEMS/DBA ACTION: This will occur only on off-load processing. The system will drop to single mode and only off-load one copy of the log. If it fails again, the off-load will be terminated until it tries again later. The log being off-loaded will not be deleted or overwritten. Make sure that any hardware or tape problems are resolved. Off-loads must be successful, or eventually the DB2 subsystem will stop.

READ I/O ERRORS ON ARCHIVE DATA SETS WHILE USING RECOVER

PROBLEM: I/O errors while reading the archive log using RECOVER.

SYMPTOM: No error message is issued, only the MVS error recovery program message in the RECOVERY job.

SYSTEM ACTION: If second copy exists, it will be used; otherwise, recovery fails.

OPERATOR ACTION: Report problem to Systems/DBA.

SYSTEMS/DBA ACTION: This will occur when a RECOVER utility is being run. The system will automatically mount the second log copy. If this also fails, one of the tapes needs to be recovered using some form of tape recovery system. Also check for failing hardware or dirty hardware.

BSDS. Following are possible scenarios and the resulting operator action based upon the problem, associated symptoms, the system action, and the operator response for DB2 systems resource failures which are associated with the bootstrap data set (BSDS).

BSDS FAILURE AT STARTUP TIME

PROBLEM: Failure of BSDS at startup time.

SYMPTOM: The following message appears:
DSNJ100I—ERROR OPENING BSDSn DSNAME = . . . , ERROR
STATUS = . . .

SYSTEM ACTION: DB2 Startup is terminated.

OPERATOR ACTION: Report to Systems/DBA.

SYSTEMS/DBA ACTION: This is a VSAM error. The error status listed above is VSAM return code/feedback. For further information, check the *VSAM Programmer's Guide*. When Dual BSDS is active, the BSDS mode will change from dual to single. Then use Access Method Services to rename or delete, and then define a new BSDS with the same name as the failing BSDS. Then issue the -RECOVER BSDS command, which will make a copy of the good BSDS into the new one. This will then reinstate the dual BSDS mode. (See Appendix 45 for JCL and Procedure data set and member name.)

If in single mode and recovery is necessary, the following must be done:

1. Find the BSDS which is associated with the most recent archive log data set (check system log—DSNJ003I message). BSDS will be first data set on log tape. Name of archive log is same as BSDS except that last data set qualifier begins with 'B' for the BSDS and 'A' for the archive log.
2. Use Access Method Services REPRO command to restore the copy of the BSDS from the archive log on tape to a VSAM data set.
3. After the BSDS restore, update it by using the Change Log Inventory to add the archive log that was used to restore the BSDS and to add to the BSDS the record of each change that occurred after the BSDS was archived.
4. Restart DB2. The log manager determines the current RBA and what active logs need to be archived.

(See Appendix 46 for JCL and procedure data set and member name definitions.)

BSDS CONTROL TIME STAMPS DIFFER

PROBLEM: Dual BSDS data sets have differing control time stamps.

SYMPTOM: The following message appears:
DSNJ120I—DUAL BSDS DATA SETS HAVE UNEQUAL TIME STAMPS

SYSTEM ACTION: DB2 startup is terminated. Perform BSDS off-line recovery.

OPERATOR ACTION: Report to Systems.

SYSTEMS/DBA ACTION: This is an error caused by either improper volume recovery without BSDS recovery, dual mode dropping to single mode without being noticed, or when BSDSs are from different systems. To resolve the first problem, do the following:
Assuming the volume has been restored to a back-level, all tablespace

data on that volume must be recovered after a successful DB2 restart. The BSDS must be recovered as described in the previous section. If an active log is on this volume, the correct version must be repro'd using Access Method Services into the version on this volume. If there is a valid version available of the log, you must recover using the procedures outlined in the 'Failure Resulting from Total or Excessive Loss of Log Data.'

In resolving the next two problems, recover the BSDS using the procedure defined in the previous section.

BSDS CONTROL RECORDS DIFFER

PROBLEM: BSDS Control Records differ.

SYMPTOM: The following message appears:
DSNJ122E—DUAL BSDS DATA SETS ARE OUT OF SYNCHRONIZATION

SYSTEM ACTION: DB2 startup processing is terminated.

OPERATOR ACTION: Report problem to Systems/DBA.

SYSTEMS/DBA ACTION: This is an error caused by improper use of the CHANGE LOG INVENTORY utility. Perform the BSDS recover procedure defined in the previous sections.

BSDS RECORDS ARE IN ERROR

PROBLEM: BSDS records are in error.

SYMPTOM: The following message appears:
DSNJ102I—LOG RBA CONTENT OF LOG DATA SET
  DSNAME = . . . ,
STARTRBA = . . . , ENDRBA = . . . ,
DOES NOT AGREE WITH BSDS INFORMATION

SYSTEM ACTION: DB2 startup processing is terminated.

OPERATOR ACTION: Report problem to Systems/DBA.

SYSTEMS/DBA ACTION: This is an error caused by improper use of the CHANGE LOG INVENTORY utility, or volume recovery has taken place. Use the PRINT LOG MAP utility and the CHANGE LOG INVENTORY utility to correct the contents of the BSDS.

DB2 database failures. Following are possible scenarios and the resulting operator action based upon the problem, associated symptoms, the system action, and the operator response for DB2 database failures.

PROBLEM: Allocation/Open problems occur.

SYMPTOM: The following message appears:

DSNB207I—DYNAMIC ALLOCATION OF DATA SET FAILED. REA-
SON = rrr. DSNAME = dsnname
If there are open problems, the following messages appear:
IEC161I . . . . REASON = xx
DSNB204I—OPEN OF DATASET FAILED. DSNAME = dsn

SYSTEM ACTION: Tablespace is stopped, and programs receive the
SQL return code -904.

OPERATOR ACTION: Ensure that related drives are available for allocation, and inform Systems/DBA.

SYSTEMS/DBA ACTION: Check reason codes and correct. Ensure that
requested disk drives are available and online. Then give the command
-START DATABASE xxxxxxxxx to get the affected tablespaces back into
DB2 as active and available.

DB2 catalog or directory input/output errors.   Following are possible scenarios and the resulting operator action based upon the problem, associated
symptoms, the system action, and the operator response for DB2 catalog or
directory input/output errors.

PROBLEM: The DB2 catalog or directory failed.

SYMPTOM: One of the following messages appears:
DSNU086I—DSNUCDA1 READ I/O ERRORS ON SPACE =
dddddddddd
   DATA SET NUMBER = nnn
   I/O ERROR PAGE RANGE = aaaaaa,bbbbbb
DSNU086I—DSNUCDA1 WRITE I/O ERRORS ON SPACE =
dddddddddd
   DATA SET NUMBER = nnn
   I/O ERROR PAGE RANGE = aaaaaa,bbbbbb

SYSTEM ACTION: DB2 remains active.

OPERATOR ACTION: Inform Systems/DBA.

SYSTEMS/DBA ACTION: Only the person with overall SYSADM authority can run the RECOVER procedure that is necessary to recover
these DB2 system catalog and directory tablespaces. The procedures below must be followed:

1. Stop the failing tablespaces and indexspaces.
2. Determine the data set(s) that failed.
   a. If more than one data set failed, perform the following steps
      on the failed tablespaces in the stated order:
      DSNDB01.SYSUTIL
      DSNDB01.DBD01

DSNDB06.SYSCOPY
SYSIBM.DSNUCH01
DSNDB01.SYSLGRNG
DSNDB06.SYSDBAUTH
SYSIBM.DSNADX01
DSNDB06.SYSUSER
DSNDB06.SYSDBASE
SYSIBM.DSNDSX01
Other catalog and directory tablespaces and indexes
User tablespaces

3. Use Access Method Services DELETE to delete the data set.

4. Use Access Method Services DEFINE to redefine the same data set.

5. Issue the command -START DATABASE ACCESS(UT) naming the tablespace involved.

6. Use the RECOVER utility to recover the tablespace that failed.

7. Give the command -START DATABASE specifying the appropriate tablespace name.
(See Appendices 40 and 30 for procedure data sets and member names for Access Method Services. Also see Appendices 54 and 55 for RECOVERY procedures.)

Tablespace or indexspace input/output errors. Following are possible scenarios and the resulting operator action based upon the problem, associated symptoms, the system action, and the operator response for DB2 user tablespace or indexspace input/output errors.

PROBLEM: A tablespace or indexspace has failed.

SYMPTOM: One of the following messages appears.
DSNU086I—DSNUCDA1 READ I/O ERRORS ON SPACE= dddddddddd
  DATA SET NUMBER= nnn
  I/O ERROR PAGE RANGE= aaaaaa,bbbbbb
DSNU086I—DSNUCDA1 WRITE I/O ERRORS ON SPACE= dddddddddd
  DATA SET NUMBER= nnn
  I/O ERROR PAGE RANGE= aaaaaa,bbbbbb

SYSTEM ACTION: DB2 remains active.

OPERATOR ACTION: Inform Systems/DBA.

SYSTEMS/DBA ACTION: Determine whether the failing space is a tablespace or indexspace.

FAILING INDEXSPACE:

1. Stop the failing indexspace using the DB2 -STOP DATABASE command.
2. Determine the data set(s) that failed.
   If the indexspace is supported by installation-managed data sets, do the following:
   a. Use Access Method Services DELETE to delete the data set.
   b. Use Access Method Services DEFINE to redefine the same data set.
   c. Issue the command -START DATABASE ACCESS(UT) naming the indexspace involved.
   d. Use the RECOVER INDEX utility.
   e. Give the command -START DATABASE specifying the indexspace name.

   If the indexspace is supported by STOGROUPS, do the following:
   a. Issue the command -START DATABASE ACCESS(UT) naming the indexspace involved.
   b. Use the RECOVER INDEX utility.
   c. Give the command -START DATABASE specifying the indexspace name.

   (See Appendix 68 for Sample JCL for Index Recovery. Also see Appendices 39, 40, 41, and 42 for Access Method Services Sample JCL.)

FAILING TABLESPACE:

1. Stop the failing tablespace using the DB2 -STOP DATABASE command.
2. Determine the data set(s) that failed.
3. Issue the command -START DATABASE ACCESS(UT) naming the tablespace involved.
4. Initiate a RECOVER utility step to recover the error range involved by using the -RECOVER TABLESPACE (tablespace) ERROR RANGE command
   If a message is received indicating that the error range recovery did not succeed, continue with Step 6.
5. Issue the command -START DATABASE to start the tablespace. Everything should be recovered, and the recovery process is over.
6. If the error range recovery of the tablespace failed because there were too few alternate tracks, or if a data set within a tablespace has been lost, proceed as follows:

a. Use the -STOP DATABASE command to stop the tablespace. If the indexspace is supported by installation-managed data sets, do the following:

    a. Use Access Method Services DELETE to delete the data set.

    b. Use Access Method Services DEFINE to redefine the same data set.

    c. Issue the command -START DATABASE ACCESS(UT) naming the tablespace involved.

    d. Use the RECOVER TABLESPACE utility.

    e. Give the command -START DATABASE specifying the tablespace name.

If the Indexspace is supported by STOGROUPS, do the following:

    a. Issue the command -START DATABASE ACCESS(UT) naming the indexspace involved.

    b. Use the RECOVER TABLESPACE utility.

    c. Give the command -START DATABASE specifying the indexspace name.

(See Appendix 42 for Procedure data sets and member names for Access Method Services. Also see Appendix 56 for recovery procedures.)

Out of space errors. Following are possible scenarios and the resulting operator action based upon the problem, associated symptoms, the system action, and the operator response for DB2 tables that run out of space.

PROBLEM: Out of space.

SYMPTOM: One of the following messages appears:

1. Demand Request Failure:
   DSNP007I—DSNPmmmm—EXTENT FAILED FOR
   data-set-name. RC = rrrrrrrr
   CONNECTION-ID = xxxxxxxx,
   CORRELATION-ID = yyyyyyyy

2. Look Ahead Warning:
   DSNP007I—DSNPmmmm—data-set-name IS WITHIN
   n KBYTES OF AVAILABLE SPACE.
   RC = rrrrrrrr
   CONNECTION-ID = xxxxxxxx,
   CORRELATION-ID = yyyyyyyy

SYSTEM ACTION: DB2 remains active but affected Demand Request Failure tablespaces will be stopped. Look Ahead Warning data sets must be expanded.

OPERATOR ACTION: Inform Systems/DBA.

SYSTEMS/DBA ACTION: Determine which of the following conditions exists and perform the resulting procedure:

Database qualifier is DSNDB07:

1. Give the command -STOP DATABASE (DSNDB07).
2. Add space for extension of the storage group by one of the following:
   a. Use SQL to alter the storage group adding additional volumes.
   b. Use SQL to create more tablespaces in database DSNDB07.
3. Give the command -START DATABASE (DSNDB07).

Data set has NOT reached maximum VSAM extents (check VTOC for this information).

1. If data set is user-defined, provide more VSAM space using Access Method Services ALTER ADDVOLUMES command or make room on current volume by deleting or moving other data sets that are on this volume.
2. If data set is defined in a storage group, add more volumes to the storage group by using the SQL ALTER STOGROUP statement.

Data set HAS reached maximum number of VSAM extents.

1. If data set is user-defined, do the following:
   a. Make sure that an image copy is done first.
   b. Use the -STOP DATABASE SPACENAM for the last data set of the object that has grown too large.
   c. Use Access Method Services DELETE to delete the data set.
   d. Use Access Method Services DEFINE to redefine the same data set (make it larger).
   e. Issue the command -START DATABASE ACCESS(UT) naming the indexspace involved.
   f. Use the RECOVER utility specifying the DSNUM option.
   g. Give the command -START DATABASE for the object.

   The REORGANIZATION utility may be the better option if the objects being expanded are small or if there is time to do it instead of the RECOVER method shown above. See 'DB2 Reorganization Utility' section of this document for more information.

2. If data set is defined in a storage group, do the following:
   a. Use SQL to create a table (B) identical to the one needing enlargement (A).

b. Use SQL to copy the data from A to B.

c. Drop the old tablespace. (Remember to get listing of existing authorizations, indexes, views, synonyms so that they can be redefined, as all of these will disappear with the drop.)

d. Redefine the tablespace, indexes, and table (New A) with a new STOGROUP and/or different PRIQTY and SECQTY values.

e. Use SQL to copy the data in B to New A.

f. Recreate all necessary views, indexes, and synonyms.

g. Regrant authorization.

(See Appendices 42, 56, 57, 58, and 64 for sample JCL.)

ICF catalog VSAM volume data set (VVDS) failure. Following are possible scenarios and the resulting operator action based upon the problem, associated symptoms, the system action, and the operator response for situations involving the failure of ICF catalog VSAM Volume Data Sets (VVDS).

PROBLEM: VSAM Volume Data Set (VVDS) is either out of space or destroyed.

SYMPTOM: The following message from DB2 will appear:
DSNP012I—DSNPSCT0—ERROR IN VSAM CATALOG LOCATE FUNCTION
FOR data-set-name
   CTLGRC = 50
   CTLGRSN = zzzRRRR
   CONNECTION-ID = xxxxxxxx,
   CORRELATION-ID = yyyyyyyy
VSAM may also issue the following message:
   IDC30009I VSAM CATALOG RETURN CODE IS 50, REASON CODE
     IS IGGOCLaa - yy
In this VSAM message, yy is 28, 30, or 32 for an out-of-space condition. Any other values indicate a damaged VVDS.

SYSTEM ACTION: Your program is terminated abnormally.

OPERATOR ACTION: Inform Systems/DBA.

SYSTEMS/DBA ACTION: Recovery of the VVDS or basic catalog structure needs to be performed by a systems programmer with appropriate knowledge. For further information, consult the following manual:
   MVS/XA Catalog User's Guide

DB2 related actions:

1. Use DB2 COPY to take image copies of all tablespaces on the affected volume(s).

2. If the COPY utility cannot be used, continue as follows:

3. Give command -STOP DATABASE for affected tablespaces, or -STOP DB2 entirely.

4. If possible, use Access Method Services to export all non-DB2 data sets off of the affected volume.

5. Use appropriate *Catalog Administration User's Guide* recovery procedures to recover all non-DB2 data sets.

6. Use Access Method Services DELETE and DEFINE commands to delete and redefine the data sets for all user-defined or installation-managed DB2 tablespaces. If they are STOGROUP defined, DB2 takes care of them automatically.

7. Issue the DB2 -START DATABASE command to restart previously stopped tablespaces. If DB2 itself was stopped, restart DB2.

8. Use DB2 RECOVER utility to recover any tablespaces and indexes. See 'DB2 Recovery Procedures' section for information.

Other recovery scenarios.   Other possible recovery scenarios are combinations of the above or are highly involved and require special processing. Further information on these and on overall recovery can be found in the following manual:

- SC26-4083 *IBM DATABASE 2 Operations and Recovery Guide (Version 1)*
- SC26-4374 *IBM DATABASE 2 System and Database Administration Guide (Version 2)*

Application program error.   Following are possible scenarios and the resulting operator action based upon the problem, associated symptoms, the system action, and the operator response.

PROBLEM: An application program placed an incorrect value in a table. (This is not for restoration of 'Old Data' that is needed from some distant past. See " 'Old Data' Restoration" section for those procedures.)

SYMPTOM: SQL SELECT returns unexpected data.

SYSTEM ACTION: None. Problem is not DB2.

OPERATOR ACTION: None. Refer to SYSTEMS/DBA.

SYSTEMS/DBA ACTION: The process involved in recovering partially or completely from an application-caused error depends upon two things:

1. When the error was noted.

2. What type of damage was done.

If it is an update error or invalid values of certain data were put into the database, the use of SQL through SPUFI or through an application program may be used to resolve the problem.

If it is an insert problem for particular rows, and if those rows are known, they can be deleted and/or updated through SPUFI, QMF, or an application program.

If the problem is that certain rows were deleted that should not have been, the recovery mode becomes very complex. Following is the scenario for a situation in which many rows were inadvertently deleted and the action was not determined to have happened for many days. In this scenario, you have the following requirements:

1. Find and reinsert the deleted records.

2. Keep records that have been added and updated since.

3. Make sure the resulting tables are what you want.

To do this, the following processes must be executed:

1. Determine which tables are in error.

2. Stop the tablespace(s) that are in error.

3. Start the tablespaces for utility-only access:
   -START DATABASE (database) SPACENAM (tablespace) AC-CESS (UT)

4. Perform full image copies on all affected tablespaces.

5. Estimate the time of the application error and find the RBA from the image copy down before that time by selecting the appropriate columns from the SYSIBM.SYSCOPY table. Execute following SQL Statement: SELECT TSNAME, DBNAME, DSNUM, ICTYPE, ICDATE, START_RBA
   FROM SYSIBM.SYSCOPY
   WHERE TSNAME = 'tablespace' ;
   Substitute the impacted tablespace names for tablespace above.

6. By using the DSN1LOGP program, you must find the RBA of the DB2 application and/or user that actually performed the delete of the needed rows. (DB2 will have to be stopped to perform this process if you have to access the current active log.) Use as a START RBA the appropriate RBA found from the query above.

7. Once the RBA of the offending application has been found, restart DB2, stop and restart the affected tablespaces as described above, and then run the RECOVER utility using the TORBA option using the RBA of the offending application.

8. Now execute a full image copy to reset each affected tablespace.

9. If the delete was found quickly and if no intervening updates occurred, you can now restart the affected tablespaces.

-START DATABASE (database) SPACENAM (tablespace) AC-
CESS (RW)

If interim updates have occurred and CANNOT be recreated, you
must now perform the process described in the " 'Old Data' Restoration" section of this manual.

'Old Data' restoration. Following are three possible procedures that can
be used in the restoration of 'old data,' or data that needs to be recovered from
some past version which makes the application error procedures impossible
or, at the least, extremely difficult to do, and in which recreation of the data
from another source is also extremely difficult or impossible. These procedures
also assume the unavailability of an application archive facility.

Each procedure is based upon availability of appropriate DB2 image copies, or,
in the case of scenario 3, the availability of system volume backups. Without these,
no recovery is possible!!!

Before this procedure is attempted, any and all data relationships that exist must
be analyzed to make sure that those relationships remain intact—otherwise database integrity could be lost!!!!!

OLD DATA—TABLE STRUCTURE UNCHANGED. This procedure for restoring old data assumes that the lost data is on an image copy that is based
upon the currently existing tables. No drops or changes to the tables have
occurred.

1. Stop tablespaces that need to be recovered.
2. Restart tablespaces for utility-only access.
3. Use DB2 COPY utility to take full image copies of all affected table-
    spaces.
4. Check the SYSIBM.SYSCOPY table for the appropriate data set name
    and volume serial number that the data to be restored from is on.
5. Use DB2 RECOVER utility using TOCOPY option specifying the ap-
    propriate image copy that is desired.
6. Unload the data that is to be restored using either the UNLOAD
    program, SPUFI, QMF, or an application program. Which one to be
    used will depend upon the amount of data, type of data, size, and what
    exactly you are trying to reload—full rows, columns, etc. This data
    needs to be placed into a sequential data set in a format in which it
    can be reloaded using the LOAD utility, SPUFI, QMF, or an application
    program.

7. Execute the standard DB2 RECOVER for the tablespaces affected. This will use the latest image copy to recover, which will be the one done in Step 3 of this section.

8. Restart the affected tablespaces normally.

9. Reinsert or update the data that was unloaded at this time in the way that was determined earlier.

OLD DATA—TABLE STRUCTURE HAS CHANGED. This procedure for restoring old data assumes that the lost data is on an image copy that is based upon a PREVIOUS table structure—a drop or change has occurred to the tables involved, and the DB2 recovery procedures CANNOT be used.

1. Create new tables to match the tables that the image copy that is selected was copied from. (To do this, you must have kept a listing of the original CREATE source, or actually save the CREATE source for every change. You also MUST KEEP the OBIDs for the original tablespace on file).

2. Execute the following SQL to determine the necessary OBIDs for the next step. This should also be executed before any tables get dropped.
SELECT DBID, PSID FROM SYSIBM.SYSTABLESPACE
   WHERE NAME = ' tablespace-name '
    AND CREATOR = ' creator-name ' ;
SELECT NAME, OBID FROM SYSIBM.SYSTABLES
   WHERE TSNAME = ' tablespace-name '
    AND CREATOR = ' creator-name ' ;
This will give you the OBIDs needed for the OBID conversion mentioned below as part of the DSN1COPY utility.

3. Check the SYSIBM.SYSCOPY table for the appropriate data set name and volume serial number that the data to be restored from is on.

4. Execute the DSN1COPY utility using the OBIDXLAT option and using the selected image copy data set as input and the new tablespace created in Setup 1 as output. The results of these SELECTs will be the input necessary for the OBIDXLAT option and the SYSXLAT input file.

5. Unload the data that is to be restored using either the UNLOAD program, SPUFI, QMF, or an application program. Which one to be used will depend upon the amount of data, type of data, size, and what exactly you are trying to reload—full rows, columns, etc. This data needs to be placed into a sequential data set in a format in which it can be reloaded using the LOAD utility, SPUFI, QMF, or an application program.

6. Restart the affected tablespaces normally.

7. Reinsert or update the data that was unloaded at this time in the way that was determined earlier.

8. After checking to make sure everything is all right, drop the tables created earlier.

OLD DATA—NO IMAGE COPY—SYSTEM BACKUP MUST BE USED. This procedure for restoring old data assumes that no image copy is available, but that a system volume backup is available from a file-based DASD backup product such as DFDSS.

1. Find the necessary backup version and file using the facilities provided with the DASD backup software.

2. Restore selected DB2 data set to a DASD volume using the RENAME option of the backup software, making sure that you do not choose a name that already exists.

3. Create new tables to match the tables that you have just restored. Also, you must have access to the OBIDs that are in this table that was just restored.

4. Execute the following SQL to determine the OBIDs that are necessary for the next step. This should also be executed before any tables get dropped.
   SELECT DBID, PSID FROM SYSIBM.SYSTABLESPACE
      WHERE NAME = ' tablespace-name '
      AND CREATOR = ' creator-name ' ;
   SELECT NAME, OBID FROM SYSIBM.SYSTABLES
      WHERE TSNAME = ' tablespace-name '
      AND CREATOR = ' creator-name ' ;
   This will give you the OBIDs needed for the OBID conversion mentioned below as part of the DSN1COPY utility.

5. Execute the DSN1COPY utility using the OBIDXLAT option and using the restored DB2 VSAM data set as input and the new tablespace created in Step 1 as output. The results of the SELECTs above will be the input necessary for the OBIDXLAT option and the SYSXLAT input file.

6. Unload the data that is to be restored using either the UNLOAD program, SPUFI, QMF, or an application program. Which one to be used will depend upon the amount of data, type of data, size, and what exactly you are trying to reload—full rows, columns, etc. This data needs to be placed into a sequential data set in a format in which it can be reloaded using the LOAD utility, SPUFI, QMF or an application program.

7. Restart the affected tablespaces normally.

8. Reinsert or update the data that was unloaded at this time in the way that was determined earlier.

9. After checking to make sure everything is all right, drop and delete (using Access Method Services) the tablespaces and data sets created earlier.

USING DB2 UTILITIES

Nonstandard DB2 utilities

DSNTIAUL—generic unload procedure. DSNTIAUL, a generic unload procedure, has been granted to all for public usage. It uses Dynamic SQL and creates DB2 LOAD utility statements.

DSNTIAD—generic dynamic SQL program. DSNTIAD is a generic Dynamic SQL program that is like SPUFI but is run in batch mode under IKJEFT01. It uses Dynamic SQL and inputs SQL statements through SYSIN.

DSNTEP2—generic dynamic SQL program. DSNTEP2 is a generic dynamic SQL program that is like SPUFI but is run in batch mode under IKJEFT01. It uses Dynamic SQL and inputs SQL statements through SYSIN.

Standard DB2 Utilities

DB2 reorganization utility (REORG). There will be the necessity from time to time to use the REORG utility to reorganize various DB2 and user tablespaces. Following is the process necessary to be performed in order to determine when to actually do a reorganization, and the procedures necessary for that process.

PURPOSE OF DB2 REORGANIZATION. The purpose of the reorganization is to improve access performance of tablespaces and to reorganize indexes so that they will be more efficiently clustered.

DETERMINING WHEN TO DO A REORGANIZATION. You can determine when to do a reorganization of either tablespaces or indexes by examining various columns in DB2 system tables and checking for certain values. This can be done by executing the following SQL statements:

```
SELECT CARD, NEARINDREF, FARINDREF
FROM SYSIBM.SYSTABLEPART
```

A resultant large number in FARINDREF indicates that I/O activity on the tablespace is high because rows are farther from their original insert area because varying length changes have caused these rows to be moved. Tables with these large values are candidates for reorganization.

Execute this SQL statement:

```
SELECT PERCDROP
FROM SYSIBM.SYSTABLEPART
```

You can thus determine which tablespaces have a large amount of 'dead' space that has been caused by tables within the tablespace being dropped. 'Dead' space from dropped tables is only recovered through the REORG utility.

Execute this SQL statement:

SELECT NEAROFFPOS, FAROFFPOS
FROM SYSIBM.SYSINDEXPART

You can thus determine if your data is clustered based upon your primary or clustered index. A high number for FAROFFPOS shows that your data is not clustered, and that a REORG of that tablespace could help performance. However, if the tablespace contains more than one table, the REORG will not help.

Execute this SQL statement:

SELECT LEAFDIST
FROM SYSIBM.SYSINDEXPART

You can thus determine if your index I/O is excessive because a distribution of index values is spread across multiple pages as far as the order in which the index is accessed. This is shown by a high number for LEAFDIST, and if the value is increasing, a reorganization of the index might help performance.

You should be aware that as this is running, you will have no access or read-only access to the affected tablespace and/or indexspace depending upon what step the REORG is in.

CHECK utility.   The CHECK utility is used to check whether indexes are consistent with the data that they index, and issues warning messages when it finds an inconsistency. DB2 allows concurrent read-only access while CHECK is executing, so you must be careful when you execute this. Large tables could result in long update lockouts.

DIAGNOSE utility.   The DIAGNOSE utility is used to generate information used in diagnosing certain problems that may occur in DB2. Use of it may be requested by the IBM Support Center in an effort to resolve particularly difficult problems.

This is run as other utilities are run (either online or batch) as the DB2 System is operational.

Authorization level for the individual running it must have REPAIR abililty as a minimum.

See Appendix 51 for sample jobstream.

LOAD utility.   The LOAD utility is used to load data into one or more tables that reside in a tablespace or partition. The LOAD DATA statement describes the data that is to be loaded and provides information necessary for allocating resources. The loaded data will be processed by any existing VALIDPROCS or EDITPROCS. No concurrent processing is allowed on the tablespace or partition being loaded.

MODIFY utility. The MODIFY utility is used to delete unwanted copies from the SYSIBM.SYSCOPY catalog table and records of related log records from the SYSIBM.SYSLGRNG directory. Records can be removed that existed before a specific date or that exceed a certain age.

DB2 Performance Monitor. The DB2 Performance Monitor is a product that extracts trace records from DB2 that are placed into the operating system's System Monitoring Facility (SMF) files. These traces are of three types: statistical, accounting, and performance. The Performance Monitor extracts the DB2 records and manipulates them to produce reports. Only a person with specific system level access can run this job.

For further information, refer to the Database 2 Performance Monitor (DB2PM) manuals.

QUIESCE utility. QUIESCE is a utility that became available with Version 2.1 of DB2. This utility establishes a quiesce point (which is defined as the current RBA) for one or more TABLESPACEs that have associated Referential Integrity dependencies and records this in the SYSIBM.SYSCOPY DB2 Catalog Table. This provides a point from which to recover effectively and correctly all related tablespaces within a referentially integrated group of tables.

This is run as other utilities are run (either online or batch) as the DB2 System is operational.

Authorization level for the individual running it must have IMAGCOPY ability as a minimum.

See Appendix 52 for sample jobstream.

REPAIR utility. The REPAIR utility is used to repair data and is to be used only in very controlled or extreme circumstances. It can be used to repair any data in DB2. Improper use can cause even further damage.

REPORT utility. The REPORT Utility produces reports about TABLESPACEs containing the following:

1. RECOVERY history.
2. Log ranges.
3. Archive data set volume serial numbers.
4. Names of all TABLESPACEs and TABLES in a TABLESPACE SET.

This is run as other utilities are run (either online or batch) as the DB2 system is operational.

Authorization level for the individual running it must have RECOVERDB ability as a minimum.

See Appendix 53 for sample jobstream.

RUNSTATS utility. The RUNSTATS utility is used to scan a tablespace or indexes to gather information about utilization of space and efficiency of indexes. This information is then recorded into the DB2 catalog and is then used by the SQL optimizer to select access paths during the BIND process. It is available to be used in evaluating data base design and in determining when tablespaces and/or indexes need to be reorganized. DB2 allows concurrent access while RUNSTATS is being run. It should be run after a LOAD, or after a large amount of insert, delete, and update activity has occurred, and after indexes have been added or dropped. All related plans should then be rebound.

STOSPACE utility. The STOSPACE utility is used to update DB2 catalog columns that tell how much space is allocated for storage groups and related tablespaces and indexes. DB2 allows concurrent access when STOSPACE is running.

DSN1PRNT service aid. The DSN1PRNT utility is used to print out any DB2 data page. This is essentially a VSAM RECORD PRINT utility.

DSN1COPY service aid. The DSN1COPY Service Aid allows the following to be performed:

- Copy DB2 VSAM data sets to Sequential Data Sets.
- Copy Sequential Data Sets to VSAM Data Sets.
- Copy VSAM to other VSAM.
- Copy Sequential to other Sequential Data Sets.
- OBID Translation when copying DB2 VSAM to another DB2 VSAM.
- Prints Hexadecimal Dumps of DB2 Data Sets.
- Perform validity checking on Data or INDEX pages.

DSN1COPY is run as an MVS jobstream and can only be run when the DB2 VSAM Data sets to be processed are not allocated to DB2.
See Appendix 67 for sample jobstream.

DSN1LOGP service aid. The DSN1LOGP Service Aid reads and formats the DB2 Recovery Log for display. Either a Detail or Summary report can be selected. It is used to find information needed primarily for a Point-in-Time Recovery process.
DSN1LOGP is run as an MVS jobstream and can only be run when DB2 subsystem to be accessed is NOT OPERATIONAL.
See Appendix 45 for sample jobstream.

DSN1CHKR service aid. The DSN1CHKR Service Aid is used to verify that the integrity of DB2 Catalog and Directory TABLESPACEs has not been compromised. It scans the requested TABLESPACE for the following:

1. Broken Links
2. Hash Chains
3. Orphans (records that are not part of any link or chain)

DSN1CHKR is run as a MVS job against a selected TABLESPACE while DB2 is operational.

See Appendix 43 for sample jobstream.

Print log map (DSNJU004) utility. The PRINT LOG MAP utility lists the following:

1. Log Data Set Name and RBA association for all active and archive log data sets.
2. Passwords for the log data sets if they exist.
3. Active Logs available for Data.
4. Status of Restart records in the Bootstrap Data Set (BSDS).
5. Contents of Checkpoint Record Queue in BSDS.

DSNJU004 is run as an MVS Job against a selected DB2 while it is operational.

See Appendix 66 for sample jobstream.

PRODUCTION TURNOVER PROCEDURES

General Issues

The following areas need to be considered and resolved in the production turnover of DB2-based applications:

1. Site production control requirements
2. Site job scheduling requirements
3. All DB2 program requirements
   a. Backup and Recovery
   b. Migration from test to production
   c. DB2 Performance Impact Document
   d. DB2 Capacity Impact Document
4. Batch DB2 requirements
5. CICS DB2 requirements
6. TSO/ISPF DB2 requirements

Production Control Requirements

Existing production control requirements. Existing production control requirements need to be followed as they are currently in existence as specified for the appropriate system—Batch, TSO/ISPF, CICS.

DB2-only production control requirements. To complete the production implementation of DB2 systems, the following additional steps need to be taken:

SPECIAL DB2 PRODUCTION LIBRARIES. As far as the standard production turnover is to be considered, two separate libraries for each production library set need to be created. These libraries are as follows:

1. DB2 RUNLIB Library
2. DB2 DBRM Library

These libraries are used in the BIND process of DB2 and in the actual execution of DB2 applications. These libraries will be the output of the PRECOMPILE/COMPILE process performed by the Production Control Group. Recommended naming conventions are as follows:

1. DB2.PROD.applid.RUNLIB.LOAD
2. DB2.PROD.applid.DBRMLIB

Note that 'applid' is the standard application ID for that application.

DB2-ONLY PRODUCTION TURNOVER PROCESS. The following steps will be followed in the production turnover of DB2-based systems:

1. Production Control receives turnover documents from applications personnel.
2. Production Control performs appropriate PRECOMPILE/COMPILE into production DB2 libraries.
   - TSO—COBOL
   - TSO/Batch—COBOL
   - CICS Command Level COBOL
3. When PRECOMPILE/COMPILE is successful, notify DB2 Systems Administrator.
4. Send DB2 Systems Administrator Migration Forms.
5. DB2 Systems Administrator will bind applications.
6. DB2 Systems Administrator will grant requested authorizations.
7. DB2 Systems Administrator will notify applications when finished.
8. CICS Systems Programmer will generate RCT for CICS (if necessary).
9. Batch DB2 jobs will be scheduled by Production Control.
10. DB2 backup jobs will be scheduled by Production Control.
11. System is successfully implemented.

Job-Scheduling Procedures

Existing policies and procedures for batch job-scheduling procedures need to be followed and executed as currently specified per company standards. The following need to be administered by the job-scheduling system:

- DB2 BATCH jobs
- DB2 Backup jobs

Requirements for all DB2 Programs

The following areas must be addressed by ALL DB2 programs and systems.

A DB2 Change Request Form will be the first page in the completed packet for DB2 service and will be part of the complete package handed out before the production turnover walkthrough in addition to any other required documentation.

Backup and recovery. The successful implementation of a system using a DBMS requires the automatic scheduling and control of the backup jobstreams. All programs and systems going into production must ensure that backup and recovery procedures are developed for each DB2 table that is implemented. In addition, the requirements for each table as far as type of recovery needed, time span necessary for recovery, and any special requirements must be defined. (See Backup and Recovery Requirements Form in Appendix 18.)

The Backup and Recovery Form for all tables must be completed and given to the corporate Database Administrator. He will ensure that the requirements can be met and that they will be implemented at the appropriate time. He will change and/or add appropriate jobstreams per standard company production control and job scheduling procedures.

Migration from test to production. All DB2 objects that are to be moved into production from test or those that require changes must be identified. These include the following:

- Tables
- Tablespaces
- Application plannames
- CICS transaction name/plan
- IMS transaction name/plan
- DBRM names
- Authorization requirements

These objects will be defined using the DB2 Migration Request Form. Additional migration issues such as table moves will be resolved using the Table Change Request.

The completed forms will be given to the corporate System Administrator for processing based on currently stated scheduling requirements.

Non-DB2 objects will be processed as they currently are.

Requirements Specifically for Batch DB2

DB2 requirements that are unique to TSO/batch processes are that the jobstream that is run in the production environment through the automated job-scheduling system must have the USERID that is defined within DB2 for the execution authorization that is necessary, or the job will fail.

Requirements Specifically for CICS DB2

The requirements for DB2 access through CICS are only that the plan-name and the authorization ID that is defined in the CICS Resource Control Table be defined correctly within DB2. If this is not correct, access to DB2 will fail.

Copy of DB2 Migration Request Form must go to the CICS Systems Programmer in charge of the RCT generation.

Requirements Specifically for TSO/ISPF DB2

The requirements for DB2 access through TSO/ISPF are different in that the TSO USERID is the key for the checking of authorization for execution of any application plan, and, in the case of any dynamic SQL calls, specific access to DB2 columns and tables. As such, the authorization list given in the DB2 Migration Request Form must be accurate. Anyone NOT on the list will NOT be able to execute the DB2 plan, and, what's worse, anyone who IS on the list but NOT supposed to be WILL be able to execute the plan.

DB2 FORMS PROCEDURES

Following are instructions on filling out the forms defined in previous sections and shown in the appendices indicated.

Logical Design Forms

The following forms are used in the logical design phase of both the application systems themselves and the DB2 data bases.

DB2 application description part 1. The DB2 Application Description Form—part 1 (Appendix 3) is used for describing the proposed DB2 application. It is in two parts. This is Part 1, which is just a description of the application from an overview standpoint.

APPLICATION NAME/CODE Application name and code for this application.
PAGE Page number of this form and total numbers of this form for this
  particular request.
DATE Date this form was filled out.

REQUESTOR Person filling out this form.
DESCRIPTION Description of this application.
DATE NEEDED Date requested service is needed by.
DATE COMPLETED Date requested service was completed.
INITIALS Initials of SYSADM/DBADM completing service request.
DATE ENTERED INTO DATA DICTIONARY Date information was entered into data dictionary/data directory.
AUTHORIZATION SIGNATURE Signature of requestor's manager.
NAME Name of requestor's manager.
Attach copy of application design and flow diagram.

DB2 application description part 2. The DB2 Application Description Form—Part 2 (Appendix 4) is used for describing the proposed DB2 application. It is in two parts. This is Part 2, which is used to estimate overall use of DB2 by this application.

APPLICATION NAME/CODE Application name and code for this application.
PAGE Page number of this form and total numbers of this form for this particular request.
DATE Date this form was filled out.
REQUESTOR Person filling out this form.
 # OF ACTIVE QMF USERS Estimates of QMF users.
TOTAL AUTHORIZED Estimate of total authorized QMF users.
AVERAGE ACTIVE Estimate of average active QMF users at one time.
PEAK ACTIVE Estimate of maximum active QMF users at one time.
 # OF OTHER DYNAMIC SQL USERS Estimates of other Dynamic SQL users.
TOTAL AUTHORIZED Estimate of total other Dynamic SQL users.
AVERAGE ACTIVE Estimate of average active other Dynamic SQL users.
PEAK ACTIVE Estimate of maximum active other Dynamic SQL users.
QUERY RATE (per hour) Dynamic SQL—Number of queries per hour.
AVERAGE Estimate of average queries per hour.
ACTIVE Estimate of peak queries per hour.
TRANSACTION RATE (per hour) Static SQL—number of transactions.
AVERAGE Estimate of average transactions executed per hour.
ACTIVE Estimate of peak transactions executed per hour.
BATCH/UTILITIES Information on batch and utility requirements.
PROCESSING WINDOW Time frames specific batch processes must be executed in.
PROCESSING REQUIREMENTS Special requirements regarding batch processing.
DATE NEEDED Date requested service is needed by.
DATE COMPLETED Date requested service was completed.
INITIALS Initials of SYSADM/DBADM completing service request.

DATE ENTERED INTO DATA DICTIONARY Date information was entered into data dictionary/data directory.

AUTHORIZATION SIGNATURE Signature of requestor's manager.

NAME Name of requestor's manager.

Data element definition. The Data Element Definition Form (Appendix 11) is used to describe and define logical data elements for input into the logical data design process and data modeling process.

APPLICATION NAME/CODE Application name and code for this application.

PAGE Page number of this form and total numbers of this form for this particular request.

DATE Date this form was filled out.

REQUESTOR Person filling out this form.

DATA ELEMENT NAME Name of logical data element.

DESCRIPTION Description of this data element.

TYPE FIELD Type of field—character, integer, decimal, etc.

FIELD SIZE Size of field.

DEFAULT Default Values—NULL, blank, zero, etc.

LOGICAL RELATIONSHIPS Relationship information of this data element to other data elements.

DATA ELEMENT NAME Name of related data element.

RELATIONSHIP TYPE Type of relationship—descriptive, secondary key, etc.

DATE NEEDED Date requested service is needed by.

DATE COMPLETED Date requested service was completed.

INITIALS Initials of SYSADM/DBADM completing service request.

DATE ENTERED INTO DATA DICTIONARY Date information was entered into data dictionary/data directory.

AUTHORIZATION SIGNATURE Signature of requestor's manager.

NAME Name of requestor's manager.

DB2 table narrative. The DB2 Table Narrative Form (Appendix 9) is used to describe and define DB2 tables.

APPLICATION NAME/CODE Application name and code for this application.

PAGE Page number of this form and total numbers of this form for this particular request.

DATE Date this form was filled out.

REQUESTOR Person filling out this form.

TABLE NAME Name of table.

TABLE TITLE Descriptive title of table.

DESCRIPTION Full description of table.

DATA ELEMENTS IN TABLE (COLUMNS) Data elements which are part of this table.

DATE NEEDED Date requested service is needed by.

DATE COMPLETED Date requested service was completed.
INITIALS Initials of SYSADM/DBADM completing service request.
DATE ENTERED INTO DATA DICTIONARY Date information was entered into data dictionary/data directory.
AUTHORIZATION SIGNATURE Signature of requestor's manager.
NAME Name of requestor's manager.

Physical Design Forms

The following forms are used in the physical design phase of the application systems and the creation of the actual DB2 table structures.

DB2 initial development checklist. The DB2 Initial Development Checklist (Appendix 14) is a checklist to be used by development personnel in the development of DB2 applications.

APPLICATION NAME/CODE Application name and code for this application.
PAGE Page number of this form and total numbers of this form for this particular request.
DATE Date this form was filled out.
REQUESTOR Person filling out this form.
SYSTEMID DB2 system ID of this request.
DESCRIPTION Description of this development request.
DATE NEEDED Date requested service is needed by.
DATE COMPLETED Date requested service was completed.
INITIALS Initials of SYSADM/DBADM completing service request.
DATE ENTERED INTO DATA DICTIONARY Date information was entered into data dictionary/data directory.
AUTHORIZATION SIGNATURE Signature of requestor's manager.
NAME Name of requestor's manager.

DB2 storage group creation request. The DB2 Storage Group Creation Request Form (Appendix 12) is used to request and record the creation of DB2 storage groups.
APPLICATION NAME/CODE Application name and code for this application.
PAGE Page number of this form and total numbers of this form for this particular request.
DATE Date this form was filled out.
STORAGE GROUP NAME Name of storage group.
REQUESTOR Person filling out this form.
SYSTEMID DB2 system ID of this request.
DESCRIPTION Description of storage group usage.
VOLUMES ASSIGNED Volumes that are to be assigned to this storage group.
DEFAULT BUFFER POOL Default buffer pool to be used for DB2 objects created using this storage group.

VCAT CATALOG NAME ICF catalog name to be used for DB2 tablespaces created using this storage group.

USE AUTHORIZATION Authorization list of those users authorized to use this storage group.

DATE NEEDED Date requested service is needed by.

DATE COMPLETED Date requested service was completed.

INITIALS Initials of SYSADM/DBADM completing service request.

DATE ENTERED INTO DATA DICTIONARY Date information was entered into data dictionary/data directory.

AUTHORIZATION SIGNATURE Signature of requestor's manager.

NAME Name of requestor's manager.

DB2 data base creation request. The DB2 Database Creation Request Form (Appendix 16) is used to request and record the creation of DB2 data bases.

APPLICATION NAME/CODE Application name and code for this application.

PAGE Page number of this form and total numbers of this form for this particular request.

DATE Date this form was filled out.

DATA BASE NAME Name of data base.

REQUESTOR Person filling out this form.

SYSTEM DB2 system ID of this request.

DBADM AUTHORITY USERID USERID to be assigned as primary DBADM for this data base.

DESCRIPTION Description of data base usage.

TOTAL # OF TABLESPACES Estimated total number of tablespaces to be created in this data base.

TOTAL # OF TABLES Estimated total number of tables to be created in this data base.

TOTAL # OF INDEXES Estimated total number of indexes to be created in this data base.

TOTAL # OF VIEWS Estimated total number of views to be created on tables in this data base.

DATE NEEDED Date requested service is needed by.

DATE COMPLETED Date requested service was completed.

INITIALS Initials of SYSADM/DBADM completing service request.

DATE ENTERED INTO DATA DICTIONARY Date information was entered into data dictionary/data directory.

AUTHORIZATION SIGNATURE Signature of requestor's manager.

NAME Name of requestor's manager.

DB2 tablespace creation request. The DB2 Tablespace Creation Request Form (Appendix 17) is used to request and record the creation of DB2 tablespaces.

APPLICATION NAME/CODE Application name and code for this application.

PAGE Page number of this form and total numbers of this form for this particular request.

DATE Date this form was filled out.

TABLESPACE NAME Name of tablespace.

REQUESTOR Person filling out this form.

SYSTEM DB2 system ID of this request.

DESCRIPTION Description of tablespace.

DATA BASE NAME Name of data base this tablespace is to be created in.

BUFFER POOL TO BE USED Buffer pool to be used for this tablespace (if the default one for the data base is not to be used).

TOTAL STORAGE ESTIMATE (in kilobytes) Estimate of total storage requirements for this tablespace in kilobytes.

DATE NEEDED Date requested service is needed by.

DATE COMPLETED Date requested service was completed.

INITIALS Initials of SYSADM/DBADM completing service request.

DATE ENTERED INTO DATA DICTIONARY Date information was entered into data dictionary/data directory.

AUTHORIZATION SIGNATURE Signature of requestor's manager.

NAME Name of requestor's manager.

DB2 table change request. The DB2 Table Change Request Form (Appendix 8) is to be used when requesting changes to existing tables.

APPLICATION NAME/CODE Application name and code for this application.

PAGE Page number of this form and total numbers of this form for this particular request.

DATE Date this form was filled out.

TABLE NAME Name of table to be changed.

CREATOR-ID Creator of table (high-level qualifier of table).

REQUESTOR Person filling out this form.

SYSTEM DB2 system ID of this request.

DESCRIPTION Description of requested change.

TYPE OF CHANGE Fill out appropriate columns relating to the change that is being requested.

DATE NEEDED Date requested service is needed by.

DATE COMPLETED Date requested service was completed.

INITIALS Initials of SYSADM/DBADM completing service request.

DATE ENTERED INTO DATA DICTIONARY Date information was entered into data dictionary/data directory.

AUTHORIZATION SIGNATURE Signature of requestor's manager.

NAME Name of requestor's manager.

DB2 view creation request. The DB2 View Creation Request Form (Appendix 10) is used for the request and recording of DB2 view creation.

APPLICATION NAME/CODE Application name and code for this application.

PAGE Page number of this form and total numbers of this form for this particular request.

DATE Date this form was filled out.

VIEW NAME Name of view.

CREATOR-ID Creator of view (high-level qualifier of view).

VIEW TITLE Descriptive title of view.

REQUESTOR Person filling out this form.

SYSTEM DB2 system ID of this request.

SYSTEMID DB2 system ID of this request.

DESCRIPTION Full description of view.

DATA ELEMENTS IN VIEW (COLUMNS) List of columns and related tables that will compose this view.

DATE NEEDED Date requested service is needed by.

SELECT REQUIREMENTS SQL SELECT requirements for this view.

DATE COMPLETED Date requested service was completed.

INITIALS Initials of SYSADM/DBADM completing service request.

DATE ENTERED INTO DATA DICTIONARY Date information was entered into data dictionary/data directory.

AUTHORIZATION SIGNATURE Signature of requestor's manager.

NAME Name of requestor's manager.

DB2 index creation request. The DB2 Index Creation Request Form (Appendix 15) is used to request and record the creation of DB2 indexes.

APPLICATION NAME/CODE Application name and code for this application.

PAGE Page number of this form and total numbers of this form for this particular request.

DATE Date this form was filled out.

INDEX NAME Name of index.

CREATOR-ID Creator of index (high-level qualifier of index).

REQUESTOR Person filling out this form.

SYSTEM DB2 system ID of this request.

TABLE NAME Name of table to be indexed.

TABLE CREATOR-ID Creator of table (high-level qualifier of table).

DESCRIPTION Full description of index.

UNIQUE Unique—Yes or No.

SORT ORDER Ascending or descending (ASC, DSC).

CLUSTERED Clustered index (only one per table).

COLUMNS TO BE INDEXED Columns to be in index.

COLUMN NAME Name of column.

KEY ORDER Sequence of column in index.

DATE NEEDED Date requested service is needed by.

DATE COMPLETED Date requested service was completed.

INITIALS Initials of SYSADM/DBADM completing service request.

DATE ENTERED INTO DATA DICTIONARY Date information was entered into data dictionary/data directory.
AUTHORIZATION SIGNATURE Signature of requestor's manager.
NAME Name of requestor's manager.

DB2 plan creation request. The DB2 Plan Creation Request Form (Appendix 19) is used to request and record the creation of DB2 application plans.

APPLICATION NAME/CODE Application name and code for this application.
PAGE Page number of this form and total numbers of this form for this particular request.
DATE Date this form was filled out.
PLAN NAME Name of application plan.
REQUESTOR Person filling out this form.
SYSTEM DB2 system ID of this request.
DESCRIPTION Description of plan.
PROGRAM NAMES Program LOAD modules which compose this plan.
DBRM LIBRARY(IES) Database Request Module (DBRM) library(ies) used in the creation of this plan.
DBRM LIST Database Request Modules (DBRMs) used in the creation of this plan.
SYNONYM LIBRARY Library synonym source resides in.
SYNONYM Synonym Library member name for synonym of table/view.
TABLE/VIEW Table/view name synonym is for.
GRANT ACCESS Grant authorization list for this plan.
USERID Authorization ID for this access.
ACCESS Access level for this authorization ID (BIND and/or EXECUTE).
DATE NEEDED Date requested service is needed by.
DATE COMPLETED Date requested service was completed.
INITIALS Initials of SYSADM/DBADM completing service request.
DATE ENTERED INTO DATA DICTIONARY Date information was entered into data dictionary/data directory.
AUTHORIZATION SIGNATURE Signature of requestor's manager.
NAME Name of requestor's manager.

DB2 object creation request. The DB2 Object Creation Request Form (Appendix 13) is a general purpose DB2 object creation request which can be used in the development environment as a change request mechanism.

APPLICATION NAME/CODE Application name and code for this application.
PAGE Page number of this form and total numbers of this form for this particular request.
DATE Date this form was filled out.
REQUESTOR Person filling out this form.
SYSTEM DB2 system ID of this request.

DESCRIPTION Description of request.
REQUEST TYPE Fill in appropriate request blanks.
DATE NEEDED Date requested service is needed by.
DATE COMPLETED Date requested service was completed.
INITIALS Initials of SYSADM/DBADM completing service request.
DATE ENTERED INTO DATA DICTIONARY Date information was entered into data dictionary/data directory.
AUTHORIZATION SIGNATURE Signature of requestor's manager.
NAME Name of requestor's manager.

DB2 Change Control Forms

DB2 change request completion notice. The DB2 Change Request Completion Notice (Appendix 5) is used to notify personnel who have requested a change to DB2 objects that the change has been completed.

APPLICATION NAME/CODE Application name and code for this application.
PAGE Page number of this form and total numbers of this form for this particular request.
DATE Date this form was filled out.
REQUESTOR Person filling out this form.
TYPE OF CHANGE REQUEST Type of change request process done.
SYSTEM DB2 System ID of this request.
DATE NEEDED Date requested service is needed by.
DATE COMPLETED Date requested service was completed.
INITIALS Initials of SYSADM/DBADM completing service request.
DATE ENTERED INTO DATA DICTIONARY Date information was entered into data dictionary/data directory.
AUTHORIZATION SIGNATURE Signature of requestor's manager.
NAME Name of requestor's manager.

DB2 change request checklist. The DB2 Change Request Checklist (Appendix 6) is to be used by personnel performing DB2 change activity in tracking and completing requested changes.

APPLICATION NAME/CODE Application name and code for this application.
PAGE Page number of this form and total numbers of this form for this particular request.
DATE Date this form was filled out.
REQUESTOR Person filling out this form.
SYSTEMID DB2 System ID of this request.
DESCRIPTION Description of change request.
TYPE OF CHANGE REQUEST Type of change request process being done.
DATE NEEDED Date requested service is needed by.
DATE COMPLETED Date requested service was completed.

INITIALS Initials of SYSADM/DBADM completing service request.
DATE ENTERED INTO DATA DICTIONARY Date information was entered into data dictionary/data directory.
AUTHORIZATION SIGNATURE Signature of requestor's manager.
NAME Name of requestor's manager.

DB2 Production Turnover Forms

DB2 backup/recovery requirements. The DB2 Backup/Recovery Requirements Form (Appendix 18) is to be used in the submission of the backup job procedures for new tablespaces.

APPLICATION NAME/CODE Application name and code for this application.
PAGE Page number of this form and total numbers of this form for this particular request.
DATE Date this form was filled out.
REQUESTOR Person filling out this form.
SYSTEMID DB2 System ID of this request.
TABLESPACE/TABLE NAMES Tablespaces to be backed up (fully qualified).
DESCRIPTION Description of necessary backup process.
RETENTION CYCLE Retention duration and/or cycle of backup tapes.
BACKUP FREQUENCY Frequency of backups.
RECOVERY PROCESS Special recovery requirements (if needed).
JOB NAMES Backup job name.
JOB DESCRIPTION Backup job description.
DATE NEEDED Date requested service is needed by.
DATE COMPLETED Date requested service was completed.
INITIALS Initials of SYSADM/DBADM completing service request.
DATE ENTERED INTO DATA DICTIONARY Date information was entered into data dictionary/data directory.
AUTHORIZATION SIGNATURE Signature of requestor's manager.
NAME Name of requestor's manager.

DB2 migration request—batch. The DB2 Migration Request—Batch Form (Appendix 20) is used to control the migration of batch DB2 systems from a development environment to a production environment and/or migration of a batch DB2 system from one DB2 subsystem to another.

APPLICATION NAME/CODE Application name and code for this application.
PAGE Page number of this form and total numbers of this form for this particular request.
DATE Date this form was filled out.
REQUESTOR Person filling out this form.
TO SYSTEM DB2 system ID where migration is going TO.
FROM SYSTEM DB2 system ID where migration is coming FROM.

DESCRIPTION Description of migration process.

HIGH-LEVEL QUALIFIER (CREATOR) of 'TO' SYSTEM Creator of tables.

SYNONYM LIBRARY DSN AND MEMBER(S) Name of data set containing SYNONYM definitions for this migration request.

TABLE CREATE LIBRARY DSN Name of data set containing TABLE CREATE definitions for this migration request.

TABLE NAMES Names of tables needed for this migration request.

DBRM LIBRARY DSN Name of data set containing DBRMs.

PLAN NAMES Names of application plans needed for this migration request.

PROGRAM NAMES Program names associated with the plans needed for this migration request.

DBRM NAMES Database Request Modules (DBRMs) associated with the plans needed for this migration request.

BATCH JOBNAME Batch jobname running this DB2 application.

EXECUTION ID Execution ID used as authorization ID.

PLAN CROSS REFERENCE Plan name associated with jobname.

DATE NEEDED Date requested service is needed by.

DATE COMPLETED Date requested service was completed.

INITIALS Initials of SYSADM/DBADM completing service request.

DATE ENTERED INTO DATA DICTIONARY Date information was entered into data dictionary/data directory.

AUTHORIZATION SIGNATURE Signature of requestor's manager.

NAME Name of requestor's manager.

DB2 migration request—CICS. The DB2 Migration Request—CICS Form (Appendix 21) is used to control the migration of CICS DB2 systems from a development environment to a production environment and/or migration of a CICS DB2 system from one DB2 subsystem to another.

APPLICATION NAME/CODE Application name and code for this application.

PAGE Page number of this form and total numbers of this form for this particular request.

DATE Date this form was filled out.

REQUESTOR Person filling out this form.

TO SYSTEM DB2 system ID where migration is going TO.

FROM SYSTEM DB2 system ID where migration is coming FROM.

DESCRIPTION Description of migration process.

HIGH-LEVEL QUALIFIER (CREATOR) of 'TO' SYSTEM Creator of tables.

SYNONYM LIBRARY DSN AND MEMBER(S) Name of Data set containing SYNONYM definitions for this migration request.

TABLE CREATE LIBRARY DSN Name of data set containing TABLE CREATE definitions for this migration request.

TABLE NAMES Names of tables needed for this migration request.

DBRM LIBRARY DSN Name of data set containing DBRMs.
PLAN NAMES Names of application plans needed for this migration request.
PROGRAM NAMES Program names associated with the plans needed for this migration request.
DBRM NAMES Database Request Modules (DBRMs) associated with the plans needed for this migration request.
CICS TRANSACTION CICS transaction associated with plan name.
PLAN CROSS REFERENCE Plan name associated with transaction.
CICS REGION NAME CICS region name transaction is in.
DATE NEEDED Date requested service is needed by.
DATE COMPLETED Date requested service was completed.
INITIALS Initials of SYSADM/DBADM completing service request.
DATE ENTERED INTO DATA DICTIONARY Date information was entered into data dictionary/data directory.
AUTHORIZATION SIGNATURE Signature of requestor's manager.
NAME Name of requestor's manager.

DB2 migration request—IMS/DC. The DB2 Migration Request—IMS/DC Form (Appendix 22) is used to control the migration of IMS/DC DB2 systems from a development environment to a production environment and/or migration of an IMS/DC DB2 system from one DB2 subsystem to another.

APPLICATION NAME/CODE Application name and code for this application.
PAGE Page number of this form and total numbers of this form for this particular request.
DATE Date this form was filled out.
REQUESTOR Person filling out this form.
DESCRIPTION Description of migration process.
TO SYSTEM DB2 system ID where migration is going TO.
FROM SYSTEM DB2 system ID where migration is coming FROM.
HIGH-LEVEL QUALIFIER (CREATOR) of 'TO' SYSTEM Creator of tables.
SYNONYM LIBRARY DSN AND MEMBER(S) Name of data set containing SYNONYM definitions for this migration request.
TABLE CREATE LIBRARY DSN Name of data set containing TABLE CREATE definitions for this migration request.
TABLE NAMES Names of tables needed for this migration request.
DBRM LIBRARY DSN Name of data set containing DBRMs.
PLAN NAMES Names of application plans needed for this migration request.
PROGRAM NAMES Program names associated with the plans needed for this migration request.
DBRM NAMES Database Request Modules (DBRMs) associated with the plans needed for this migration request.
IMS/DC TRANSACTION IMS/DC transaction associated with plan name.
PLAN CROSS REFERENCE Plan name associated with transaction.

IMS/DC REGION NAME CICS region name transaction is in.
DATE NEEDED Date requested service is needed by.
DATE COMPLETED Date requested service was completed.
INITIALS Initials of SYSADM/DBADM completing service request.
DATE ENTERED INTO DATA DICTIONARY Date information was entered into data dictionary/data directory.
AUTHORIZATION SIGNATURE Signature of requestor's manager.
NAME Name of requestor's manager.

DB2 migration request—DBEDIT. The DB2 Migration Request—DBEDIT Form (Appendix 34) is used to control the migration of DBEDIT DB2 systems from a development environment to a production environment and/or migration of a DBEDIT DB2 system from one DB2 subsystem to another.

APPLICATION NAME/CODE Application name and code for this application.
PAGE Page number of this form and total numbers of this form for this particular request.
DATE Date this form was filled out.
REQUESTOR Person filling out this form.
TO SYSTEMID DB2 system ID where migration is going TO.
FROM SYSTEMID DB2 system ID where migration is coming FROM.
DESCRIPTION Description of migration process.
HIGH-LEVEL QUALIFIER (CREATOR) of 'TO' SYSTEM Creator of tables.
TABLE CREATE LIBRARY DSN Name of data set containing TABLE CREATE definitions for this migration request.
TABLE NAMES Names of tables needed for this migration request.
PANELS TO BE MIGRATED Names of DBEDIT panels to be migrated.
DATE NEEDED Date requested service is needed by.
DATE COMPLETED Date requested service was completed.
INITIALS Initials of SYSADM/DBADM completing service request.
DATE ENTERED INTO DATA DICTIONARY Date information was entered into data dictionary/data directory.
AUTHORIZATION SIGNATURE Signature of requestor's manager.
NAME Name of requestor's manager.

DB2 migration request—QMF. The DB2 Migration Request—QMF Form (Appendix 23) is used to control the migration of QMF DB2 systems from a development environment to a production environment and/or migration of a QMF DB2 system from one DB2 subsystem to another.

APPLICATION NAME/CODE Application name and code for this application.
PAGE Page number of this form and total numbers of this form for this particular request.
DATE Date this form was filled out.
REQUESTOR Person filling out this form.

TO SYSTEM DB2 system ID where migration is going TO.

FROM SYSTEM DB2 system ID where migration is coming FROM.

DESCRIPTION Description of migration process.

HIGH-LEVEL QUALIFIER (CREATOR) of 'TO' SYSTEM Creator of tables.

TABLE CREATE LIBRARY DSN Name of data set containing TABLE CRE-ATE definitions for this migration request.

TABLE NAMES Names of tables needed for this migration request.

PROCEDURE NAME Name of QMF procedures to be migrated.

QUERY NAMES QMF Queries that need to be migrated.

FORM NAMES QMF Forms that need to be migrated.

PROCEDURE Name of QMF procedure.

TABLE(S) ACCESSED Tables used by this QMF procedure.

DATE NEEDED Date requested service is needed by.

DATE COMPLETED Date requested service was completed.

INITIALS Initials of SYSADM/DBADM completing service request.

DATE ENTERED INTO DATA DICTIONARY Date information was entered into data dictionary/data directory.

AUTHORIZATION SIGNATURE Signature of requestor's manager.

NAME Name of requestor's manager.

DB2 migration checklist. The DB2 Migration Checklist Form (Appendix 25) is to be used by personnel performing a migration as a checklist and change record form.

APPLICATION NAME/CODE Application name and code for this application.

PAGE Page number of this form and total numbers of this form for this particular request.

DATE Date this form was filled out.

REQUESTOR Person filling out this form.

SYSTEM DB2 system ID where migration took place.

DESCRIPTION Description of migration. Check appropriate block.

DATE NEEDED Date requested service is needed by.

DATE COMPLETED Date requested service was completed.

INITIALS Initials of SYSADM/DBADM completing service request.

DATE ENTERED INTO DATA DICTIONARY Date information was entered into data dictionary/data directory.

AUTHORIZATION SIGNATURE Signature of requestor's manager.

NAME Name of requestor's manager.

DB2 utility/DXT usage. The DB2 Utility/DXT Usage Form (Appendix 28) is to be used for the use of DXT and other DB2 utilities.

APPLICATION NAME/CODE Application name and code for this application.

PAGE Page number of this form and total numbers of this form for this particular request.

DATE Date this form was filled out.

REQUESTOR Person filling out this form.

SYSTEM DB2 system ID where utility usage will occur.

DESCRIPTION Description of Utility/DXT process.

LOAD How many LOADs are needed and when.

REORG How many REORGs are needed and when.

RUNSTATS How many RUNSTATs are needed, when, and frequency.

DXT USAGE What type of DXT usage is necessary.

DESCRIPTION Description of DXT usage.

RESTRUCTURING DESCRIPTION Description restructuring of files using DXT (if necessary).

TABLES TO BE LOADED Tables to be loaded using DXT.

TABLE NAME Name of table to be loaded using DXT input.

EXTRACT RATE If extract, what is rate/frequency?

UPDATE/REFRESH Will there be update and/or refresh?

DATE NEEDED Date requested service is needed by.

DATE COMPLETED Date requested service was completed.

INITIALS Initials of SYSADM/DBADM completing service request.

DATE ENTERED INTO DATA DICTIONARY Date information was entered into data dictionary/data directory.

AUTHORIZATION SIGNATURE Signature of requestor's manager.

NAME Name of requestor's manager.

DB2 End-User Request Forms

DB2 report request. The DB2 Report Request Form (Appendix 7) is to be used for requesting particular system catalog reports.

APPLICATION NAME/CODE Application name and code for this application.

PAGE Page number of this form and total numbers of this form for this particular request.

DATE Date this form was filled out.

REQUESTOR Person filling out this form.

SYSTEM DB2 system ID where migration took place.

DESCRIPTION Description of report requested.

TYPE OF REPORT Place X in blank next to desired reports.

DATE NEEDED Date requested service is needed by.

DATE COMPLETED Date requested service was completed.

INITIALS Initials of SYSADM/DBADM completing service request.

DATE ENTERED INTO DATA DICTIONARY Date information was entered into data dictionary/data directory.

AUTHORIZATION SIGNATURE Signature of requestor's manager.

NAME Name of requestor's manager.

DB2 Performance and Capacity Planning Forms

DB2 performance impact analysis. The DB2 Performance Impact Analysis Form (Appendix 26) is to be filled out in the attempt to analyze all SQL calls in a program so that the performance impact can be analyzed. This will be done during each of the design review phases and be updated as more information becomes available. This form is set up to accept information from the EXPLAIN subcommand on the BIND command.

APPLICATION NAME/CODE Application name and code for this application.

PAGE Page number of this form and total numbers of this form for this particular request.

DATE Date this form was filled out.

PLAN NAME Name of application plan being analyzed.

TYPE Type of plan (TSO, batch, CICS).

REQUESTOR Person filling out this form.

SYSTEM DB2 system ID where plan executes.

PLAN EXPLAIN INFORMATION The information in this section is extracted from the EXPLAIN PLAN process in the BIND. (See EXPLAIN description earlier in this manual.)

EXECUTION INFORMATION The information in this section is primarily an estimate in the initial development cycle, and as the plan is actually executed, more accurate information can be obtained.

QUERY # Match with above if possible; else leave blank.

QUERY TYPE Type of query.

ESTIMATED # OF ROWS Estimated number of rows accessed.

 # OF EXECUTIONS of SQL STATEMENTS BY TIME PERIOD Estimated number of times SQL will be executed in specified time period.

DATE NEEDED Date requested service is needed by.

DATE COMPLETED Date requested service was completed.

INITIALS Initials of SYSADM/DBADM completing service request.

DATE ENTERED INTO DATA DICTIONARY Date information was entered into data dictionary/data directory.

AUTHORIZATION SIGNATURE Signature of requestor's manager.

NAME Name of requestor's manager.

DB2 capacity planning impact analysis. The DB2 Capacity Planning Impact Analysis Form (Appendix 27) is to be filled out to aid in capacity planning in the areas of DASD utilization and CPU utilization. This will also be done during each of the design review phases and be updated as more information becomes available.

APPLICATION NAME/CODE Application name and code for this application.

PAGE Page number of this form and total numbers of this form for this particular request.

DATE Date this form was filled out.

TABLESPACE NAME Name of tablespace.

REQUESTOR Person filling out this form.

SYSTEM DB2 System ID where allocation will be done.

DESCRIPTION Description of tablespace.

DATA BASE NAME Name of data base tablespace is in.

BUFFER POOL TO BE USED Name of buffer pool to be used.

INITIAL STORAGE ESTIMATE (in kilobytes) Initial storage needs for this tablespace in kilobytes.

GROWTH STORAGE ESTIMATE (in kilobytes) Growth storage needs for this tablespace in kilobytes (per month).

MAXIMUM STORAGE ESTIMATE (in kilobytes) Maximum storage needs for this tablespace in kilobytes.

ACCESS INFORMATION Access to be done on this tablespace.

ACCESS TYPE Type of access to be done on this tablespace.

ESTIMATED # OF ROWS Estimated number of rows per access type.

# of ACCESSES PER TIME PERIOD Number of times this access is to be done in specified time periods.

DATE NEEDED Date requested service is needed by.

DATE COMPLETED Date requested service was completed.

INITIALS Initials of SYSADM/DBADM completing service request.

DATE ENTERED INTO DATA DICTIONARY Date information was entered into data dictionary/data directory.

AUTHORIZATION SIGNATURE Signature of requestor's manager.

NAME Name of requestor's manager.

DB2 SQL statement processing. The DB2 SQL Statement Processing Form (Appendix 30) is used to analyze the structure and impact of SQL Statements that are created.

APPLICATION NAME/CODE Application name and code for this application.

PAGE Page number of this form and total numbers of this form for this particular request.

DATE Date this form was filled out.

REQUESTOR Person filling out this form.

SYSTEM DB2 system ID where query will be run.

DESCRIPTION Description of SQL statement.

EXECUTION RATE/HOUR Execution rate of this SQL statement per hour.

 # OF USERS AUTHORIZED Number of users authorized to run this SQL.

TABLES USED BY THIS QUERY Tables used in this SQL statement.

TABLE NAME Name of table used in this query.

NUMBER OF ROWS: Retrieved Number of rows selected by this SQL statement.

NUMBER OF ROWS: Updated Number of rows updated by this SQL statement.

NUMBER OF ROWS: Inserted Number of rows inserted by this SQL statement.

NUMBER OF ROWS: Deleted Number of rows deleted by this SQL statement.

SQL STATEMENT LISTING Listing of SQL statement.

OUTPUT Estimated total number of rows returned.

DATE NEEDED Date requested service is needed by.

DATE COMPLETED Date requested service was completed.

INITIALS Initials of SYSADM/DBADM completing service request.

DATE ENTERED INTO DATA DICTIONARY Date information was entered into data dictionary/data directory.

AUTHORIZATION SIGNATURE Signature of requestor's manager.

NAME Name of requestor's manager.

QMF procedure processing. The QMF Procedure Processing Form (Appendix 29) is used to analyze the structure and impact of QMF procedures that are created.

APPLICATION NAME/CODE Application name and code for this application.

PAGE Page number of this form and total numbers of this form for this particular request.

DATE Date this form was filled out.

REQUESTOR Person filling out this form.

SYSTEM DB2 system ID where query will be run.

QMF PROCEDURE NAME Name of QMF procedure.

PROCEDURE TITLE Descriptive title of QMF procedure.

DESCRIPTION Description of QMF procedure.

EXECUTION RATE/HOUR Execution rate of this procedure per hour.

 # OF AUTHORIZED USERS Number of authorized users.

RESPONSE TIME REQUIREMENT Required response time for the procedure.

AUXILIARY TABLES CREATED BY THIS PROCEDURE Auxiliary tables created by this procedure.

TABLE NAME Name of auxiliary table.

SIZE Size of auxiliary table (in kilobytes).

DURATION Duration of auxiliary table.

PROCEDURE LISTING Listing of procedures, including QUERIES and FORMs used in the procedure as well as EXPORT/IMPORT, TSO CLISTS, and ISPF processes.

DATE NEEDED Date requested service is needed by.

DATE COMPLETED Date requested service was completed.

INITIALS Initials of SYSADM/DBADM completing service request.

DATE ENTERED INTO DATA DICTIONARY Date information was entered into data dictionary/data directory.

AUTHORIZATION SIGNATURE Signature of requestor's manager.

NAME Name of requestor's manager.

DB2 QMF query processing. The DB2 QMF Query Processing Form (Appendix 31) is used to analyze the structure and impact of QMF queries that are created.

APPLICATION NAME/CODE Application name and code for this application.

PAGE Page number of this form and total numbers of this form for this particular request.

DATE Date this form was filled out.

REQUESTOR Person filling out this form.

SYSTEM DB2 system ID where query will be run.

QMF QUERY NAME Name of QMF query.

QUERY TITLE Descriptive title of QMF query.

DESCRIPTION Description of QMF query.

EXECUTION RATE/HOUR Execution rate of this query per hour.

 # OF AUTHORIZED USERS Number of authorized users.

RESPONSE TIME REQUIREMENT Required response time for the query.

QMF QUERY INFORMATION Information about query structure.

QUERY LISTING Listing of query including form used (if any).

DATE NEEDED Date requested service is needed by.

DATE COMPLETED Date requested service was completed.

INITIALS Initials of SYSADM/DBADM completing service request.

DATE ENTERED INTO DATA DICTIONARY Date information was entered into data dictionary/data directory.

AUTHORIZATION SIGNATURE Signature of requestor's manager.

NAME Name of requestor's manager.

Production Control Forms for DB2 Applications

Production control migration request for DB2 applications. The Production Control Migration Request Form (Appendix 32) is used to control the production turnover of DB2 applications by production control personnel.

APPLICATION NAME/CODE Application name and code for this application.

PAGE Page number of this form and total numbers of this form for this particular request.

DATE Date this form was filled out.

REQUESTOR Person filling out this form.

SYSTEM DB2 system ID where query will be run.

DESCRIPTION Description of what is going into production.

PROGRAM TYPE Types of program(s) going into production.

PROGRAM LANGUAGE Languages of program(s) going into production.

DEVELOPMENT SOURCE FILE DSN Development data set containing source code.

PRODUCTION SOURCE FILE DSN Production data set containing source code.

PRODUCTION DBRM LIBRARY DSN Production data set containing DBRM members.

PRODUCTION DCLGEN LIBRARY DSN Production data set containing DCLGEN members.

PRODUCTION DB2 LOAD LIBRARY DSN Production data set containing DB2 load library members.
DCLGENS TO BE CREATED DCLGEN members that need to be created for this production turnover process.
SYNONYMS TO BE CREATED SYNONYMS that need to be created for this production turnover process.
SOURCE NAME/DBRM NAME Source program names and associated DBRM names for this production turnover process.
PLAN NAME/DBRM MEMBER NAMES Application plan names and associated DBRM names for this production turnover process.
DATE NEEDED Date requested service is needed by.
DATE COMPLETED Date requested service was completed.
INITIALS Initials of SYSADM/DBADM completing service request.
DATE ENTERED INTO DATA DICTIONARY Date information was entered into data dictionary/data directory.
AUTHORIZATION SIGNATURE Signature of requestor's manager.
NAME Name of requestor's manager.

Production control checklist for DB2 applications. The Production Control Checklist Form (Appendix 33) is used to check off the tasks necessary to place DB2 applications into production.

APPLICATION NAME/CODE Application name and code for this application.
PAGE Page number of this form and total numbers of this form for this particular request.
DATE Date this form was filled out.
REQUESTOR Person filling out this form.
SYSTEM DB2 system ID where query will be run.
DESCRIPTION Description of what is going into production.
PROGRAM TYPE Type(s) of program(s) going into production.
PROGRAM LANGUAGE Language(s) of program(s) going into production.
CHECKLIST Check off appropriate task as it is finished.
DATE NEEDED Date requested service is needed by.
DATE COMPLETED Date requested service was completed.
INITIALS Initials of SYSADM/DBADM completing service request.
DATE ENTERED INTO DATA DICTIONARY Date information was entered into data dictionary/data directory.
AUTHORIZATION SIGNATURE Signature of requestor's manager.
NAME Name of requestor's manager.

Security Administration Forms for DB2 Applications

DB2 security authorization request. The DB2 Security Authorization Request Form (Appendix 24) is used to request and record security authorization requests within a DB2 subsystem.

APPLICATION NAME/CODE Application name and code for this application.

PAGE Page number of this form and total numbers of this form for this particular request.

DATE Date this form was filled out.

REQUESTOR Person filling out this form.

SYSTEM DB2 system ID where authorization is needed.

DESCRIPTION Description of why this authorization is necessary.

DB2 OBJECT NAME Name of DB2 object authorization is requested for.

OBJECT TYPE Type of DB2 object (plan, table, view, etc.).

AUTHORIZATION LEVEL Authorization level desired.

ID Authorization ID needing authorization listed above.

TYPE Type of ID (TSO USERID, CICS TXID, CICS USERID, etc.).

DATE NEEDED Date requested service is needed.

DATE COMPLETED Date requested service was completed.

INITIALS Initials of SYSADM/DBADM completing service request.

DATE ENTERED INTO DATA DICTIONARY Date information was entered into data dictionary/data directory.

AUTHORIZATION SIGNATURE Signature of requestor's manager.

NAME Name of requestor's manager.

DB2 Standards   6

INTRODUCTION

The institution of standards is just as important in DB2 as it is in any other system. In fact, it is more important because of the probable amount of data-sharing and ad hoc usage that will take place. Also, the avoidance of following a certain few SQL design standards can make the difference between an application or query running in seconds or running in hours.

The following areas are considered to be important enough to have standards defined for them.

1. Allocation of DB2 resources
2. Naming conventions
3. DB2 table-design considerations
4. Application-design considerations
5. SQL creation considerations
6. Application-programming techniques
7. Using DB2 utilities
8. Using other DB2-related products

ALLOCATION OF DB2 RESOURCES

DB2 Security

- To use any DB2 features, a user must be granted authorization for that privilege.
- A GRANT or REVOKE SQL statement controls the usage of a DB2 data base or any DB2 resources.

- Authorization levels should be layered to correspond with DB2's structured authorization layers.
- Group security-level relationships should be developed where possible in order to simplify DB2 security authorization processes.
- SYSADM authority should be severely restricted. A combination of other authorities should be sufficient for all non-System Administrator level personnel.

DB2 General Rules

- ALWAYS use SYNONYMS.
- Logical data design necessary.
- Table design should be done by DBA using logical data-modeling techniques.
- Programmers should ask for views of elements.
- Row lengths should never exceed 4,056 characters.
- Do NOT use special characters in column names.
- Reuse threads as much as possible.
- Avoid use of Dynamic SQL.
- Avoid use of DDL statements in applications. Use of DDL statements decreases concurrency.
- Forms will be created and used to track requests for creation of DB2 objects (tables, grants, views, etc.) and for requests for migration.
- Programs will use views when possible and synonyms always.
- Character fields should not exceed 254 characters.
- Execute RUNSTATS often for high-usage and updated tables. Then do not forget to REBIND.
- Think in terms of element-level access, not record of low-level access.

Storage groups.

- Storage groups may have a maximum of 133 DASD volumes.
- All volumes defined in a storage group must be of the SAME DEVICE TYPE (i.e., all 3380s); otherwise, a dynamic allocation error occurs if you try to create a tablespace or index.
- Do not use the system default storage group, SYSDEFLT.
- Assign EACH partition of a partitioned tablespace in DIFFERENT storage groups.
- Production tablespaces should NOT use storage groups.
- A volume may belong to more than one storage group.
- Volumes are filled in order.
- Use of storage groups must be granted.
- To improve performance, assign frequently accessed DB2 objects (databases, tablespaces, and indexes) to different storage groups on different volumes.

- Storage groups will be created and assigned by the DB2 System Administrator.

Data base.

- Group related data in DIFFERENT data bases.
- Do not use the DB2 default data base name, DSNDB04.

Tablespace.

- A tablespace name is always qualified by a data base name.
- A tablespace can contain only 127 rows per page.
- If you omit the data base name, DB2 defaults to the DB2 default database name, DSNDB04. Do not use the DB2 system default database.
- When a sequential scan is required, DB2 scans the entire tablespace —another reason for one table per tablespace.
- Caution should be taken when planning for a partitioned tablespace. The size of the tablespace and the nature of processing should be taken into consideration during analysis.
- Specify CLOSE NO for frequently used tables. This eliminates the closing of all data sets supported by the tablespace when there are no current users of the tablespace.
- Use FREEPAGE and PCTFREE parameters for High-Update and Insert tables especially around a clustered index.
- Use LOCKSIZE ANY. Let DB2 track locking.

Table.

- Use unqualified table names in programs and queries and then use synonyms for production and test.
- Do not use Buffer Pool BP32K. Use of this buffer pool will result in greatly increased CPU usage and, especially, I/O and main storage.
- Reduce number of tables to be joined. Too many table JOINS will lead to bad DB2 performance. In most cases, the degree of normalization may have been carried out to the point that there are more tables in the application than DB2 can efficiently handle. As a result, a DE-NORMALIZATION process is suggested.
- A COMMENT ON statement should be added to each table.

Views.

- Views should be used as much as possible in application development because of security access requirements and data and program independence considerations.
- A COMMENT ON statement should be added to each view.

Indexes.

- The first character of the index name must be an alpha. All others can be alphanumeric.
- Do not define an index for FREQUENTLY accessed read-only tables less than five pages. DB2 will use more time accessing the index than just scanning the entire tablespace.
- Do not define an index for INFREQUENTLY accessed read-only tables less than 10 pages.
- Do not define an index for a table with a low update rate (UPDATE, INSERT, or DELETE) if it has less than 15 data pages.
- A large number of indexes can add significantly to the I/O time for update and insert operations on columns participating in an index. Additional DASD space is also required for all the indexes. However, the performance impact will probably override those considerations. In fact, certain indexes will reduce I/O on certain updates and deletes.
- Not enough indexes will sometimes result from a tablespace scan; this will be inefficient when only a few rows are necessary to satisfy the request.
- Indexes are used by DB2 internally only in access path selection during the bind process. A user or application program CANNOT explicitly specify use of an index, and, in fact, unless large numbers of rows are being accessed, the index will actually impair performance.
- Good candidates for indexes are the following:
    - Columns frequently referenced by SELECT, JOIN, GROUP BY, or ORDER BY.
    - Columns frequently checked for EXISTENCE of certain values using the WHERE Clause.
    - Columns that are considered to be keys.
- Bad candidates for indexes are the following:
    - Columns that are frequently updated.
    - Columns with few distinct values such as the first or only column.
    - Columns longer than 40 bytes build indexes with multiple levels, thereby requiring additional I/O.
- Only the first eight bytes of the first column of a multiple-column index are considered by DB2 when determining first key cardinality.
- In a multiple-column index, the index is ONLY used when the high order column is coded with an '=' in the WHERE clause (e.g., WHERE col1 = 'ABC' and col2 = 123 and col3 > 456).
- If clustering is necessary, create the index using the CLUSTER parameter before loading the data. This will group the data and result in improved performance in queries involving the indexed column(s).
- A unique key is the best choice for a cluster index.

- You can determine whether or not DB2 will use an index by using the EXPLAIN option of the BIND command.
- A table can have several indexes but only one can be clustered.

Column.

- Use NOT NULL WITH DEFAULT as default.
- Avoid use of nullable columns. This causes greater CPU usage.
- VARCHAR should only be used when the length of the column varies by more than 20 bytes—probably even more. Use of VARCHAR results in very little savings when comparing extra CPU and programming time with DASD space utilization.
- Do not use VARCHAR for a column that is less than 20 characters long.
- Specify NOT NULL, or NOT NULL WITH DEFAULT, on all columns not requiring the null attribute.
- When using indexes to enforce uniqueness, remember that if you use NOT NULL WITH DEFAULT, only ONE row will be allowed to default.
- The data types of columns used in the WHERE clause comparison MUST be the SAME data types (e.g., comparisons in joining two tables).
- If two CHARACTER-type columns will be compared, they should be the same length.
- Columns defined as DECIMAL should always use ODD PRECISION —e.g., DECIMAL (7,2) instead of DECIMAL (6,2). This data definition will not require more space and will enable DB2 to process more efficiently.
- A COMMENT ON statement should be used for each column.

Synonym.

- Synonyms should be the same as the table or view for which the synonym has been created.
- Synonyms are valid for ONE user only and the USERID is always appended to the synonym name.

Plan.

- Plannames must be UNIQUE within a single DB2 subsystem.
- A planname is not qualified with a prefix.

BIND options.

- Plans will be bound with CS (Cursor Stability) option (unless deferred-update processing).
- Lock duration will be USE and COMMIT.

- Authorization check should be at bind time.
- AVOID execution time validation.
- Use EXPLAIN to determine access path and indexes used.

Referential integrity.

- Do not update primary keys.
- Create indexes for foreign keys.
- Remember referential integrity in backup/recovery.
- Do not place tables with referential ties to other tables in same tablespace with tables they are not related to. (Causes potential recovery problems.)

NAMING CONVENTIONS

Standard Conventions

Following is a naming standard that can be implemented to take into account all aspects of a data processing installation.

Assume 8-Character Length Limitation: **AABYXXXX**

AA—Alphanumeric Project ID

B—Resource Type (Non-DB2)

'C' = TSO Command List/Procedure
'D' = Dsect/Copybook/Data Structure
'E' = Data Element/Field
'F' = File/Database/Dataset
'I' = Index
'J' = Job/Jobstep
'K' = Document/Report
'L' = Project Function
'M' = Macro
'N' = Module
'O' = Object
'P' = Program
'Q' = Partition Element
'R' = Record/Segment
'S' = ISPF Screen
'T' = Transaction (CICS and IMS)
'Z' = System

YXXXX—Free-form project naming convention

BY—Resource Type (DB2)

B is always '2' for DB2 resources

'2B' = Tablespace
'2C' = DCLGEN Member
'2D' = Database
'2E' = Element (or Column)
'2G' = Storage Group
'2I' = Index
'2L' = Plan *
'2P' = Program
'2T' = Table
'2V' = View

Synonym will be same name as table/view.
XXXX—Free-form naming convention (except for plan)

* Last character for plan will be as follows:

'D' Development
'T' Test Integration
'S' Systems Integration
'P' Production Implementation

Other Recommendations

- Synonyms for tables and views have the same name as the table/views they are synonyms for except for the fourth character ('S' instead of 'V' or 'T').
- Program names should be same as plan name except for the fourth character ('P' instead of 'L'), and the eighth character in the program name should be blank.
- As one table per tablespace is the recommendation, the table and the tablespace should also have the same name except for the fourth character ('T' for table and 'B' for tablespace).

DB2 VSAM Data Sets

The data base name and tablespace name are included in the data set name that DB2 dynamically allocates. All DB2 data sets created by DB2 will have the following attributes. VSAM data sets that are created by DBA and SYSADM personnel must have the following attributes so that DB2 will find the necessary tables. If the data sets are not allocated as shown, DB2 will NOT be able to locate the tables necessary for processing requests.

on

catname.DSNDBx.dbname.tsname.I001.Annn

where:

catname = ICF catalog name
x   = C—VSAM cluster
x   = D—VSAM data component
dbname = DB2 DATABASE name (8 char)
tsname = Tablespace or Indexspace (8 char)
nnn   = 001 for single Tablespace.
           001,002, . . . for first partition, second partition
           and so on. If the size of the simple table space
           approaches 2 gigabytes, DB2 defines another
           data set and gives it the same name as the
           first DSN, and the number 002.

on

Another Naming Convention Just for DB2

First character determines DB2 object type.

- 'T' for table
- 'V' for view
- 'S' for tablespace

Synonym equals table name or view name.

DB2 Source Files Naming Convention

All DB2 source files should follow a standard naming convention that allows quick and easy location and usage in developed procedures for ease of use.

- Standard
- USERIDs (high-level qualifier) on each system
  - DBAXXX—System X
  - DBAYYY—System Y
- File Names/Descriptions
  - USERID.DB2.TABLES   — DB2 Table CREATE Source
  - USERID.DB2.VIEWS   — DB2 View CREATE Source
  - USERID.DB2.SYNONYMS — DB2 Synonym CREATE Source

– USERID.DB2.DCLGEN	– DBA Created DCLGEN Source
– USERID.DB2.SQL	– Various SQL Source
– USERID.DB2UTIL.CNTL	– DB2 Utility JCL

- DB2 Database Names/Creator Names

– XXXDEVDB/XXXDEV	– Project XXX Development
– XXXPRDDB/XXXPROD	– Project XXX Production
– INTTSTDB/INTTEST	– Integration Testing
– SYSTSTDB/SYSTEST	– Systems Testing

DB2 TABLE DESIGN CONSIDERATIONS

Logical Database Design Overview

Logical data base design affects many areas of application development and design. In addition, it is critical to ensuring effective use of overall system resources. Following is a list of areas impacted and how:

1. Data Requirements Definition
   a. Validates user-needs to data existence
   b. Validates that correct data relationships exist
   c. Reduces rework because of missed data relationships
   d. Reduces rework because of physical structure changes
2. Database Design
   a. Reduces narrow view of design
   b. Increases probability of valid physical data base design
   c. Allows design based upon system requirements
3. System Impact
   a. Allows data base design to reflect performance requirements
   b. Allows data base design to reflect system-wide needs
4. Standards Enforcement
   a. Allows extra level of standards enforcement

The Logical Design Process

The logical design process consists of the following five steps:

1. Data element definition
2. Data element relationships definition
3. Data model creation
4. Data flow definition
5. Data flow diagram creation

Each of the above will be described as to the processes and steps involved, and the forms and tools needed to perform each step. First, we will describe the naming conventions and structure icons that will be used in the processes and what they mean.

Definitions

A logical data base is a conceptual-level representation of either an entire organization's data or some standalone portion of an organization's data. It represents a single, unified view of the data that can be shared and understood by different entities within an organization, thus promoting data consistency and standardization.

In the icon scheme that will be used here, each data item will be represented by a box that shows what type of data item it is and some information about its relationship. In addition, an indication of its frequency requirements and mandatory/optional status will be shown. Before this can be achieved, every element within the organizational entity and all of its relationships must be defined.

Following is a description of terminology that will be used in the discussions.

Data element definition.   In the data-element definition process, each unique data element is defined and categorized. The definition process includes determining the following information about each data element:

- Name
- Description
- Type
- Size
- Editing characteristics
- Mandatory values (if any)

Data element relationships.   After the data elements themselves are defined, it is necessary to define the relationships that exist between each data element and other data elements. The result of this will be the data groups (otherwise known as tables, files, data bases, etc.). A data group is a group of data elements which all have some type of relationship to a key element defined in that group.

MANY-TO-MANY RELATIONSHIP.   If a data element has a many-to-many relationship with another data element, this is defined so that any value of it can be related to multiple values of another element, and multiple values of the other element can be related to multiple values of this data element.

EXAMPLE: Many different engines have the same parts in them. This is a many-to-many relationship.

MANY-TO-ONE RELATIONSHIP.   A data element has a many-to-one relationship with another data element when many values of it can be related to a single UNIQUE value of the related data element.

EXAMPLE: Parts in a single engine have a many-to-one relationship to that engine.

ONE-TO-MANY RELATIONSHIP. A data element has a one-to-many relationship with another data element when a single value of it can be related to multiple UNIQUE values of the related data element.

EXAMPLE: An engine with a specific serial number has a one-to-many relationship to the parts which are in that engine.

ONE-TO-ONE RELATIONSHIP. A one-to-one relationship exists when a data element which has been defined as a key is related to a single value of another data element which has been defined as a key.

EXAMPLE: The registration number of an automobile has a one-to-one relationship to the vehicle identification number.

COMPOUND KEYS. Compound keys are key elements which are composed of multiple data elements, each of which has certain definitions.

EXAMPLE: The order item number on a purchase order is composed of two elements: (1) the order number, and (2) the line item number on the order.

PRIMARY KEY. A primary key data element is the definitive data element in a group of data elements which defines a data group. Any element that has a one-to-many, many-to-one, or many-to-many relationship will be a primary key in a table.

EXAMPLE: The customer number in a customer data base containing information about the customer would be a primary key.

FOREIGN KEY. A foreign key data element is a data element in a group that is defined as a primary key in another table and is defined to have either a one-to-many, many-to-one, many-to-many, or one-to-one relationship to the primary key in this table.

EXAMPLE: The customer number in an order data base containing information about orders made by that customer would be a foreign key in this data base.

DESCRIPTIVE DATA ELEMENT. A descriptive data element is a data element in a group that only describes some aspects of the primary key of that data group and/or supplies additional information about that same key. This data element is not used in any other data group.

EXAMPLE: The customer name in a customer data base would be supplying additional information about the customer number that is the primary key within this data group.

INTEGRITY RULES. The integrity rules concerning each data element need to be defined to ensure that the required relationships are valid whenever data is added to the physical data structure containing the data base.

These integrity rules include the following:

- Entity integrity—Primary key must always be there.
- Referential integrity—Foreign keys are mandatory or optional.
- User-defined integrity—Other data-related rules.

Data model creation. After all of the relationships have been defined, the data model can be created. This model will graphically show each resultant data group, the contents of each data group, and any foreign-key relationships that exist.

Data structure icon representation. The icon representation that can be used for the data model Creation is as follows:

- Primary Key

```
*************
*   Primary   *
*     Key      *
*    Name      *
*************
```

- Descriptive Element

```
.......................
:    Descriptive    :
:     Element       :
:      Name         :
.......................
```

- Foreign Key—Many-to-Many Relationship

- Foreign Key—One-Many Relationship

```
              MMMMMMMMMM
          /    Primary Key    /  M
      1111111111111111         M
      1                  1     M
      1      Foreign     1     M
      1        Key       1     M
      1        Name      1     M
      1                  1
      1111111111111111
```

- Foreign Key—Many-One Relationship

```
          1111111111111111
          /    Primary Key    /  1
      MMMMMMMMMM               1
      M               M        1
      M     Foreign   M        1
      M       Key     M        1
      M       Name    M        1
      M               M
      MMMMMMMMMM
```

- Foreign Key—One-One

```
          1111111111111111111111
          /   Primary Key Name   /  1
      1111111111111111111111        1
      1                      1      1
      1        Foreign        1      1
      1          Key          1      1
      1          Name         1      1
      1                      1
      1111111111111111111111
```

• Compound Key

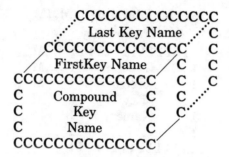

```
                              .CCCCCCCCCCCCCCC
                      .       Last Key Name  . C
                .CCCCCCCCCCCCCCC'     C
                     FirstKey Name  / C   C
            CCCCCCCCCCCCCCC'     C   C
            C      Compound     C   C
            C        Key        C   C.
            C        Name       C   /
            CCCCCCCCCCCCCCC'
```

The entity requirement of whether an entry is mandatory or optional can be designated by placing an (M) for mandatory, or an (O) for optional in the data element box.

EXAMPLE:

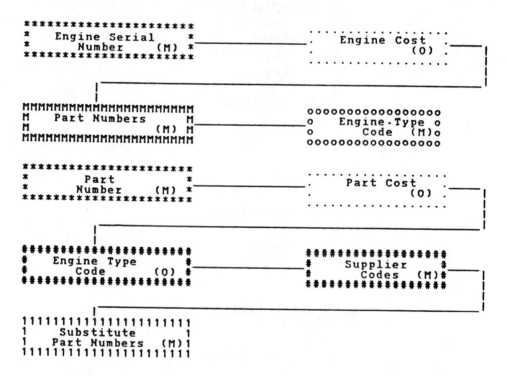

```
************************                      . . . . . . . . . . . . . . . .
*    Engine Serial     *                      .    Engine Cost    .
*         Number    (M) *_____.               (O) ._____
************************                      . . . . . . . . . . . . . . . . |
                                                                              |
        |_____|
        |
MMMMMMMMMMMMMMMMMMMMMMMM                       OOOOOOOOOOOOOOOOOOOO
M     Part Numbers    M                        O    Engine·Type  O
M              (M)    M_____  O       Code   (M)O
MMMMMMMMMMMMMMMMMMMMMMMM                        OOOOOOOOOOOOOOOOOOOO

************************                       . . . . . . . . . . . . . .
*        Part          *                       .    Part Cost    .
*        Number    (M) *_____ .             (O) ._____
************************                       . . . . . . . . . . . . . . |
                                                                           |
        |_____|
        |
#######################                        ####################
#     Engine Type     #                        #     Supplier     #
#         Code    (O) #_____  #     Codes   (M)#_____
#######################                        ####################     |
                                                                        |
        |_____|
        |
11111111111111111111111
1     Substitute       1
1     Part Numbers  (M)1
11111111111111111111111
```

Data-Element-Based Design

After the logical data model has been developed, it is easy to translate the model into the DB2 physical design. Because of the similarity between logical data modeling and the DB2 relational structure, the first cut at the physical design is almost a direct transformation.

If the logical data model was created using the techniques defined above, a data-element-based design has been done.

Denormalization for Performance Considerations

After the first design attempt has resulted in a physical DB2 structure (tables), the process of denormalization can begin. This involves knowing how much data will be input into each table and in finding out how the data will be accessed. With this knowledge, the creation of indexes and the combination of specific tables and/or columns into other tables can begin. This combining process is known as 'denormalization for performance considerations.'

The prime consideration for combining tables is whether the amounts of data to be input into certain tables is small, and the relationships of the data to other table data is not large. The data can then be combined, as the usage of DASD is much less a factor compared to access time and CPU requirements.

Another way to denormalize DB2 structures is to keep the tables intact, with their data groups composed of only the primary key and descriptive data elements, and to create cross-reference tables which are composed of just secondary keys that have relationships to each other.

EXAMPLE: In the engine example listed previously, you would build a parts table, an engine serial number table, and an engine type table. Then a cross-reference table would be created which would contain part number, engine type code, and engine serial number. Then, depending upon which relationship you were accessing, you would read the cross-reference file, extract the keys you need, and then read the needed master file.

Remembering Views in Design

When doing DB2 table design, you need to remember the view capability so that you do NOT design into the DB2 structure particular access requirements based upon application needs. In most cases, a particular application requirement can be satisfied by creating a logical table or view of the necessary data without changing the physical structure in its relationship to the logical structure.

Referential Integrity Using Data-Driven Methodology

After the logical design has been completed, the implementation of Referential Integrity is simple:

1. Defined PRIMARY KEYS become DB2 PRIMARY KEYS
2. Defined FOREIGN KEYS become DB2 FOREIGN KEYS
3. PRIMARY KEY Definitions become DB2 BASE TABLES

4. Many-to-Many Relationships become DB2 CROSS REFERENCE TABLES

APPLICATION DESIGN CONSIDERATIONS

The design of application systems depends upon what type of access to DB2 is going to be done, that is, whether it will be TSO/ISPF, CICS, IMS/DC, the CALL ATTACH facility, or batch. The considerations of good design in each of those subsystems should continue to be followed.

Deciding What to Use—TSO/ISPF, CICS, IMS/DC, or Call Attach

In some cases, there will exist various options as to what system you will write DB2 applications in. Each of the options has its pros and cons, and many times the decision will be based upon the level of expertise and the resources available. If there is, in fact, an option, the following characteristics need to be taken into account.

Thread utilization. The thread concept is how applications access DB2 data. This thread is used to do the following:

- Identify the user
- Allocate DB2 resources
- Execute user requests

One of the most important aspects of application design is the minimizing of the times a thread is allocated to an application. In this way, the total number of threads that can be allocated at any point in time can increase, thus improving total system throughput.

High-volume, repetitive transactions require that allocation overhead is minimized. This is accomplished by the following:

- Using ACQUIRE (ALLOCATE) BIND option
- Using RELEASE (DEALLOCATE) BIND option
- Reusing the thread

A large number of plan allocations will use significant amounts of CPU. The options described above will reduce this.

For thread reuse, the transaction manager will determine what particular considerations need to be analyzed for effective thread usage.

TSO/ISPF THREAD CHARACTERISTICS. In a TSO environment, threads cannot be reused by multiple users because a thread is created for each TSO address space accessing DB2. A TSO application will hold the thread from the first SQL call until the application is terminated. Therefore, the application needs to be designed so that the total logical process is completed for a given application during a single transaction with no terminal interaction, else the thread will be unavailable as well as being unused.

CICS THREAD CHARACTERISTICS. In CICS, a thread is used from the time of the first SQL call until a COMMIT is issued, or the transaction terminates. Minimize time for thread use by NOT doing the following when a thread has been allocated:

- NO conversational processing
- NO synchronous writes to the terminal
- NO other CICS or DL/I time-consuming services

Thread reuse needs to be considered for high-volume transactions. Thread reuse can only be done among transactions of the same Resource Control Table (RCT) entry. Because of thread reuse, you may try to group logical transactions into a single application plan and allocate dedicated RCT entries to this group of transactions. If you do this, however, you must handle transaction-level security within CICS as far as the DB2 authorization requirements are considered.

IMS/DC THREAD CHARACTERISTICS. In IMS, there is only ONE thread per dependent region. If you can reduce application elapsed time, you can then reduce the number of IMS regions, and thus the number of overall threads. IMS itself allocates threads from the first SQL call in the IMS schedule through program termination.

High-volume IMS transactions should be defined as 'Wait for Input' (WFI) transactions. This will cause the thread to be reused continually without reallocating it. Because each of the WFI-type transactions requires its own address space, grouping of related logical transactions into a single application program identified to IMS as 'one transaction group' is recommended.

Using Dynamic vs. Static SQL

The overwhelming factor to consider in the comparison of Dynamic vs. Static SQL is that all Dynamic SQL calls must do the BIND process for every call. This can have a tenfold or more increase in the number of instructions created for the run-time module. Also, more I/O is done in satisfying the authorization check and path selection process requirements. If the design seems to call for a Dynamic SQL process, analyze it for possible multiple static calls instead. Many seemingly Dynamic SQL requirements turn out to be a finite set of static calls instead.

Using QMF Instead of Custom Code

In many cases, it is possible to use the QMF instead of writing application code. This can be done without the personnel using the system having to even learn QMF. They can use the ISPF Dialog Manager to front-end the actual QMF procedures and queries that can be created, or just have the user select pre-created QMF procedures and/or queries by using QMF synonyms or executing the QMF procedures from an ISPF selection panel. If the queries are not high-usage queries, this can be an aid to developing systems quickly.

Application Restart for TSO Batch

DB2 batch programs run under TSO batch. As such, there are no checkpoint/restart capabilities built into the system. Therefore, in order to provide a restart capability, you must use the OS CHECKPOINT/RESTART facility.

If you do use this facility, it is recommended that you at least perform a COMMIT for each checkpoint. Remember that the cursor position is lost when a COMMIT statement is issued.

A suggestion for large update systems is to group the updates by some set of keys, with each update call followed by a COMMIT. Also make sure that the program itself has an error routine that performs all necessary clean-up and provides the necessary information required for a successful recovery and/or restart.

SQL CREATION CONSIDERATIONS

Advantage of SQL

The big advantage of using SQL in combination with a good DB2 table design and views is that correctly defined SQL can eliminate the need for a large percentage of customized program code. This is done because of the ability to join different data from different tables, and through the judicious use of the WHERE clause and other SQL clauses, DB2 will perform a great many of the processes that formally had to be coded in other systems. These powerful capabilities also can result in very bad performance and incorrect results if the SQL is not correct. As such, while life as far as coding goes is much simpler, the necessity to learn the intricacies of SQL becomes more pronounced.

General SQL 'Rules of Thumb'

Following are some considerations and standards to follow in the creation of SQL statements:

1. Design SQL statements to take advantage of indexes.
2. Use of IN, LIKE, and OR will not take advantage of any indexes created for columns that use those predicates.

3. Use joins instead of subqueries.
4. Use redundant information in joins.
5. Analyze usage of temporary tables in joins.
6. Avoid numeric conversion.
7. Avoid string truncation.
8. Do not use an arithmetic expression as an operand to be compared to a column in a WHERE clause.
9. Do not use SELECT *, especially when ordering rows. Select only the columns that you need.
10. Do not use the NOT predicate. It should be used only for negating very complex predicates.
11. Use DISTINCT in conjunction with columns that have indexes.
12. Use ORDER BY and GROUP BY in conjunction with the columns that have indexes.

Cursor Operations

Most application programs will be using one or more cursors to work on sets of rows. When using these cursors, the following should be remembered:

- Cursor Stability (CS) option does not lock pages for non-X locks.
- Repeatable Read (RR) option locks all pages.
- Cursor positioning is LOST on COMMIT or ROLLBACK.
- In tablespace scan, cursor repositioning causes another full tablespace scan.
- If application needs to compare rows from same table, open two (or more) cursors for the same table.

Single-Row Operations

In any case when a row is unique, do NOT use a cursor. Use a standard SELECT statement. This is more efficient than opening a cursor. This applies for UPDATE and DELETE also unless the row must be read before the row is updated. In this case, use a cursor.

Multiple-Row Update/Delete

The most effective way of performing multiple-row UPDATE and/or DELETE processes is by using the set capability of the SQL language. This requires a knowledge of the data and the correct creation of an SQL statement with all the necessary predicates. This is not possible if the application must examine the data to make a decision. The cost of the process increases as follows:

- One Update/Delete statement
- One cursor operation

- Multiple Update/Delete statements
- Multiple Cursor operations

Aggregate Functions

The SQL SELECT statement has five built-in functions or aggregations. These functions can be used to reduce the code that is necessary to be written to perform the same function. The SQL aggregation in most cases will be less expensive to run than to have the application do it.

Columns with null values that are used in aggregate functions will be ignored. However, those defined as 'not null with default' will all be included in the aggregate function.

The aggregate functions are:

- COUNT
- AVG
- MAX
- MIN
- SUM

GROUP BY

Using GROUP BY is cheaper than using application code.

Using and Understanding EXPLAIN

Selecting the EXPLAIN option of the BIND process shows the access path which will be selected for the SQL statements defined in your application plan. This is the only way to determine what the execution of your DB2 application will actually do as far as DB2 is concerned.

The information that can be determined is:

- Access order of tables
- Indexes that will be used
- Methods used for joins and sorts
- Processing costs of SQL statements

What must be remembered is that this information is based upon the amount of data and indexes that exist at the time the EXPLAIN is requested. If the indexes in existence or the amounts of data change and you have reexecuted RUNSTATS, the EXPLAIN must be done again.

EXPLAIN can be executed as an option for the BIND and REBIND statements for an entire application plan, or it can be executed as a statement by itself on either a specific plan, all plans that you have created, or on a specific SQL statement.

Creating the PLAN_TABLE EXPLAIN TABLE. To use the EXPLAIN option, you must first have a PLAN_TABLE table defined for your TSO USERID. The sample for this CREATE table resides in the DB2 DSNSAMP data set with the member name of DSNTESC. The CREATE TABLE statement is:

```
        CREATE TABLE USERID.PLAN_TABLE
(   QUERYNO               INTEGER NOT NULL,
    QBLOCKNO              SMALLINT NOT NULL,
    APPLNAME              CHAR(8) NOT NULL,
    PROGNAME              CHAR(8) NOT NULL,
    PLANNO                SMALLINT NOT NULL,
    METHOD                SMALLINT NOT NULL,
    CREATOR               CHAR(8) NOT NULL,
    TNAME                 CHAR(18) NOT NULL,
    TABNO                 SMALLINT NOT NULL,
    ACCESSTYPE            CHAR(2) NOT NULL,
    MATCHCOLS             SMALLINT NOT NULL,
    ACCESSCREATOR         CHAR(8) NOT NULL,
    ACCESSNAME            CHAR(18) NOT NULL,
    INDEXONLY             CHAR(1) NOT NULL,
    SORTN_UNIQ            CHAR(1) NOT NULL,
    SORTN_JOIN            CHAR(1) NOT NULL,
    SORTN_ORDERBY         CHAR(1) NOT NULL,
    SORTN_GROUPBY         CHAR(1) NOT NULL,
    SORTC_UNIQ            CHAR(1) NOT NULL,
    SORTC_JOIN            CHAR(1) NOT NULL,
    SORTC_ORDERBY         CHAR(1) NOT NULL,
    SORTC_GROUPBY         CHAR(1) NOT NULL,
    TSLOCKMODE            CHAR(3) NOT NULL,
    TIMESTAMP             CHAR(16) NOT NULL,
    REMARKS               VARCHAR(254) NOT NULL
```

IN database.tablespace;

PLAN_TABLE description. The definitions of the columns in the PLAN_

TABLE are as follows:

- QUERYNO
  If SET QUERYNO = n was used, this value will be n. Otherwise, the value is set by DB2 and corresponds to the SQL statement number in the appropriate DBRM.
- QBLOCKNO
  The QBLOCKNO is the number that identifies subselects in an explainable SQL-statement. The top-level subselect is numbered 1.

- APPLNAME

  APPLNAME is the application plan name. It is blank for dynamically created EXPLAIN and for SQL statement-only EXPLAIN request.

- PROGNAME

  PROGNAME is the name of the DBRM in which the EXPLAIN statement is embedded.

- PLANNO

  The PLANNO number identifies which step of the application plan the subselect identified when QBLOCKNO was processed. Each new table defined for access requires a new step in the plan.

- METHOD

  The METHOD number indicates the method used in this step. The possible values and meanings are:

  - 0—Access a first table (PLANNO = 1)
  - 1—Nested loop JOIN
  - 2—Merge scan JOIN
  - 3—Additional sorts

- CREATOR

  Creator of the new table accessed in this step.

- TNAME

  Table name accessed in this step.

- TABNO

  TABNO is a number used to distinguish different references to the same table.

- ACCESSTYPE

  ACCESSTYPE is the method used to access this table. Possible values are:

  - I—By an index
  - R—Tablespace scan of ALL pages
  - Blank—QBLOCKNO 1 of an INSERT statement or UPDATE and DELETE statements that use WHERE CURRENT

- MATCHCOLS

  Use MATCHCOLS for ACCESSTYPE I number of columns used in index to match predicate. Otherwise, it is 0.

- ACCESSCREATOR

  Use ACCESSCREATOR for ACCESSTYPE I only—Creator of index.

- ACCESSNAME

  Use ACCESSNAME for ACCESSTYPE I only—Name of index.

- INDEXONLY

  'Y' if only index must be accessed, enter 'N' if data must also be accessed.

- SORTN_UNIQ

  'Y' if a sort is performed to remove duplicate rows from new table. Otherwise, 'N'.

- SORTN_JOIN

'Y' if a sort is performed on new table for Method 2 JOIN. Otherwise, 'N'.

- SORTN_ORDERBY

  'Y' if a sort is performed on new table for ORDER BY. Otherwise, 'N'.
- SORTN_GROUPBY

  'Y' if a sort is performed on new table for GROUP BY. Otherwise, 'N'.
- SORTC_UNIQ

  'Y' if a sort is performed to remove duplicate rows from composite table. Otherwise, 'N'.
- SORTC_JOIN

  'Y' if a sort is performed on composite table for Method 2 JOIN. Otherwise, 'N'.
- SORTC_ORDERBY

  'Y' if a sort is performed on composite table for ORDER BY. Otherwise, 'N'.
- SORTC_GROUPBY

  'Y' if a sort is performed on composite table for GROUP BY. Otherwise, 'N'.
- TSLOCKMODE

  TSLOCKMODE is lock mode applied to the tablespace containing the new table. Possible Values are:

  - IS (Intent Share)

    Intent is to read data but NOT change it. Other programs may both read AND change.
  - IX (Intent Exclusive)

    Intent is to read data AND change it.
  - S (Share)

    Read only. NO ONE can update data.
  - X (Exclusive)

    Read and update. NO ONE else can access data, either read or update.
  - SIX (Share with Intent Exclusive)

    Read and update intent. NO ONE can update data, but anyone can read the data.
- TIMESTAMP

  Timestamp of EXPLAIN processing.
- REMARKS

  Remarks is an empty string. Can be updated by user.

Analyzing EXPLAIN results. You analyze the EXPLAIN results by using SQL to create statements that access the particular rows and columns in the PLAN_TABLE that you are interested in. The primary column, called QUERYNO, defines all rows that pertain to a particular SQL statement.

The purposes and uses of the EXPLAIN output are:

- Assist in application design by
  - Determining chosen access path
  - Identifying large SORT bottlenecks
- Determine when PLAN REBIND is needed
- Determine bottlenecks
- Assist in database design
- Show need for additional indexes
- Show unneeded indexes

The items to analyze are:

- All sorts
- All ACCESSTYPE = 'R'
- LOCK modes (especially 'S')

Changing DB2 catalog entries for EXPLAIN. With Version 2.1 the capability exists to change certain of the DB2 catalog entries in an attempt to better evaluate the EXPLAIN results without creating full size tables and associated data. By changing the appropriate column values, a BIND can be performed with EXPLAIN which will show potential performance problems in a full-blown production environment without having to create that environment.
The following columns can be changed:

in SYSIBM.SYSTABLES:

CARD Total number of ROWS in table

NPAGES Total number of pages on which rows appear.

PCTPAGES For nonsegmented tablespaces contains percentage of total pages of the tablespace which contain rows of the selected table.

For segmented tablespaces contains the percentage of total pages in the set of segments assigned to the table which contains rows for this table.

The columns above would be the ones to be changed to effect the SIZE-based parameters within the Optimizer.

in SYSIBM.SYSCOLUMNS:

HIGH2KEY Second highest column value

LOW2KEY Second lowest column value

COLCARD Number of distinct values of column

in SYSIBM.SYSTABLESPACE:

NACTIVE Number of active pages in a tablespace

The column above would also be changed to effect the SIZE-based parameters within the Optimizer.

in SYSIBM.SYSINDEXES:

CLUSTERRATIO Shows percentage of rows in table in clustering Order

FIRSTKEYCARD Number of distinct values of first key column

FULLKEYCARD Number of distinct values of key

NLEAF Number of Active Leaf Pages

NLEVELS Number of Levels in the Index Tree

The columns above would be the ones to be changed to effect the INDEX-based parameters upon SIZE within the Optimizer.

APPLICATION PROGRAMMING TECHNIQUES

Rules of Thumb

- Do NOT use SELECT *.
- Use views whenever possible.
- Programs should be as small as possible.
- SQL statements embedded in applications programs should follow the SQL guidelines.
- Dynamic SQL should be avoided if at all possible.
- COMMIT should be issued at the end of each logical unit of work. This will free all tablespace and page locks caused by the program.
- Do not specify repeatable read [ISOLATION (RR)] at bind time unless your application must read multiple rows in order to make an update decision, or if a given row must not change until the end of a logical unit of work. Repeatable read will force DB2 to lock every page accessed and to hold the lock until a COMMIT is issued. This results in less concurrency. Specify cursor stability (CS) to ensure application concurrency.
- All applications should have an error routine that checks the SQLCODE (return code) to determine whether an SQL statement was successfully executed, and should also use the IBM-supplied DSNTIAR SQL error routine.
- Use the LOCK TABLE statement with care. It locks up ALL the tables in the tablespace, the locks are held until COMMIT or DEALLOCATION occurs, and all other users are locked out of the tablespace. Another reason for one table per tablespace.

SQL Return Code Processing

Because of the complexity of the DB2 system, return codes may have many meanings. In addition, many of these return codes have multiple subcodes that are necessary to fully determine what problem has occurred. Following sections include information on implementation in the currently available environments (batch, TSO, CICS), locations and descriptions of the sample routines, and a listing of each of the two supplied routines (one for COBOL and one for PLI) and their related data areas.

The basis of each routine, no matter in which environment or language it is used, is a call to the IBM-supplied DSNTIAR routine which is composed of the DSNTIAR SQLCA formatting module and the DSNTIAM SQLCA formatting routine. These are routines written in assembler which are part of the DB2 sample library. The resultant load module is located in the following library:

- DSN120.DSNSAMP

For further information on and a listing of this procedure, refer to the following manual:

- SC26-4086 *IBM DATABASE 2 Sample Application Guide*

Environmental Usage

The call to DSNTIAR can occur in any environment if the appropriate linkage editor steps have been taken. Where the results of the call to DSNTIAR go is dependent upon where the programmer decides to send them. Following are recommendations based on each environment.

1. Batch
   In a batch environment, the results of the call should go to a predefined error and/or status file that is defined within the program for that purpose.
2. TSO
   In a TSO environment, the results of the call should also go to a predefined error and/or status file and to the terminal executing the DB2 program if possible, but at least always to an external file so that the data is not lost through screen erasure or an inability of the program to communicate with the executing terminal.
3. CICS
   In a CICS environment, the results of the call should also go to a predefined CICS region-wide error and/or status file and to the user on the terminal that was executing the DB2 program, if possible, but at least always to the external file within CICS so that the data is not lost through screen erasure or an inability of the program to communicate with the executing terminal.
4. Programming Languages
   Programming languages are supplied CICS and PLI routines which call the DSNTIAR SQLCA formatting routine and process to results.

These can be included in a programmer's program and can be modified to fit specific output requirements. When using these, remember that they are tied into the use of the SQLWARNING and SQLERROR statements. These particular samples use common data areas which are also shown.

Location of Samples

The sample code and data areas listed are members in the following data sets:

- COBOL Common Area Sample — DSN120.DSNSAMP (DSN8MCCA)
- COBOL Code Sample — DSN120.DSNSAMP (DSN8MCXX)
- PLI Common Area Sample — DSN120.DSNSAMP (DSN8MPCA)
- PLI Code Sample — DSN120.DSNSAMP (DSN8MPXX)

DB2 Application Referential Integrity Considerations

Before Version 2.1 of DB2, it did not support referential integrity and these requirements had to be written into the applications. Because this facility is now part of DB2, any built-in application code can now be removed or not written at all, as long as the referential integrity was defined in the tables.

DB2 AND SQL LIMITS

The following tables list limits imposed by DB2 and SQL:

DB2 Object Length Limits

ITEMS	LIMITS
TABLE	1 - 18 characters
INDEX	1 - 18 characters
VIEW	1 - 18 characters
COLUMN	1 - 18 characters
SYNONYM	1 - 18 characters
CORRELATION-NAME	1 - 18 characters
PLAN NAME	1 - 18 characters
STORAGE GROUP	1 - 8 characters
DATABASE	1 - 8 characters
TABLESPACE	1 - 8 characters
AUTHORIZATION -ID	1 - 8 characters

DB2 Data Length Limits

TABLE LENGTH (including overhead bytes)	for 4k PAGES - 4056 for 32K PAGES-32714
CHAR value	1 - 254
GRAPHIC value	1 - 127
VARCHAR or VARGRAPHIC column	for 4k PAGES - 4046 for 32K PAGES-32704
LONG VARCHAR or LONG VARGRAPHIC	calculated by DB2
INTEGER value	-2147483648 to +2147483647
SMALLINT value	-32768 to +32767
FLOAT value	-7.2E+75 to +5.4E-79

DECIMAL(m,n) value	m=total # of digits
	  +999999999999999
	to -999999999999999
	n=digits/fraction
	  >0 and <=m

Longest SQLDA and the largest number of HOST and INDICATOR VARIABLES pointed to in an SQLDA	32767 bytes
HOST VARIABLE used for insert or update	32704 bytes
Longest SQL statement	32765 bytes

DB2 Object Amount Limits

TABLE names in an SQL statement (In a complex SELECT, the number of TABLES can be joined nay be less)	1 - 15, depending on the SQL statement
NUMBER OF COLUMNS IN A TABLE OR VIEW (the value depends on the complexity of CREATE VIEW statement)	1 - 300
HOST VARIABLES in a PRECOMPILED PROGRAM	system storage
HOST VARIABLES in an SQL statement	system storage
ELEMENTS in a SELECT list	1 -300
FUNCTIONS in a SELECT list	system storage
PREDICATES in a WHERE or HAVING clause	1 - 300
Total length of COLUMNS in a GROUP BY clause	1 - 4044
Total length of COLUMNS in an ORDER BY clause	1 - 4044
Number of COLUMNS in an INDEX KEY	1 - 16
INDEX KEY for a NON-PARTITIONED TABLE SPACE	1 - 255 bytes less the # of key columns that allow nulls
INDEX KEY for a partitioned TABLESPACE	1 - 40 bytes less the # of key columns that allow nulls
INDEXES on a TABLE	system storage
PARTITIONS in a PARTITIONED TABLESPACE	1 - 64
VOLUME IDs in a STORAGE GROUP	1- 133

DB2 and Related-Products Usage Guide

7

USING DB2 UNDER THE TIME SHARING OPTION (TSO)

DB2 can be accessed under the time-sharing option of TSO in three ways:

- Interactive System Productivity Facility (ISPF) under TSO
- Native TSO
- Batch TSO

In using DB2 in online mode under native TSO or ISPF, the user must have allocated to him a TSO log-on procedure which has in it the appropriate DB2 and related-products (QMF, DBEDIT, DBMAUI, DXT, etc.) data sets. In batch mode, the appropriate data sets are defined in the Job Control Language (JCL) used to execute the TSO batch program known as IKJEFT01.

DB2 Applications Using TSO/ISPF

Applications using the ISPF Dialog Manager and DB2 can be written and run under the TSO/ISPF session. Batch applications can also be written but must be run using the batch TSO program IKJETF01 executing the TSO DSN Command Processor.

Using DB2 Under TSO/ISPF

DB2 can be used under the ISPF through the selection of it from one or more ISPF menu panels.

A sample ISPF Primary Option menu panel is shown below.

```
|--------------------------------------------------------------------------|
|------------ ------------- ISPF/PDF Primary Option Menu -----------------  |
|OPTION ===>                                                    USERID  -   |
|                                                                           |
|0 ISPF PARMS   Specify terminal and user parameters            PREFIX  -   |
|1 BROWSE       Display source data or output listings          TIME    -   |
|2 EDIT         Create or change source data (default)          DATE    -   |
|3 UTILITIES    Perform utility functions                       JUL DATE -  |
|4 FOREGROUND   Invoke language processors in foreground        TERMINAL -  |
|5 BATCH        Submit job for language processing              PF KEYS  -  |
|6 COMMAND      Enter TSO command or CLIST                                  |
|7 TEST         Perform dialog testing                                      |
|8 SDSF         Display your job queues and job output                      |
|                                                                           |
|D *DB2*        Display  DB2  Options                                       |
|                                                                           |
|T TUTORIAL     Display  ISPF/PDF  information                              |
|                                                                           |
|X EXIT         Using LIST/LOG defaults                                     |
|Press END KEY to terminate ISPF                                           |
|                                                                           |
|--------------------------------------------------------------------------|
```

Accessing DB2 through a menu panel set as above would be done by entering 'D' in the option field and depressing the Enter key. This would result in another menu panel being presented, something like the DB2 Selection menu panel shown below.

DB2 Selection Menu

Depending upon the number of DB2 products installed and available to you, a menu of DB2-related products would be shown to you after selecting the DB2 products entry in the Primary Option menu.

```
|--------------------------------------------------------------------------|
|------------------------- DB2 SELECTION MENU ---------------------------   |
|OPTION  ===>                                                               |
|                                                                           |
|   D - DB2         - DB2 Perform DATABASE 2 interactive functions          |
|  QP - QMF PROD    - QMF Query Management Facility (PROD)                   |
|  QT - QMF TEST    - QMF Query Management Facility (TEST)                   |
|  QM - QMF MSG     - QMF Message Tool                                       |
|  QS - QMF SQL     - QMF SQL Building Application                          |
|   P - DB2PM       - DB2PM Interactive Report Facility                     |
|  MP - DBMAUI P    - DB2 Migration Aid Utility (PROD)                      |
|  MT - DBMAUI T    - DB2 Migration Aid Utility (TEST)                      |
|  EP - DBEDIT P    - DB2 Edit Facility (PROD)                              |
|  ET - DBEDIT T    - DB2 Edit Facility (TEST)                              |
|  DA - DXT ADMIN   - Invoke DXT V2 Administrative Dialogs                  |
|  DE - DXT END US  - Invoke DXT V2 End User Dialogs                        |
|                                                                           |
|--------------------------------------------------------------------------|
```

From this menu, you would select the desired DB2 function or related product. The option you select will determine the next panel or screen that you see.

DB2I Primary Option Menu

If you select 'D', you will see the DB2 Interactive (DB2I) Primary Option menu. This menu includes the various functions that are part of the DB2 product itself.

```
r----------------------------------------------------------------------------
|                         DB2I PRIMARY OPTION MENU
|===>
|
|Select one of the following DB2 functions and press ENTER.
|  1   SPUFI                    (Process SQL statements)
|  2   DCLGEN                   (Generate SQL and source language declarations)
|  3   PROGRAM PREPARATION      (Prepare a DB2 application program to run)
|  4   PRECOMPILE               (Invoke DB2 precompiler)
|  5   BIND/REBIND/FREE         (BIND, REBIND, or FREE application plans)
|  6   RUN                      (RUN an SQL program)
|  7   DB2 COMMANDS             (Issue DB2 commands)
|  8   UTILITIES                (Invoke DB2 utilities)
|  D   DB2I DEFAULTS            (Set global parameters)
|  X   EXIT                     (Leave DB2I)
|
|
|
|
|
|
|PRESS:  END to exit         HELP for more information
|
L----------------------------------------------------------------------------
```

From this menu, you would select the desired DB2 function that you need.

Selecting the DB2 online tutorial. You can view an online tutorial of information about DB2 and the DB2I by depressing the Help (PF1) key from this panel. This tutorial is a subset of information extracted from the various DB2 reference manuals and is designed to provide reference information as well as instruction for the online user.

DB2 ONLINE HELP

```
r----------------------------------------------------------------------------
|
|                 HELP for DB2I PRIMARY OPTION MENU              Page
|===>
|
|he DB2I (DB2 Interactive) task panels allow you to perform programmer,
|dministrator, and operator tasks interactively, by filling in fields
|n task panels.
|
|his panel is an example of the HELP panels available with task panels,
|hich you see when you press the HELP PF key.
|
|ome HELP panels, like this one, show you a list of topics. For informat
|n any of the topics, enter its number on the command line and press ENT
|o begin to see all topics in order, press ENTER only.
|
|opics:
|  A   Using the HELP panels
|  B   Overview of DB2I
|  C   Using PF keys with the task panels
|  D   Default values on the task panels
|
|RESS:  END to exit      UP for the DB2I tutorial menu
|
|
L----------------------------------------------------------------------------
```

SPUFI—SQL processor using file input. If you select the SPUFI option (1) from the DB2I Primary Option menu, you will see the panel below, which is the entry panel to use the SQL Processor Using File Input (SPUFI) function within DB2. This function allows the submission of Structured Query Language (SQL) statements into DB2. These statements must exist in a sequential data set or as a member of a partitioned data set (PDS).

```
------------------------------------------------------------------------------
|                               SPUFI                                         |
| ===>                                                                        |
|                                                                             |
|Enter the input data set name:          (Can be sequential or partitioned)   |
| 1  DATA SET NAME ... ===> DB2.SQL(CHKINDEX)                                  |
| 2  VOLUME SERIAL ... ===>               (Enter if not cataloged)            |
| 3  DATA SET PASSWORD ===>               (Enter if password protected)       |
|Enter the output data set name:         (Must be a sequential data set)      |
| 4  DATA SET NAME ... ===> DB2.LISTA                                         |
|                                                                             |
|Specify processing options:                                                  |
| 5  CHANGE DEFAULTS    ===> NO           (Y/N - Display SPUFI defaults panel?)|
| 6  EDIT INPUT ......  ===> YES          (Y/N - Enter SQL statements?)        |
| 7  EXECUTE .........  ===> YES          (Y/N - Execute SQL statements?)      |
| 8  AUTOCOMMIT ......  ===> YES          (Y/N - Commit after successful run?) |
| 9  BROWSE OUTPUT ...  ===> YES          (Y/N - Browse output data set?)      |
|                                                                             |
|                                                                             |
|                                                                             |
|PRESS: ENTER to process    END to exit    HELP for more information          |
------------------------------------------------------------------------------
```

Current SPUFI default panel.   If you place YES in the CHANGE DE-FAULTS field in the SPUFI panel above, you will receive the panel below. In this panel, you select your SPUFI processing defaults. The defaults below are recommended. You only have to set the defaults once. Once they are set, you can set the CHANGE DEFAULTS field to NO to keep from receiving this default panel every time you process some SQL.

```
------------------------------------------------------------------------------
|                        CURRENT SPUFI DEFAULTS                               |
| ===>                                                                        |
|                                                                             |
|Enter the following to control your SPUFI session:                           |
| 1  ISOLATION LEVEL    ===> CS          (RR=Repeatable Read, CS=Cursor Stability|
| 2  MAX SELECT LINES   ===> 10000       (Maximum number of lines to be        |
|                                          returned from a SELECT)            |
|Output data set characteristics:                                             |
| 3  RECORD LENGTH ...  ===> 133         (LRECL=Logical record length)        |
| 4  BLOCK SIZE ......  ===> 3990        (Size of one block)                  |
| 5  RECORD FORMAT ...  ===> FBA         (RECFM=F, FB, FBA, V, VB, or VBA)     |
| 6  DEVICE TYPE .....  ===> SYSDA       (Must be DASD unit name)             |
|Output format characteristics:                                               |
| 7  MAX NUMERIC FIELD  ===> 20          (Maximum width for numeric fields)   |
| 8  MAX CHAR FIELD ..  ===> 200         (Maximum width for character fields) |
| 9  COLUMN HEADING ..  ===> NAMES       (NAMES, LABELS, ANY or BOTH)         |
|                                                                             |
|                                                                             |
|                                                                             |
|PRESS: ENTER to proceed    END to exit    HELP for more information          |
------------------------------------------------------------------------------
```

DCLGEN.   If you select the DCLGEN (Declarations Generation) function (2) from the DB2I menu, you will receive the panel below. You would select this panel if you needed to generate SQL Declaration statements for your applications.

```
r----------------------------------------------------------------------------
I                              DCLGEN
I===>
I
IEnter table name for which declarations are required:
I  1   SOURCE TABLE NAME ===> 'TECHSPT.TCBTCSBS'
I
IEnter destination data set:             (Can be sequential or partitioned)
I  2   DATA SET NAME ... ===> 'USERID.DB2.DCLGEN(TCBTCSBS)'
I  3   DATA SET PASSWORD ===>            (If password protected)
I
IEnter options as desired:
I  4   ACTION .......... ===> REPLACE  (ADD new or REPLACE old declarations)
I  5   COLUMN LABEL .... ===> YES      (Enter YES for column label)
I  6   STRUCTURE NAME .. ===> TCBTCSBS-TABLE                     (Optional)
I  7   FIELD NAME PREFIX ===>                                   (Optional)
I
I
I
I
IPRESS: ENTER to process     END to exit      HELP for more information
I
L----------------------------------------------------------------------------
```

Online program preparation.   If you select the online PROGRAM PREP-ARATION (3) function from the DB2I menu, you will receive the panel below. You would select this panel if you were preparing DB2 application programs to run. The options that you will enter on this panel will depend upon what process you are trying to do, what language you are using, and what other specialized interfaces you need.

```
r----------------------------------------------------------------------------
I                       DB2 PROGRAM PREPARATION
I===>
I
IEnter the following:
I  1   INPUT DATA SET NAME .... ===> 'USERID.DB2.SOURCE(MEMBER)'
I  2   DATA SET NAME QUALIFIER  ===> TEMP      (For building data set names)
I  3   PREPARATION ENVIRONMENT  ===> FOREGROUND (FOREGROUND, BACKGROUND, EDITJCL)
I  4   RUN TIME ENVIRONMENT ... ===> TSO       (TSO, CICS, IMS)
I  5   STOP IF RETURN CODE >=   ===> 8         (Lowest terminating return code)
I  6   OTHER OPTIONS ===>
I
ISelect functions:               Display panel?        Perform function?
I  7   CHANGE DEFAULTS ........ ===> Y  (Y/N)
I  8   PL/I MACRO PHASE ....... ===> Y  (Y/N)          ===> N  (Y/N)
I  9   PRECOMPILE ............. ===> Y  (Y/N)          ===> N  (Y/N)
I 10   CICS COMMAND TRANSLATION .... Y  .....          ===> N  (Y/N)
I 11   BIND ................... ===> Y  (Y/N)          ===> N  (Y/N)
I 12   COMPILE OR ASSEMBLE .... ===> Y  (Y/N)          ===> N  (Y/N)
I 13   LINK ................... ===> Y  (Y/N)          ===> N  (Y/N)
I 14   RUN .................... ===> Y  (Y/N)          ===> N  (Y/N)
I
IPRESS:  ENTER to process       END to exit      HELP for more information
I
L----------------------------------------------------------------------------
```

ONLINE PROGRAM PREPARATION—PRECOMPILE.   If you choose to dis-play the PRECOMPILE panel from the online PROGRAM PREPARATION panel, you will receive the following screen. On this screen, you would enter your DB2 PRECOMPILE options.

```
+-----------------------------------------------------------------------------+
|                              PRECOMPILE                                      |
|===>                                                                         |
|Enter precompiler data sets:                                                 |
|  1   INPUT DATA SET .... ===> 'USERID.DB2.SOURCE(TCSBSOC1)'                 |
|  2   INCLUDE LIBRARY ... ===> 'USERID.DB2.DCLGEN'                           |
|                                                                             |
|  3   DSNAME QUALIFIER .. ===> TEMP        (For building data set names)     |
|  4   DBRM DATA SET ..... ===> 'USERID.DB2.DBRMLIB.DATA'                     |
|Enter processing options as desired:                                         |
|  5   WHERE TO PRECOMPILE ===> FOREGROUND  (FOREGROUND, BACKGROUND, or EDITJCL) |
|  6   OTHER OPTIONS ..... ===>                                               |
|                                                                             |
|                                                                             |
|                                                                             |
|                                                                             |
|PRESS:   ENTER to process    END to exit    HELP for more information        |
|                                                                             |
+-----------------------------------------------------------------------------+
```

ONLINE PROGRAM PREPARATION—COMPILE, LINK, RUN.   If you choose to display either the COMPILE, LINK, and/or RUN option from the online PROGRAM PREPARATION panel, you will receive the following screen. On this screen, you would enter your COMPILE or ASSEMBLE options, LINK options, and/or RUN options. The options that you will enter on this panel will depend upon what process you are trying to do, what language you are using, and what other specialized interfaces you need.

```
+-----------------------------------------------------------------------------+
|              PROGRAM PREPARATION: COMPILE, LINK, AND RUN                     |
|===>                                                                         |
|Enter compiler or assembler options:                                         |
|  1   INCLUDE LIBRARY ===>                                                   |
|  2   INCLUDE LIBRARY ===>                                                   |
|  3   OPTIONS ....... ===>                                                   |
|Enter linkage editor options:                                                |
|  4   INCLUDE LIBRARY ===>                                                   |
|  5   INCLUDE LIBRARY ===>                                                   |
|  6   INCLUDE LIBRARY ===>                                                   |
|  7   LOAD LIBRARY .. ===> DB2.RUNLIB.LOAD                                   |
|  8   OPTIONS ....... ===>                                                   |
|Enter run options:                                                           |
|  9   PARAMETERS .... ===>                                                   |
| 10   SYSIN DATA SET  ===> TERM                                             |
| 11   SYSPRINT DS ... ===> TERM                                             |
|                                                                             |
|PRESS: Enter to proceed    END to exit    HELP for more information          |
|                                                                             |
+-----------------------------------------------------------------------------+
```

ONLINE PROGRAM PREPARATION—BIND.   If you choose to display the BIND panel from the online PROGRAM PREPARATION panel, you will receive the following screen. On this screen you would enter your BIND options.

```
.-----------------------------------------------------------------------------.
|                              BIND                                           |
|===>                                                                         |
|                                                                             |
|Enter DBRM data set name(s):                                                 |
| 1   LIBRARY(s)  ===> 'USERID.DB2.DBRMLIB.DATA'                              |
| 2   MEMBER(s)   ===> TCSBSOC1                                               |
| 3   PASSWORD(s) ===>                                                        |
|                                                                             |
| 4   MORE DBRMS? ===> NO                       (YES to list more DBRMs)      |
|                                                                             |
|Enter options as desired:                                                    |
| 5   PLAN NAME ................ ===> TCSBSOC1  (Required to create a plan)   |
| 6   ACTION ON PLAN ........... ===> REPLACE   (REPLACE or ADD)              |
| 7   RETAIN EXECUTION AUTHORITY ===> YES       (YES to retain user list)     |
| 8   ISOLATION LEVEL .......... ===> CS        (RR or CS)                    |
| 9   PLAN VALIDATION TIME ..... ===> BIND      (RUN or BIND)                 |
|10   RESOURCE ACQUISITION TIME  ===> USE       (USE or ALLOCATE)             |
|11   RESOURCE RELEASE TIME .... ===> COMMIT    (COMMIT or DEALLOCATE)        |
|12   EXPLAIN PATH SELECTION ... ===> NO        (NO or YES)                   |
|                                                                             |
|                                                                             |
|PRESS:   ENTER to process       END to exit    HELP for more information     |
'-----------------------------------------------------------------------------'
```

PRECOMPILE.   If you select the PRECOMPILE function (4) from the DB2I menu, you will receive the same panel shown in the PROGRAM PREPARATION PRECOMPILE section previously.

BIND/REBIND/FREE.   If you select the BIND/REBIND/FREE function (5) from the DB2I menu, you will receive the panel below. You would select this panel if it is necessary to BIND ADD or REPLACE, REBIND, or FREE any or all application plans over which you have BIND authority.

```
.-----------------------------------------------------------------------------.
|                         BIND/REBIND/FREE                                    |
|===>                                                                         |
|                                                                             |
|Select one of the following and press ENTER:                                 |
|                                                                             |
| 1   BIND            (Add or replace an application plan)                    |
|                                                                             |
| 2   REBIND          (Rebind existing application plan or plans)             |
|                                                                             |
| 3   FREE            (Erase application plan or plans)                        |
|                                                                             |
|                                                                             |
|                                                                             |
|                                                                             |
|                                                                             |
|                                                                             |
|                                                                             |
|PRESS:    END to exit       HELP for more information                        |
'-----------------------------------------------------------------------------'
```

BIND.   If you select the BIND option from the BIND/REBIND/FREE panel, you will receive the panel below. You would select this panel if it is necessary to BIND ADD or BIND REPLACE any or all application plans over which you have BIND authority.

```
,--------------------------------------------------------------------------.
|                               BIND                                       |
| ===>                                                                     |
| Enter DBRM data set name(s):                                             |
|  1   LIBRARY(s)   ===> 'APL2.SYMBLIB'                                    |
|  2   MEMBER(s)    ===> AP2DBRM2                                          |
|  3   PASSWORD(s)  ===>                                                   |
|                                                                          |
|  4   MORE DBRMS?  ===> NO                     (YES to list more DBRMs)   |
|                                                                          |
| Enter options as desired:                                               |
|  5   PLAN NAME ................ ===> APL2PLN2  (Required to create a plan)|
|  6   ACTION ON PLAN ........... ===> REPLACE   (REPLACE or ADD)          |
|  7   RETAIN EXECUTION AUTHORITY ===> YES       (YES to retain user list) |
|  8   ISOLATION LEVEL .......... ===> RR        (RR or CS)                |
|  9   PLAN VALIDATION TIME ..... ===> RUN        (RUN or BIND)            |
| 10   RESOURCE ACQUISITION TIME  ===> USE       (USE or ALLOCATE)         |
| 11   RESOURCE RELEASE TIME .... ===> COMMIT     (COMMIT or DEALLOCATE)   |
| 12   EXPLAIN PATH SELECTION ... ===> NO         (NO or YES)              |
|                                                                          |
|                                                                          |
| PRESS:   ENTER to process      END to exit     HELP for more information |
|                                                                          |
`--------------------------------------------------------------------------'
```

REBIND.   If you select the REBIND option from the BIND/REBIND/FREE
panel, you will receive the panel below. You would select this panel if it is
necessary to REBIND any or all application plans over which you have BIND
authority.

```
,--------------------------------------------------------------------------.
|                              REBIND                                      |
| ===>                                                                     |
| Enter plan name(s) to be rebound, or * for all authorized plans:        |
|  1   ===> PLANNAME   4   ===>        7   ===>        10   ===>           |
|  2   ===>            5   ===>        8   ===>        11   ===>           |
|  3   ===>            6   ===>        9   ===>        12   ===>           |
| Enter options as desired:                                               |
| 13   ISOLATION LEVEL .......... ===> SAME     (SAME, RR, or CS)          |
| 14   PLAN VALIDATION TIME .... ===> SAME     (SAME, RUN, or BIND)        |
| 15   RESOURCE ACQUISITION TIME ===> SAME     (SAME, ALLOCATE, or USE)    |
| 16   RESOURCE RELEASE TIME ... ===> SAME     (SAME, DEALLOCATE, or COMMIT)|
| 17   EXPLAIN PATH SELECTION .. ===> SAME     (SAME, NO, or YES)          |
|                                                                          |
|                                                                          |
|                                                                          |
|                                                                          |
|                                                                          |
| PRESS:   ENTER to process      END to exit     HELP for more information |
|                                                                          |
`--------------------------------------------------------------------------'
```

FREE.   If you select the FREE option from the BIND/REBIND/FREE panel,
you will receive the panel below. You would select this panel if it is necessary
to FREE any or all application plans over which you have BIND authority.

```
r--------------------------------------------------------------------------------1
|                               FREE                                             |
|===>                                                                            |
|Enter plan name(s) to be freed or * for all authorized plans:                   |
|  1  ===>              4  ===>              7  ===>              10  ===>         |
|  2  ===>              5  ===>              8  ===>              11  ===>         |
|  3  ===>              6  ===>              9  ===>              12  ===>         |
|                                                                                |
|                                                                                |
|                                                                                |
|                                                                                |
|                                                                                |
|                                                                                |
|                                                                                |
|                                                                                |
|PRESS: ENTER to process     END to exit   HELP for more information             |
|                                                                                |
L--------------------------------------------------------------------------------J
```

RUN.   If you select the RUN function (6) from the DB2I menu, you will receive the panel below. You would select this panel if you needed to execute a DB2 application that has already been successfully precompiled, bound, compiled, and linked.

   You must have previously allocated any files needed by the program to your TSO session.

```
r--------------------------------------------------------------------------------1
|                               RUN                                              |
|===>                                                                            |
|Enter the name of the program you want to run:                                  |
|  1   DATA SET NAME ===>                                                         |
|  2   PASSWORD .... ===>              (Required if data set is password protected)|
|Enter the following as desired:                                                 |
|  3   PARAMETERS .. ===>                                                         |
|  4   PLAN NAME ... ===>              (Required if different from program name)  |
|  5   WHERE TO RUN  ===> FOREGROUND (FOREGROUND, BACKGROUND, or EDITJCL)         |
|                                                                                |
|                                                                                |
|                                                                                |
|                                                                                |
|                                                                                |
|NOTE : Information for running command processors is on the HELP panel.          |
|PRESS: ENTER to process     END to exit     HELP for information                |
|                                                                                |
L--------------------------------------------------------------------------------J
```

DB2 commands.   If you select the DB2 COMMANDS option (7) from the DB2I menu panel, you will receive the panel below. You would select this panel if it is necessary to issue a DB2 system command of some type.

```
---------------------------------------------------------------------
|                           DB2 COMMANDS                              |
| ===>                                                                |
| Enter a single DB2 command on up to 4 lines below:                  |
|  1  ===> -DISPLAY THREAD(*)                                         |
|  2  ===>                                                            |
|  3  ===>                                                            |
|  4  ===>                                                            |
|                                                                     |
|                                                                     |
|                                                                     |
|                                                                     |
|                                                                     |
|                                                                     |
| PRESS:  ENTER to process      END to exit    HELP for more information |
---------------------------------------------------------------------
```

DB2 utilities.   If you selected the UTILITIES option (8) from the DB2I menu panel, you will receive the panel below. You would select this panel if you needed to create DB2 utility Job Control Language (JCL).

```
---------------------------------------------------------------------
|                          DB2 UTILITIES                              |
| ===>                                                                |
| Select from the following:                                          |
|  1 FUNCTION ===> EDITJCL   (SUBMIT job, EDITJCL, DISPLAY, or TERMINATE) |
|  2 JOB ID   ===> USERID        (A unique job identifier string)     |
|  3 UTILITY  ===> RECOVER   (LOAD, REORG, COPY, MERGECOPY, RECOVER, REPAIR, |
|                             RUNSTATS, STOSPACE, CHECK, or MODIFY)    |
|  4 CONTROL CARDS DATA SET  ===> DB2.UTIL(DSNAUH01)                   |
|  5 RECDSN  (LOAD, REORG)   ===>                                     |
|  6 DISCDSN (LOAD)          ===>                                     |
|  7 COPYDSN (COPY, MERGECOPY) ===>                                   |
| To RESTART a utility, specify starting point, otherwise enter NO.   |
|  8 RESTART  ===> NO           (NO, At CURRENT position, or beginning of P |
|                                                                     |
|                                                                     |
| PRESS:  ENTER to process      END to exit    HELP for more information |
---------------------------------------------------------------------
```

DB2I defaults.   If you select the DEFAULTS option (D) from the DB2I menu panel, you will receive the panel below. You would select this panel if you needed to change the DB2I function defaults.

```
r-------------------------------------------------------------------------------,
I                            DB2I DEFAULTS                                       I
I===>                                                                            I
IChange defaults as desired:                                                     I
I  1   DB2 NAME ............. ===> DB2T        (Subsystem identifier)             I
I  2   DB2 CONNECTION RETRIES ===> 0           (How many retries for DB2 connect) I
I  3   APPLICATION LANGUAGE   ===> COBOL       (COBOL, COB2, FORT, ASM, ASMH, PLI)I
I  4   LINES/PAGE OF LISTING  ===> 60          (A number from 5 to 999)           I
I  5   MESSAGE LEVEL ........ ===> I           (Information, Warning, Error,      I
I  6   COBOL STRING DELIMITER ===> '           (DEFAULT, ' or ")                  I
I  7   SQL STRING DELIMITER   ===> '           (DEFAULT, ' or ")                  I
I  8   DECIMAL POINT ........ ===> .           (. or ,)                           I
I                                                                                I
I  9   DB2I JOB STATEMENT:   (Optional if your site has a SUBMIT exit)           I
I      ===> //DBAJOB1 (DB2U),DBA,CLASS=X                                         I
I      ===> //*                                                                  I
I      ===> //*                                                                  I
I      ===> //*                                                                  I
I                                                                                I
I                                                                                I
IPRESS: ENTER to save and exit      END to exit      HELP for more information   I
L-------------------------------------------------------------------------------'
```

Using DB2 Under Native TSO

The following TSO commands are DB2 commands that can be executed under Native TSO and Option 6 of ISPF.

- DSN

  The TSO command DSN invokes the DSN command processor which sets up the TSO attachment to DSN and will then process the following subcommands:

  – ABEND

  Used in problem diagnosis of DB2 problems.

  – BIND

  Does the bind and builds the application plan.

  – DCLGEN

  Produces the SQL DECLARE statement for a table or view.

  – END

  Ends the TSO attachment thread to DB2.

  – FREE

  Deletes application plans from DB2.

  – REBIND

  Rebinds existing application plan. Use when SQL has NOT changed.

  – RUN

  Executes an application program under DB2.

  – SPUFI

  Executes SPUFI and CAN ONLY BE DONE UNDER ISPF OPTION 6.

- DSNH

  DSNH is a TSO command list (CLIST) that performs the PROGRAM PREPARATION functions of DB2. The options of this CLIST will perform the following functions:

- PRECOMPILE
- BIND
- COMPILE
- PLI Macro Expansion
- CICS Command-Level PRECOMPILE
- LINK
- RUN
- DSNU

  DSNU is a TSO CLIST that generates the JCL needed to invoke
  the DSNUPROC procedure that is used to execute DB2 utilities as
  batch jobs.

Using DB2 Under Batch TSO

All of the above commands described in 'Using DB2 under Native TSO'
can be executed as input to the batch TSO program—IKJEFT01.

Batch Program Preparation

Execution of the procedures listed below use standard MVS batch JCL.
Refer to the appropriate appendix listing for a sample of the batch JCL and
procedures to be used. Procedures are in the appendix for the following language compilers with DB2 precompilers. The end results of the use of these
supplied procedures will be a DB2 application that is ready to be executed
after a bind for the appropriate plan has been done.

- COBOL II (Appendix 69)
- VS/COBOL (Appendix 70)
- PLI (Appendix 71)
- Assembler (Appendix 72)
- Fortran (Appendix 73)

Other combinations of processing will require custom-made JCL procedures or the use of the DSNH TSO command, or the background processor
selection from the DB2I Program Preparation System (which uses DSNH). See
Appendix 74 for a sample of the DSNH batch process.

Batch DB2 Program Execution

Execution of DB2 applications requires the use of the IKJEFT01 TSO
batch procedure. Refer to Appendix 76 for a sample of the batch JCL.

Using DB2 Under CICS

The CICS attachment facility which comes with DB2 allows the access
to DB2 from CICS regions. The programming of CICS applications to access

DB2 remains the same except that the access calls will be embedded SQL calls for data requests to DB2.

The installation and interface of DB2 and CICS requires that the CICS attachment be installed in the selected CICS region along with the creation of a new CICS table called the Resource Control Table (RCT). The CICS Attachment Facility inside CICS provides the control and program functionality needed by CICS to process DB2 requests from CICS transactions while the Resource Control Table provides the structure of information about the connection to DB2 and all transactions and programs that will be issuing calls to DB2.

DB2 commands can be issued from the attached CICS regions using the DB2-provided CSMT CICS Transaction.

Recovery is coordinated by both DB2 and the associated CICS region.

A single CICS region can attach to only 1 DB2 subsystem.

The CICS Attachment capability gives another way to access DB2 data. It is structured different from the TSO Attachment in that a single CICS region will be managing multiple requests to DB2 through multiple thread attachments to DB2 while a single TSO User session has a single thread attachment to DB2.

The program development and application BINDing itself must still be done through the use of the TSO and ISPF facilities provided with DB2.

Using DB2 Under IMS/DC

The IMS attachment facility which comes with DB2 allows the access to DB2 from IMS/DC regions. The programming of IMS Applications to access DB2 remains the same except that the access calls will be embedded SQL calls for data requests to DB2. The use of Data Language I (DL/I) and Fast Path Calls can be used as well with DB2 calls.

The installation and interface of DB2 and IMS requires that the IMS/DC attachment be installed in the selected IMS/DC region along with the definition of DB2 to the IMS/VS region. The IMS attachment facility inside IMS provides the control and program functionality needed by IMS to process DB2 requests from IMS transactions.

Recovery is coordinated by both DB2 and the associated IMS region. Within IMS the recovery can be coordinated through an Extended Recovery Facility (XRF). To do this, though, all DB2 data sets must be placed on sets of DASD shared between the Primary and Alternate XRF processors and global serialization must be active and each processor must be in the global serialization ring.

A single IMS region can attach to more than one DB2 subsystem.

The IMS attachment capability gives another way to access DB2 data. It is structured different from the TSO attachment in that a single IMS region will be managing multiple requests to DB2 through multiple thread attachments to DB2 while a single TSO user session has a single thread attachment to DB2.

DB2 Commands can be issued from the attached IMS regions using the DB2-provided /SSR IMS Command.

The program development and application BINDing itself must still be done through the use of the TSO and ISPF facilities provided with DB2.

Using the DB2 Call Attach Facility

Most TSO applications can accomplish everything that is needed through the use of the TSO attachment facility which used the DSN TSO Command Processor. This provides automatic connection and control over errors. This requires that the application run under control of the DSN processor. This might provide a limitation in some cases, and the Call Attach Facility (CAF) is provided as an alternative connection for TSO, ISPF, and batch applications which require tight control over the session environment. CAF provides explicit control over the state of the connections to DB2.

The Call Attach Facility provides the capability to access DB2 from MVS address spaces without TSO, IMS/VS, or CICS, access the DB2 Instrumentation Facility Interface, run when DB2 is down, run with or without the TSO Terminal Monitor Program (TMP), and run without the DSN command processor. It can establish both 'explicit' and 'implicit' connections to DB2 and intercept all return codes, reason codes, and abend codes from DB2 and translate them as needed.

Programs CAF must be coded in assembler which can then be called by other non-assembler programs such as Cobol and PLI.

Restrictions in using CAF are as follows:

1. Cannot use CICS or IMS/VS (except Batch)
2. Cannot use DB2 Program Preparation System
3. Cannot invoke DSN or be invoked by DSN
4. Cannot invoke DB2 from an MVS Service Request Block (SRB)
5. Cannot invoke DB2 while in Cross-Memory Mode

Using CAF provides you the capability to manage your connection to DB2 in great detail if you can afford the extra code required and the maintenance headaches that can result. Using CAF allows you to change your PLANNAME and reconnect to DB2 at will. It does, however, eliminate compatibility with the Systems Application Architecture because it is written in assembler and only fits the MVS environment. Suggestion: Do Not Use It.

USING OTHER DB2-RELATED PRODUCTS

Other DB2-related products provided by IBM that may prove to be useful and, in some cases, mandatory are as follows:

1. Query Mangement Facility (QMF)
2. Data Extract (DXT)

3. DBEDIT
4. DBMAUI
5. DB2 Performance Monitor (DB2PM)

These products provide particular extra functions that are not supplied by the base DB2 product itself.

Query Management Facility (QMF)— Test and Production

If you select either the QMF Test or QMF Production option from the DB2 Selection menu, you will receive the panel below. The difference between QMF Test and QMF Production is that QMF Test will be pointing to the Test DB2 subsystem and QMF Production will be pointing to the Production DB2 subsystem.

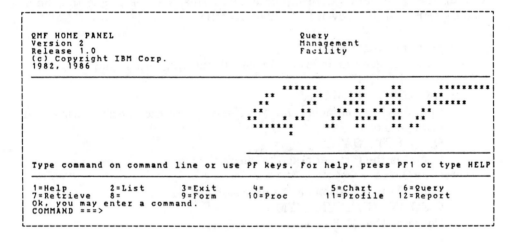

Introduction to QMF. The IBM Query Management Facility (QMF) is a query-and-report-generation system designed to use DB2 databases. It is an online (it can be executed in batch) system that allows the manipulation and formatting of data in DB2 tables. It uses the Structured Query Language (SQL) and another access language called Query By Example (QBE).

QMF is composed of the following four entities:

- Queries
  A QMF query is an SQL statement that processes DB2 tables.
- Forms
  A QMF form is a report-formatting module that manipulates the data which results in the execution of a query.
- Procedures
  QMF procedures are combinations of SQL queries, forms, and/or TSO

and/or ISPF command processors and lists which are stored together to be executed as a single process.
* Command Synonyms
Command synonyms are installation-defined synonyms for other commands, procedures, queries, etc.

The possible modes of operation using QMF:

* Log on to QMF and execute QMF procedures.
* Create your own ad hoc queries and reports.
* Create the QMF procedures and queries for someone else.
* Execute QMF queries and procedures in batch mode.
* Execute QMF queries and procedures from ISPF panels.

QMF structure. Each user creates a QMF temporary workspace that will contain the QMF data, queries, procedures, forms, and the profile that he is using. QMF itself has seven DB2 tables as follows:

* Q.OBJECT_DIRECTORY
Contains general information on all queries, forms, and procedures defined to QMF.
* Q.OBJECT_REMARKS
Contains the comments that were saved with the queries, forms, and procedures.
* Q.OBJECT_DATA
Contains the text defining the queries, forms, and procedures.
* Q.PROFILES
Contains information on the user-session profiles.
* Q.COMMAND_SYNONYMS
Contains the QMF command synonyms.
* Q.ERROR_LOG
Contains information on errors that occurred in the system, other resources, and unexpected condition errors.
* Q.RESOURCE_TABLE
Contains information on the resource and limit values used by the QMF governor.

Learning to use QMF. If you have not had any formal training using QMF, an excellent way to learn the basics is to procure and go through the following manual. It is well written and does not assume any data processing knowledge other than knowing how to sign on to TSO/ISPF and then into QMF itself.

* *Query Management Facility: Learner's Guide*—SC26-4231

This book will explain how to use QMF and what to expect concerning screen formats and overall system usage.

After going through the learner's guide online using QMF, the next manual that will be helpful is the following:

- *Query Management Facility: User's Guide and Reference—SC26-4232*

After becoming familiar with the QMF commands, instead of using the large user's guide referenced above, you will want to get a copy of the reference summary booklet:

- *Query Management Facility: Reference Summary—SX26-3752*

QMF enrollment. Enrollment in QMF can be restricted or open. Open enrollment exists when there is a system row in Q.PROFILES. This is a default profile for all users of QMF. If this row does not exist, a restricted environment exists, and each user must be formally enrolled using an SQL INSERT statement similar to the one listed below:

```
INSERT INTO Q.PROFILES
    (CREATOR, LANGUAGE, SPACE, TRANSLATION, PFKEYS,
    SYNONYMS, RESOURCE_GROUP )
VALUES
    ('creator', 'SQL or QBE', 'default.tablespace', 'ENGLISH',
    'Q.PFKEY_DEFINITIONS', 'Q.COMMAND_ SYNONYMS',
    'groupname')
```

By not assigning a value, otherwise using null, the value of the column will use a default value.

English for TRANSLATION column must always be used, or the profile will be ignored.

QMF guidelines.
- When using the SAVE command, use the following parameters:

```
SHARE = YES
COMMENT = 'any text'
COMMAND  ⇒ SAVE  QUERY  AS  QUERY1  (COM = 'QUERY
    NO.1',SHARE = YES
or
on  the  SAVE  panel  enter:  COMMENTS = QUERY  NO.1  RE-
    STRICTED = N
```

QMF governor. The QMF Governor is a process in QMF that places limits on the resource usage of a QMF query and/or process on the following:

- Execution time
- Number of rows fetched

QMF will send a message as a warning at one point in time and ask if you want the query or procedure to be continued or cancelled.

This message looks like the following:

DSQUE00 Your QMF command is suspended!
   Command has executed for xxxxxxxxxx seconds of CPU time and fetched yyyyyyyyy rows of data.
   ⇒ To continue QMF command press the ENTER key.
   ⇒ To cancel QMF command type CANCEL then press the ENTER key.
   ⇒ To turn off prompting type NOPROMPT then press the ENTER key.

At the next threshold, the query or procedure will be cancelled.

These thresholds are set by the installation based upon the QMF resource group that the QMF user is placed in.

The default thresholds are as follows:

* First Notice
   – Execution time
   – Number of rows fetched
* Termination
   – Execution time
   – Number of rows fetched

For additional information on the IBM-supplied governor and on writing your own governor, refer to the following manual:

* *Query Management Facility: Planning and Administration Guide for MVS—SC26-4235*

QMF resource table definition.   The IBM-Default QMF Resource Table is defined as follows:

Column Name	Data Type	Length in Bytes	Nulls Allowed
Resource__Group	Cha	16	no
Resource__Option	Char	16	no
Intval	Integer	4	yes
Floatval	Float	8	yes
Charval	Varchar	80	yes

The definitions of each column are as follows:

- RESOURCE_GROUP—Name of each defined resource group.
- RESOURCE_OPTION—Contains governor assigned name.
  IBM-Defaults are
  - SCOPE determines whether governing will occur. Non-Zero value inhibits governing.
  - TIMEPROMPT specifies amount of CPU time that can elapse on a governing cycle before a cancellation prompt.
  - TIMELIMIT specifies amount of CPU time to be used before UN-CONDITIONAL cancellation occurs.
  - CHECKTIME specifies maximum amount of CPU time between time checks for both prompting and cancellation.
  - ROWPROMPT specifies number of rows that can be retrieved before a cancellation prompt occurs.
  - ROWLIMIT specifies maximum number of rows that can be fetched before UNCONDITIONAL cancellation occurs.

The following values have whatever meaning the governor routine assigns to them. The default governor uses INTVAL as the value for the actual limits set for the options listed above.

- Intval—Integer Value
- Floatval—Floating Value
- Charval—Character Value

QMF resource group definition. You define a resource group using the default governor values by issuing various INSERT statements to the QMF Q.RESOURCE _TABLE which contains the groupname desired and appropriate RESOURCE_OPTION value and INTVAL as defined above.

```
INSERT INTO Q.RESOURCE_TABLE
    (RESOURCE_GROUP, RESOURCE_OPTION, INTVAL)
    VALUES
    ('groupname', 'option', intval) ;
```

One INSERT for each desired value of RESOURCE_OPTION is necessary.

QMF user resource group assignment. You assign a resource group to a user by issuing the following SQL UPDATE statement to the QMF Q.PROFILES table.

```
UPDATE Q.PROFILES
    SET RESOURCE_GROUP = 'groupname'
    WHERE CREATOR = 'USERID' AND
    TRANSLATION = 'ENGLISH' ;
```

When a user is formally enrolled into QMF and you fail to place an entry into the RESOURCE_GROUP column of Q.PROFILES, the user's resource group will be null, which results in NO governing for that user.

Application development using QMF. Applications can be developed using a combination of the following:

- TSO CLISTs
- ISPF Dialog Manager
- Batch QMF
- Application code

For additional information on application development using QMF, refer to the following manual:

- *Query Management Facility: Application Development Guide for MVS* —SC26-4237

QMF batch-mode processing. QMF batch-mode processing can be invoked by executing the DSQBATCH procedure. The following control card must be added to the SYSTSIN data set of your job:

```
ISPSTART PGM(DSQQMFE) NEWAPPL(DSQE)
PARM(M = B,S = DB2,I = userid.procname)
     where M = B (Batch mode processing)
           S = DB2 Subsystem name
           I = Invoked procedure name
               userid = TSO Userid
               procname = QMF procedure name
               (could be Command Synonym)
```

QMF Batch-Mode Procedure Example:

```
SET PROFILE (CONFIRM = NO ←——— REQUIRED
RUN QUERYA (F = FORMA
PRINT REPORT (PR = "
EXIT ←——— OPTIONAL
```

Data Extract (DXT)

Introduction to DXT. The Data Extract (DXT) licensed product from IBM provides the capability to extract data from the following:

- IMS/VS DL/I databases under MVS
- DB2 databases

- Physical sequential data sets
- Virtual Storage Access Method (VSAM) files

DXT will then format the data for the following:

- Loading into a DB2 database
- Loading into an SQL/DS database under VM/SP
- Storage into an Integration Exchange Facility file (IEF) under MVS or VM/SP
- Storage in a physical sequential data set
- Storage in a CMS file under VM/SP

DXT will also create the necessary MVS JCL and control cards that are necessary for the load process that was requested.

DXT structure. DXT's structure is as follows:

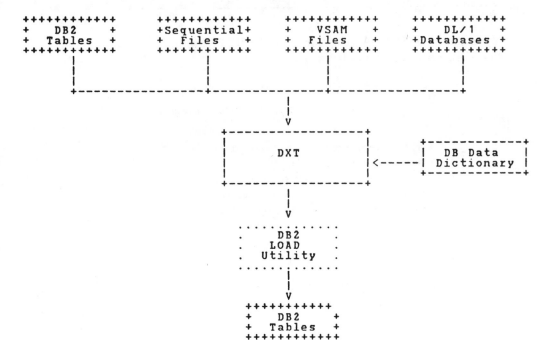

Usage

DXT dialogs. The DXT Dialogs is an ISPF-based system that allows you to interactively build jobs that create the requested extract and data description requests. DXT Dialogs runs under the Interactive System Productivity Facility (ISPF) in TSO of MVS or the Conversational Monitor System (CMS) of the VM operating system.

DXT ADMINISTRATIVE DIALOGS. If you select the DXT Administrative Dialogs option from the DB2 Selection menu, you will receive the panel below.

```
,----------------------------------------------------------------------------,
|                                                                            |
|                            DXT ADMINISTRATIVE DIALOGS                      |
|SELECT OPTION ===>                                                          |
|                                                                            |
|                                                                            |
|            1    EXTRACT        Build and maintain extract requests.        |
|            2    DESCRIPTION    Build and maintain data description requests |
|            3    JCL            Build and maintain Job Control Language.     |
|            4    PROFILE        Specify Dialogs processing options.         |
|            5    ADMINISTER     End User Dialogs Administration.            |
|                                                                            |
|                                                                            |
|                                                                            |
|Press:   ENTER to select    END key to exit    HELP key for information     |
|                                                                            |
`----------------------------------------------------------------------------'
```

If you select the EXTRACT option from the DXT Administrative Dialog panel, you will receive the panel below.

```
,----------------------------------------------------------------------------,
|                                                                            |
|                      BUILD AND MAINTAIN EXTRACT REQUESTS                    |
|SELECT OPTION ===>         _                                                |
|                                                                            |
|            1     BUILD or UPDATE/INSPECT an extract request.               |
|            2     ERASE an extract request.                                |
|            3     SEND an extract request for execution.                    |
|            4     IMPORT or EXPORT an extract request.                      |
|            5     Check STATUS of an extract request sent for execution.    |
|            6     CANCEL an extract request sent for execution.             |
|            7     LIST extract requests sent for execution.                 |
|                                                                            |
|                                                                            |
|Press:   ENTER to select   END key to return   HELP key for information     |
|Useful Commands:   END    HELP    CANCEL    KEYS                            |
|                                                                            |
`----------------------------------------------------------------------------'
```

If you select the DESCRIPTION option from the DXT Administrative Dialog panel, you will receive the panel below.

```
                          BUILD AND MAINTAIN DATA DESCRIPTION REQUESTS
SELECT OPTION ===>
                   _

         1    BUILD or UPDATE/INSPECT a CREATE request.
         2    ERASE a CREATE request.
         3    SEND a CREATE request for execution.
         4    IMPORT or EXPORT a CREATE request.
         5    PRINT or PUNCH data description(s).
         6    DELETE data description(s).
         7    Invoke the DAP (Dictionary Access Program).



Press:    ENTER to select   END key to return   HELP key for information
Useful Commands:   END   HELP   CANCEL   KEYS
```

If you select the JCL option from the DXT Administrative Dialog panel, you will receive the panel below.

```
                          BUILD AND MAINTAIN JCL FILES
SELECT OPTION ===>
                   _

         1    BUILD or UPDATE/INSPECT a JCL file.
         2    ERASE a JCL file.
         3    IMPORT or EXPORT a JCL file.






Press:    ENTER to select   END key to return   HELP key for information
Useful Commands:   END   HELP   CANCEL   KEYS
```

If you select the PROFILES option from the DXT Administrative Dialog panel, you will receive the panel below.

```
r---------------------------------------------------------------------------
I                                                                          I
I                           DIALOGS PROFILE OPTIONS                  Panel I
ICOMMAND ===>                                                              I
ISpecify default names to be used by all DXT Dialogs:                      I
I                                                                          I
I   UIM JCL        ===> DVRJDXTE            Enter JCL file name to invoke  I
I                       -                                                  I
I   DAP JCL        ===> DVRJDAPI            Enter JCL file name to invoke  I
I   REM JCL (MVS) ===> DVRJREMM            Enter JCL file name to invoke  I
I                                           on an MVS system.              I
I   REM JCL (VM)  ===> DVRJREMV            Enter JCL file name to invoke  I
I                                           on a VM system.               I
I   Enter a ? in any field to display                                     I
I   a list of names.                                                      I
I                                                                          I
I                                                                          I
IPress:    ENTER to continue    END key to return    HELP key for informati I
IUseful Commands:    END    HELP    SAVE    CANCEL    KEYS                 I
I                                                                          I
L---------------------------------------------------------------------------J
```

If you select the ADMINISTER option from the DXT Administrative Dialog panel, you will receive the panel below.

```
r---------------------------------------------------------------------------
I                                                                          I
I                          END USER DIALOGS ADMINISTRATION                 I
ISELECT OPTION ===>                                                        I
I                                                                          I
ISelect option number desired and press ENTER:                            I
I                                                                          I
I        1    Request Source Table Descriptions                           I
I        2    Update the End-User Table                                   I
I        3    Restart Master Index Table Update                           I
I                                                                          I
I                                                                          I
I                                                                          I
I                                                                          I
I                                                                          I
IPress:    ENTER to select    END key to return    HELP key for information I
IUseful Commands:    END    HELP    CANCEL    KEYS                         I
I                                                                          I
L---------------------------------------------------------------------------J
```

DXT END USER DIALOGS. If you select the DXT V2 End User Dialogs option from the DB2 Selection menu, you will receive the panel below.

```
|---------------------------------------------------------------------------|
|                                                                           |
|                        DXT END USER DIALOGS                               |
|Select ONE of the following options,                                       |
|  or use the PF Keys:                                                      |
|                                                                           |
|      1     TABLES           -   Display table and DXTVIEW                  |
|                                 names available for extract               |
|      2     COLUMNS          -   Display  column  names  of                 |
|                                 tables or DXTVIEWs selected               |
|      3     CONDITIONS       -   Specify conditions on the                  |
|                                 columns                                   |
|      4     JOIN             -   Specify join condition if more            |
|                                 than one table or DXTVIEW selected        |
|      5     TARGET           -   Specify the target for loading            |
|                                 extracted data                            |
|      6     DB ACCESS        -   Specify relational data base access       |
|                                 information                               |
|Available Commands:   Send, Save, Display, Status, Cancel, Reset, Check.   |
|                                                                           |
|PF23=EXT LIST                                                              |
|OPTION ===>                                                                |
|                                                                           |
|---------------------------------------------------------------------------|
```

If you select the TABLES option from the DXT End User Dialogs panel, you will receive the panel below.

```
|---------------------------------------------------------------------------|
|                                                                           |
|             SELECT TABLES/DXTVIEWS FOR EXTRACT                             |
|Enter an S under SELECT to select table(s) or dxtview(s) you wish to ex    |
|from. Remember to select items from the same LOCATION and of the same T    |
|SELECT TABLE/DXTVIEW      CREATOR   LOCATION   TYPE     DESCRIPTION         |
|  S       NAME                                                             |
|**************************** BOTTOM OF DATA ************************        |
|                                                                           |
|                                                                           |
|                                                                           |
|                                                                           |
|                                                                           |
|                                                                           |
|                                                                           |
|PF23=EXT LIST                                                              |
|COMMAND ===>                                                SCROLL ==       |
|---------------------------------------------------------------------------|
```

If you select the COLUMNS option from the DXT End User Dialogs panel, you will receive the panel below.

```
----------------------------------------------------------------------------
|                       SELECT COLUMNS FOR EXTRACT                          |
|Do you wish to select ALL columns for extract, Yes or No?    ===> N        |
|If not, enter an S under SELECT to select specific columns for extract     |
|SELECT COLUMN                    DXTVIEW                  DESCRIPTION       |
|   S    NAME                     NAME                                       |
|*****************************  BOTTOM OF DATA  ************************     |
|                                                                           |
|                                                                           |
|                                                                           |
|                                                                           |
|                                                                           |
|                                                                           |
|PF23=EXT LIST                                                              |
|COMMAND ===>                                                  SCROLL ==     |
----------------------------------------------------------------------------
```

If you select the CONDITIONS option from the DXT End User Dialogs panel, you will receive the panel below.

```
----------------------------------------------------------------------------
|                          SPECIFY CONDITIONS                               |
|Enter a CONDITION to be met by all rows as comparison operator followed    |
|by value(s).  Press HELP key for syntax on conditions.                     |
|COLUMN                   COLUMN   COLUMN    CONDITION                       |
| NAME                    TYPE     LENGTH                                    |
|*****************************  BOTTOM OF DATA  ************************     |
|                                                                           |
|                                                                           |
|                                                                           |
|                                                                           |
|                                                                           |
|                                                                           |
|PF23=EXT LIST                                                              |
|COMMAND ===>                                                  SCROLL ==     |
----------------------------------------------------------------------------
```

If you select the JOINS option from the DXT End User Dialogs panel, you will
receive the panel below.

```
|----------------------------------------------------------------------------|
|                                                                            |
|                              SPECIFY JOINS                                 |
|When  multiple tables are selected for extract, the columns to be joine     |
|be specified.  Enter the number from the COLUMN NUMBER field for one of     |
|columns into the JOIN COLUMN field for the other column.                    |
|COLUMN   JOIN   COLUMN                  TABLE/DXTVIEW          CREATOR   COLU |
|NUMBER   COLUMN  NAME                       NAME                         TYP |
|*****************************  BOTTOM OF DATA  ************************       |
|                                                                            |
|                                                                            |
|                                                                            |
|                                                                            |
|                                                                            |
|                                                                            |
|PF23=EXT LIST                                                               |
|COMMAND ===>                                                  SCROLL ==      |
|----------------------------------------------------------------------------|
```

If you select the EXTRACT option from the DXT End User Dialogs panel, you
will receive the panel below.

```
|----------------------------------------------------------------------------|
|                                                                            |
|                   NAME TARGET FOR EXTRACT OUTPUT                           |
|Target Type          ===> D               D= DB2 S= SQLDS I= IXF M=         |
|Target Table Name    ===>                 Specify for DB2, SQL/DS           |
|  Table Qualifier    ===> USERID          Prefix for target table n         |
|Specify when Target is SQL/DS:                                              |
|SQL/DS Table Option ===>                  A= Add To C= Create R= Re         |
|                                                                            |
|Change the TARGET COLUMN NAMEs where appropriate.                           |
|INPUT COLUMN           ACCEPTS NULL     TARGET COLUMN                        |
|    NAME               (Y,N, or D)         NAME                             |
|*****************************  BOTTOM OF DATA  ************************       |
|                                                                            |
|                                                                            |
|                                                                            |
|PF23=EXT LIST                                                               |
|COMMAND ===>                                                  SCROLL ==      |
|----------------------------------------------------------------------------|
```

If you select the RELATIONAL option from the DXT End User Dialogs panel, you will receive the panel below.

```
------------------------------------------------------------------------
|                                                                        |
|                    RELATIONAL DATA BASE ACCESS                         |
|                                                                        |
|Source information when source is DB2 or SQL/DS:                        |
|Node ID    ===>                        Location of table(s) to be ex    |
|User ID    ===> USERID                 User ID to access source tabl    |
|Password   ===>                        Access password of above User    |
|                                                                        |
|Target information when source is SQL/DS:                               |
|Network ID ===> RSCS                   Net ID to route extracted out    |
|Node ID    ===>                        Location for extracted output    |
|User ID    ===> JOB                    User ID to execute the job wh    |
|                                       loads the extracted data.        |
|                                                                        |
|Press ENTER to save the required information.                           |
|                                                                        |
|                                                                        |
|PF23=EXT LIST                                                           |
|COMMAND ===>                                                            |
------------------------------------------------------------------------
```

DXT Assist

Introduction. Data Extract Assist (DXTA) is a front-end product to the Data Extract product. It is menu driven and provides the capability for the person with NO knowledge of DXT itself to generate DXT Extract requests. It runs in the MVS environment but can create requests for both the VM and MVS environment.

Features and functions. DXTA provides the following:

- Builds and edits tables and table design
- Generates DXT JCL
- Creates relational tables
- Extracts data from:
  - IMS/VS databases
  - Sequential files
  - VSAM files
- Loads data into DB2 and SQL/DS tables

DBEDIT

Introduction to DBEDIT. The Database Edit Facility (DBEDIT) is an IBM program offering that gives quick and easy access to tables defined within a DB2 subsystem. It is designed for easy use by inexperienced end users without data processing expertise. DBEDIT provides full-screen data retrieval, update, insert, and delete capabilities through the use of DB2 and MVS/TSO. It provides the following features:

- Panel-driven data/edit facility
- Generates SQL for user
- Provides capability for field-edit rules
- Reduces development time
- Allows quick entry of test data

Basic structure. DBEDIT has three major functional components:

- HOME component
  Provides access point to other functions and Help facility
- PQUERY component
  Allows usage of DBEDIT panels and systems previously created
- PFORM component
  Provides DBEDIT panel and system creation capability

These components are related as follows:

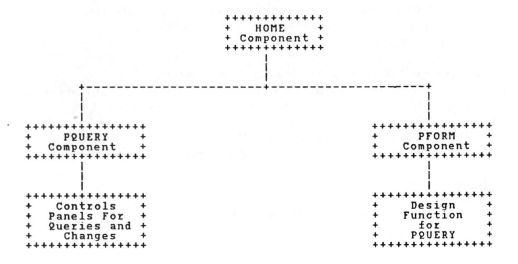

DBEDIT uses the following three DB2 tables:

- DBE.PNLTBL1
  Contains single control row for each DBEDIT panel
- DBE.PNLTBL2
  Defines specifications for each field on a DBEDIT panel
- DBE.REFLIST
  Contains reference list values for fields in a DBEDIT panel

Usage.   Access to DBEDIT can be gained by either selecting it from an ISPF DB2 menu selection panel as shown earlier, or by executing the DBEDIT TSO (CLIST) under Native TSO or Option 6 of ISPF.

DBEDIT manuals.   For further information on using DBEDIT refer to the following manuals:

* *Database Edit Facility for MVS/TSO Program Description/Operations Manual,* SH20-0076
* *Database Edit Facility User's Guide,* SH20-6522
* *Database Edit Facility Quick User's Guide to PQUERY,* SH20-6523

DBMAUI

Introduction.   The Database Migration Aid Utility I (DBMAUI) program is a set of functions designed to be used by DB2 system and database administrators.

In general, it is to be used when the following needs to be done:

* Redefine/Rename data and tables in existing DB2 subsystem
* Migration of data and SQL DDL from one DB2 to another
* Migration of DB2 authorization levels

DBMAUI runs using the TSO attachment facility of DB2.

If you selected either the DBMAUI Test or DBMAUI Production option from the DB2 Selection menu, you will receive the screen below. This is NOT an ISPF screen. This is a set of lines written out to the terminal from a TSO command list and command processor. The difference between the DBMAUI Test and the DBMAUI Production is that the DBMAUI Test will be pointing to the Test DB2 subsystem and the DBMAUI Production will be pointing to the Production DB2 subsystem.

DB MIGRATION AID UTILITY VERSION 1.1 COMPILED 6 JAN 86 10.10.30

ENTER. . .
FUNCTION NAME :
    DBAS—BUILD DATABASE CREATE DDL
    FLAT—FLAT FILE TABLE DUMP AND LOAD CONTROL
    GRANT—DUMP TABLE GRANTS
    PLAN—DUMP PLAN GRANTS
    SPACE—BUILD TABLESPACE CREATE DDL
    STORG—BUILD STORAGE GROUP CREATE DDL
    TDEF—BUILD TABLE AND INDEX CREATE DDL
    USE—DUMP USE GRANTS

VIEW—BUILD VIEW CREATE DDL
SYN—BUILD SYNONYM CREATE DDL
SYSP—DUMP SYSTEM PRIVILEGE GRANTS
.TSO < CMD >—TO EXECUTE COMMANDS:
QUIT—TO EXIT

On this panel, you select the function that is desired. The result of the selected function will be a sequential data set containing the SQL statements for creating the desired DB2 objects.

DBMAUI functions. The functions that can be selected from above are as follows:

- DBSTOG—STORG—Builds Storage Group Create DDL
- DBDBAS—DBAS—Builds Database Create DDL
- DBSPAC—SPACE—Builds Tablespace Create DDL
- DBDEF—TDEF—Builds Table and Index Create DDL
- DBVIEW—VIEW—Builds View Create DDL
- DBFLAT—FLAT—Relational Data Extractor
- DBGRNT—GRANT—Creates Table/View Grant DDL
- DBPLAN—PLAN—Creates Plan Grant DDL
- DBUSE—USE—Creates Use Grant DDL
- DBSYN—SYN—Builds Synonym Create DDL
- DBSYSP—SYSP—Creates System Authority Grant DDL

Each function will ask for its appropriate DB2 object name (such as a storage group, database, tablespace, creator, table, grantor, planname, view, etc.) or the default of ALL can be taken.

DBMAUI output files. DBMAUI will output a fixed-length data set with the following structure for the

DBSTOG function
USERID.DBSTOG.owner.ALL if owner is entered
USERID.DBSTOG.owner.stogroup   if owner and stogroup name are entered

USERID.DBSTOG.ALL.stogroup   if only stogroup name is entered
USERID.DBSTOG.ALL.ALL if nothing is entered
DBMAUI entered

DBMAUI will output a fixed-length data set with the following structure for the DBDBAS function:

USERID.DBDBAS.owner.ALL if owner is entered
USERID.DBDBAS.owner.dbname   if owner and database name are entered

USERID.DBDBAS.ALL.dbname	if only database name is entered
USERID.DBDBAS.ALL.ALL	if nothing is entered

DBMAUI will output a fixed-length data set with the following structure for the DBSPAC function:

USERID.DBSPAC.owner.ALL	if owner is entered
USERID.DBSPAC.owner.tsname	if owner and tablespace name are entered
USERID.DBSPAC.ALL.tsname	if only tablespace name is entered
USERID.DBSPAC.ALL.ALL	if nothing is entered

DBMAUI will output a fixed-length data set with the following structure for the DBDEF function:

USERID.DBDEF.owner.ALL	if owner is entered
USERID.DBDEF.owner.tname	if owner and table/index name are entered
USERID.DBDEF.ALL.tname	if only table/index name is entered
USERID.DBDEF.ALL.ALL	if nothing is entered

DBMAUI will output a fixed-length data set with the following structure for the DBVIEW function:

USERID.DBVIEW.owner.ALL	if owner is entered
USERID.DBVIEW.owner.viewname	if owner and view name are entered
USERID.DBVIEW.ALL.viewname	if only view name is entered
USERID.DBVIEW.ALL.ALL	if nothing is entered

DBMAUI will output a fixed-length data set with the following structure for the DBGRNT function:

USERID.DBGRNT.grantor.ALL	if grantor is entered
USERID.DBGRNT.grantor.tname	if grantor and table name are entered
USERID.DBGRNT.ALL.tname	if only table name is entered
USERID.DBGRNT.ALL.ALL	if nothing is entered
USERID.DBGRNT.GRANTEE.grantee	if grantee is entered

DBMAUI will output a fixed-length data set with the following structure for the DBUSE function:

USERID.DBUSE.grantor.ALL	if grantor is entered
USERID.DBUSE.grantor.name	if grantor and object name are entered

USERID.DBUSE.ALL.name	if only object name is entered
USERID.DBUSE.ALL.ALL	if nothing is entered
USERID.DBUSE.GRANTEE.grantee	if grantee is entered

DBMAUI will output a fixed-length data set with the following structure for the DBSYN function:

USERID.DBSYN.grantor.ALL	if grantor is entered
USE- RID.DBSYN.grantor.synonynname	if grantor and synonyn name are en- tered
USERID.DBSYN.ALL.synonynname	if only synonym name is entered
USERID.DBSYN.ALL.ALL	if nothing is entered

DBMAUI will output a fixed-length data set with the following structure for the DBPLAN function:

USERID.DBPLAN.grantor.ALL	if grantor is entered
USERID.DBPLAN.grantor.pname	if grantor and plan name are entered
USERID.DBPLAN.ALL.pname	if only plan name is entered
USERID.DBPLAN.ALL.ALL	if nothing is entered
USERID.DBPLAN.GRANTEE.grantee	if grantee is entered

DBMAUI will output a fixed-length data set with the following structure for the DBSYSP function:

USERID.DBSYSP.grantor.ALL	if grantor is entered
USERID.DBSYSP.grantor.dbname	if grantor and database name are en- tered
USERID.DBSYSP.ALL.dbname	if only database name is entered
USERID.DBSYSP.ALL.ALL	if nothing is entered
USERID.DBSYSP.GRANTEE.grantee	if grantee is entered

DBMAUI manuals. For more detailed information on using DBMAUI, refer to the following manual:

* *Database Migration Aid Utility User's Guide,* SH20-9232

Database Relational Application Directory (DBRAD)

Introduction. Database Relational Application Directory (DBRAD) is an IBM software product designed to provide the following for DB2 or SQL/DS systems:

* Acts as directory of information about
  Application objects
    – Where used

- Where stored
- Existing relationships
Data element definitions
* Provides DB2 catalog information

  - Where objects are used
  - Existing relationships
  - Authorization revoke impact
* Supports COBOL, PL/1, and Cross System Product (CSP)

  - Provides single consistent interface
* Generates 'MODEL' SQL statements

  - Produces source from DB2 or SQL/DS catalog tables
  - Produces source from DBRAD tables
* Provides reports

  - Object
  - Relationship
  - Program profiles
  - Summary and/or detailed
* Uses interactive dialogs
* Promotes integrated application development environment

DBRAD does NOT, however, support the following:

* Does NOT make DB2 catalog completely active
* Does NOT assist in design phase of development
* Does NOT contain source definitions
* Does NOT support versioning
* Does NOT store validation rules

Structure.   DBRAD supports the following object types:

* System
* Application
* Job
* Transaction
* Program
* Application
* CSP
* ALF
* Process
* Report
* Map
* File
* IMS PSB

- Record
- Item
- Table
- Column

Other object types can be added through an extensibility feature.

Other features.   DBRAD runs under the following:

- TSO
- CMS
- CICS

DBRAD also provides an IMPORT function which does the following:

- Transfers source information into DBRAD
- Loads components
- Loads catalog tables
- Provides application data information
- Transfers DB2 catalog data into DBRAD
- Imports CSP objects, relationships, and applications

DBRAD is designed to provide a directory for the applications and systems development environment and to work as an application development tool in the IBM DB2 and SQL/DS relational database environment.

DB2 VSAM Transparency

Introduction.   DB2 VSAM transparency is a software tool provided by IBM to allow a migration of VSAM-based applications into a DB2 environment without an immediate rewrite of the application programs. This is NOT a permanent solution, however. The program code should be rewritten as soon as possible.

Features and functions.   DB2 VSAM transparency provides the following capabilities:

- Attachments
  - TSO
  - Batch
  - CICS
- Supports KSDS and ESDS VSAM, no RRDS
- Supports variable and fixed-length
- Provides backward processing
- Supports following languages

- COBOL
- PL/1
- Fortran
- Basic
- Assembler
- Provides mixed-application support in same program
  - Native VSAM calls
  - DB2/VSAM transparency calls
  - SQL-only calls

Implementation. To implement the DB2 VSAM transparency, the following needs to be done:

- Move VSAM data to DB2 tables (can use DXT or AMS UNLOAD and DB2 LOAD)
- Some JCL changes required
- Run existing unmodified VSAM programs against DB2

How it works. DB2 VSAM transparency works basically by intercepting the VSAM call, then converting the call into a Dynamic SQL call. DB2 return codes are then converted into VSAM codes and passed back to the calling routine.

BECAUSE THIS IS DYNAMIC SQL, CONSIDER THE RAMIFICA-TIONS!!!

DB2 VSAM transparency limitations. DB2 VSAM transparency does NOT support the following:

- VSAM Relative Record Data Sets (RRDS)
- VSAM Share option
- VSAM Shared DASD
- MVS Checkpoint/Restart
- VSAM RBA calculations—RBA access IS supported
- Control Interval (CI) processing
- Direct access to index component

DB2 VSAM transparency will run ONLY in the MVS/XA environment and only in TSO and CICS DB2 applications.

DB2 Performance Monitor (DB2PM)

Introduction. The IBM Database 2 Performance Monitor (DB2PM) is a performance-monitoring and analysis tool for DB2. With DB2PM, reports can be obtained that show both system-wide and application-level information regarding various performance factors as well as usage information.

This information can be obtained in varying degrees of detail and within different time frames.

Basic structure. DB2PM processes the data that is created by the DB2 TRACE facility. This data is placed in one of the following files by DB2:

- System Monitoring Facility (SMF) file
- Generalized Trace Facility (GTF) file
- Internal System Trace file

The data itself is of the following types:

- Statistical
- Accounting
- Performance

The reports themselves are created by batch jobs run in background mode using whichever data file has been decided. These reports are grouped into sets by function and include the following:

- Accounting
- DB2PM summaries
- Graphics
- I/O activity
- Locking
- Record Trace
- SQL traces
- Statistics
- System parameters
- Transit time

These reports will give the following information:

- DB2 system-wide activity summary
- Summary of work by and application
- Transit time by application
- Application-related I/O by DB2 application
- Logging I/O by data set
- Locking activity by application
- SQL activity by application
- Application usage by USERID
- Total SQL calls by USERID
- Many others

These reports are used in the management of performance and capacity, and are also used in some areas of problem determination.

Usage. Usage of DB2PM is accomplished through the execution of batch jobs using the DB2PM JCL procedure and supplying the appropriate Report Control cards. These control cards can be produced manually or through the use of the online DB2PM Interactive Report Facility (IRF) (see Appendix 59 for example JCL).

The type of control cards to be selected would depend upon the report desired and upon the time frame for the desired report.

The Interactive Report Facility also allows graphical reports to be created if the user has already selected the appropriate data and has the Graphical Data Display Manager (GDDM) installed and an appropriate GDDM graphics terminal.

Interactive report facility (IRF). If you select DB2PM from the DB2 Selection menus, you will receive the panel below. From this panel, you will select the type of report creation that is desired. The results of this will be a batch job to produce a report or create a report set for processing either in a batch mode or online graphics mode.

```
---------------------------------------------------------------------------------
I                                                                                 I
I                      IBM DATABASE 2 PERFORMANCE MONITOR                         I
I                                PRIMARY MENU                                     I
I                                                                                 I
I          DDDDDDDD     BBBBBBBB    22222    PPPPPPPP    MM         MM             I
I          DD     DD    BB    BB   22    22  PP     PP   MMM       MMM             I
I          DD     DD    BB    BB        22   PP     PP   MMMM     MMMM             I
I          DD     DD    BBBBBBBB        22   PPPPPPPP    MM MM MM MM               I
I          DD     DD    BB    BB       22    PP         MM   MMM    MM             I
I          DD     DD    BB    BB      22     PP         MM    M     MM             I
I          DDDDDDDD     BBBBBBBB    2222222   PP        MM          MM             I
I                                                                                 I
ISelect one of the following and press ENTER.                                     I
I    1   REPORT SELECTION    Select report sets and processing options            I
I    2   JOB GENERATION      Generate and submit job stream                       I
I    3   GRAPHICS            Process graphs                                       I
I                                                                                 I
I                                                                                 I
ISelect  ===>                                                                     I
I                                                                                 I
IPF1=Help  3=End                                                                  I
ICommand ===>                                                                     I
I                                                                                 I
---------------------------------------------------------------------------------
```

If you select the Job Generation option from the DB2PM main menu panel, you will receive the panel below.

```
 ----------------------------------------------------------------------
|                    DB2PM JOB GENERATION PRIMARY MENU                  |
| Select one of the following and press ENTER.                          |
|                                                                       |
|      1   CREATE    Create a new job                                   |
|      2   RECALL    Recall a previously saved job                      |
|                                                                       |
|                                                                       |
|                                                                       |
|                                                                       |
|                                                                       |
|                                                                       |
|                                                                       |
|                                                                       |
| Select   ===>                                                         |
| PF1=Help 3=End                                                        |
| Command ===>                                                          |
 ----------------------------------------------------------------------
```

If you select RECALL from the Job Generation primary menu above, you will receive the panel below.

```
 ----------------------------------------------------------------------
|                  DB2PM RECALL PREVIOUSLY SAVED JOB STREAM             |
| Specify Input Dataset where Job Stream was Saved and Press ENTER      |
| to receive a list of previously SAVED members.                        |
|                                                                       |
|      PROJECT ===> _____                                            |
|      GROUP   ===> _____                                            |
|      TYPE    ===> _____                                            |
|                                                                       |
| OTHER INPUT PARTITIONED DATA SET:                                     |
|              ===> _____            |
|   Note - above data set name must be in quotes if fully qualified.    |
|                                                                       |
|                                                                       |
|                                                                       |
| PF1=Help 3=End                                                        |
| Command ===>                                                          |
 ----------------------------------------------------------------------
```

If you select CREATE from the Job Generation primary menu above, you will receive the panel below.

```
r----------------------------------------------------------------------------
I                      DB2PM JOB GENERATION OPTIONS                      ROW
I
IType Data Set Names.  Press PF4 to Continue Job Generation, PF3 to Exit
IDefault DSN is ONLY substituted for missing dataset names indicated by
IDEFAULT DSN  => _____
I
IDDNAME         DATA SET NAME                              REPORTS  SELEC
I                                                         I  L   S  A  T
IINPUTDD      ?
ICORRELDD     ?
IDPMOUTDD     ?
IJOBSUMDD     ?
IMSGRPTDD     ?
ISYSPRINT     ?
ISYSUDUMP     ?
I************************************ BOTTOM OF DATA ************************
I
I
I
ICommand ===>                                                 SCROLL ==
L----------------------------------------------------------------------------
```

If you select the Report Selection option from the DB2PM main menu panel, you will receive the panel below.

```
r----------------------------------------------------------------------------
I                      DB2PM REPORT SELECTION MENU
ISelect one of the following.  Specify Default or User Specified
IREPORT FUNCTIONS if 1 - 5 is selected.  Press ENTER.
I
I
I    REPORT SETS                          PROCESSING OPTIONS
I       1    I/O ACTIVITY                   8    GLOBAL
I       2    LOCKING                        9    GROUP
I       3    STATISTICS                    10    LIST
I       4    ACCOUNTING                    11    DISTRIBUTE
I       5    TRANSIT TIME                  12    FIELD DEFINITION
I       6    RECORD TRACE
I       7    SQL TRACE
I
I
ISelect  ===> __      REPORT FUNCTIONS ===>  _   D=Default  U=User Speci
IPF1=Help 3=End 4=View  5=Save 6=Recall                    11=Delete
ICommand ===>
L----------------------------------------------------------------------------
```

If you select the Graphics option from the DB2PM main menu panel, you will receive the panel below.

```
r----------------------------------------------------------------------
|                      DB2PM GRAPHIC SUBSYSTEM
|                            MAIN MENU
|Select one of the following and press ENTER..
|    1    GRAPHICS         Perform DB2PM graphics.
|    2    RECALL           Recall previous saved graphs.
|    3    CHART            Transfer to GDDM Chart Utility.
|
|
|OTE TO ALL GRAPHIC USERS:
|  The DB2PM Graphics Subsystem data is generated from data REDUCED by
|  background processing.  To generate input data, press PF3.
|
|
|SELECT ===> _
|
|PF1=Help 3=End
|COMMAND ===>
|
L----------------------------------------------------------------------
```

If you select the Graphics option from the Graphic subsystem panel, you will receive the panel below.

```
r----------------------------------------------------------------------
|                      DB2PM GRAPHIC SUBSYSTEM
|                         PERFORM GRAPHICS
|  Select one of the following and press ENTER.
|   1   ACCOUNTING BY FIELD ID          Plot Field ID's by a DB2 Identifier
|   2   ACCOUNTING BY DB2 IDENTIFIER    Plot DB2 Identifier by a Field ID
|   3   STATISTICS                      Plot Field ID's
|   4   FREQUENCY DISTRIBUTION          Plot a Field ID by a DB2 Identifier
|
|
|
|
|
|
|SELECT ===> _
|
|PF1=Help 3=End                                      12=Menu
|COMMAND ===>
|
L----------------------------------------------------------------------
```

If you select Option 1 from the Graphic subsystem panel above, you will receive the panel below.

```
.--------------------------------------------------------------------.
|                     DB2PM GRAPHIC SUBSYSTEM                         |
|                     ACCOUNTING BY FIELD ID                         |
| Type in the following information and press ENTER.                 |
|              HH.MM.SS.TH                              MM/DD/YY      |
|     START TIME =>  _  _  _  _         START DATE =>  _  _  _        |
|     STOP  TIME =>  _  _  _  _         STOP  DATE =>  _  _  _        |
|     INPUT DATA SET NAME(R) ==>                                     |
|                                     (in quotes if fully qualified) |
|     GRAPH TITLE         ==> _____        |
|     INTERVAL            ==> _____        |
|     DAY                 ==> _                                      |
|     FIELD ID(s)    (R)  1  _____    2 _____                   |
|                         3  _____    4 _____                   |
|     Type an 'X' next to                VALUE                       |
|        the IDENTIFIER    AUTH  _    _____                      |
|        TYPE(s) and enter CONN  _    _____    1 - 3 IDENTIFIER TYPES |
|        the VALUE(s):     CNAM  _    _____       may be selected |
|                          CNUM  _    _____                      |
|                          PLAN  _    _____                      |
| REQUIRED DATA                                                      |
| PF1=Help 3=End                                                     |
| COMMAND ===>                          5=Save 6=Graph 12=Menu       |
'--------------------------------------------------------------------'
```

If you select Option 2 from the Graphic subsystem panel above, you will receive the panel below.

```
.--------------------------------------------------------------------.
|                     DB2PM GRAPHIC SUBSYSTEM                         |
|                     ACCOUNTING BY DB2 IDENTIFIER                   |
| Type in the following information and press ENTER.                 |
|              HH.MM.SS.TH                              MM/DD/YY      |
|     START TIME =>  _  _  _  _         START DATE =>  _  _  _        |
|     STOP  TIME =>  _  _  _  _         STOP  DATE =>  _  _  _        |
|     INPUT DATA SET NAME    (R) ==>  _____            |
|                                     (in quotes if fully qualified) |
|     GRAPH TITLE              ==> _____   |
|     INTERVAL                 ==> _____                           |
|     DAY                      ==> _                                 |
|     FIELD ID          (R) ==> _                                    |
|                                          DB2 IDENTIFIER TYPES      |
|     DB2 IDENTIFIER:                 AUTH  CNUM  PLAN  CNAM  CONN    |
|              TYPES  (R) ==>  _____   _  _____  _  _____           |
|              VALUES (R)   1  _____   _  _____  _  _____           |
|                           2  _____   _  _____  _  _____           |
|                           3  _____   _  _____  _  _____           |
|                           4  _____   _  _____  _  _____           |
| PF1=Help 3=End                                                     |
| COMMAND ===>                          5=Save 6=Graph 12=Menu       |
'--------------------------------------------------------------------'
```

If you select Option 3 from the Graphic subsystem panel above, you will receive
the panel below.

```
----------------------------------------------------------------------------
|                        DB2PM GRAPHIC SUBSYSTEM                            |
|                            STATISTICS                                    |
| Type in the following information and press ENTER.                       |
|               HH.MM.SS.TH                             MM/DD/YY           |
|   START TIME => __ __ __ __          START DATE => __ __ __              |
|   STOP  TIME => __ __ __ __          STOP  DATE => __ __ __              |
|                                                                          |
|   INPUT DATA SET NAME(R) ==> _____              |
|                              (in quotes if fully qualified)              |
|   GRAPH TITLE          ==> _____                |
|   INTERVAL             ==> __                                            |
|   DAY                  ==> _                                             |
|                                                                          |
|   FIELD ID(s)      (R)  1  _____      2  _____                    |
|                         3  _____      4  _____                    |
|                                                                          |
|                                                                          |
| PF1=Help 3=End                        5=Save 6=Graph 12=Menu            |
| COMMAND ===>                                                             |
----------------------------------------------------------------------------
```

If you select Option 4 from the Graphic subsystem panel above, you will receive
the panel below.

```
----------------------------------------------------------------------------
|                        DB2PM GRAPHIC SUBSYSTEM                            |
|                        FREQUENCY DISTRIBUTION                            |
| Type in the following information and press ENTER.                       |
|               HH.MM.SS.TH                             MM/DD/YY           |
|   START TIME => __ __ __ __          START DATE => __ __ __              |
|   STOP  TIME => __ __ __ __          STOP  DATE => __ __ __              |
|                                                                          |
|   INPUT DATA SET NAME (R) ==> _____             |
|                               (in quotes if fully qualified)             |
|   GRAPH TITLE           ==> _____               |
|   FIELD ID        (R) ==> _____                                      |
|                                                                          |
|   DB2 IDENTIFIER          TYPE      VALUE       DB2 IDENTIFIER TYPES     |
|        TYPES and VALUES  1 ___     _____     AUTH CONN CNAM CNUM      |
|                          2 ___     _____     PLAN DSET DTBS PSET      |
|                          3 ___     _____                             |
|                                                                          |
| PF1=Help 3=End                        5=Save 6=Graph 12=Menu            |
| COMMAND ===>                                                             |
----------------------------------------------------------------------------
```

If you select RECALL from the Graphic menu subsystem panel above, you will receive the panel below.

```
,--------------------------------------------------------------------------------,
|                                                                                |
|                    RECALL PREVIOUSLY SAVED GRAPHICS VARIABLES                   |
|                                                                                |
| Specify Input Dataset where Graphics Variables were SAVED and Press            |
| ENTER to receive a list of previously SAVED Members.                           |
|                                                                                |
|    PROJECT ===>                                                                |
|    GROUP   ===>                                                                |
|    TYPE    ===>                                                                |
|                                                                                |
|                                                                                |
|OTHER INPUT PARTITIONED DATA SET:                                               |
|            ===>                                                                |
| Note - above data set name must be in quotes if fully qualified.               |
|                                                                                |
|                                                                                |
|                                                                                |
|                                                                                |
|                                                                                |
|PF1=Help 3=End                                                                  |
|Command ===>                                                                    |
'--------------------------------------------------------------------------------'
```

DB2 Online Monitors

In any high-usage environment, real-time, on-line monitors are a necessity for the day-to-day support and problem determination. The DB2 environment is no exception. IBM itself has only provided DB2PM, which is definitely NOT a real-time monitor. Candle Corporation has again provided a monitor for the DB2 world in their OMEGAMON line of products. It is called Omegamon/DB2. Another company called Data Base Utility Group has a DB2 Monitor as well.

In either case, the product provides the capability to show the status of DB2 at the point in time that the problem is occurring, and if you are intent on providing proper support of DB2, this capability is mandatory.

Other DB2-Related Topics

8

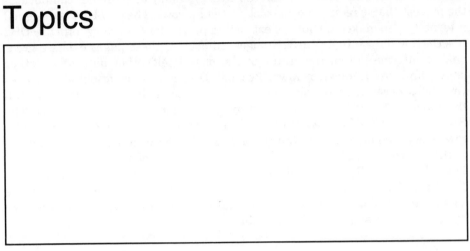

GENERIC DB2 APPLICATION ARCHIVE FACILITY

There is, in many installations, the need to guarantee recovery of individual rows and/or values of specific columns within those rows. This generic DB2 application ARCHIVE facility is a design for a system that can be developed and placed into a DB2 subsystem.

Overview of Requirements

Data recoverability. The primary reason for the creation of the ARCHIVE facility revolves around the potential requirement that some of the data within any DB2 table may be updated and/or deleted and must be recovered for some reason in the future. The need for recovery may have been caused by one of the following:

1. Application program error
2. User error
3. Improper use of SPUFI or QMF

If one of these situations occurs, particular parts of data or possibly complete rows may need to be recovered and restored. This requires the use of an ARCHIVE facility.

Why not use DB2 recovery? The DB2 BACKUP, RECOVERY AND LOGGING facility is designed to recover complete tables up to either a previous point in time or to the present. The system is not designed to recover only certain rows or data within a particular table. Also, the DB2 system logs and records data for ALL tables within the DB2 system, which further complicates the process that is required to extract particular rows. The way DB2 is designed internally also makes the idea of extracting particular rows very difficult. DB2 inserts row data into 4K or 32K pages. In each of these pages exists a great deal of information on the status of the page itself, other data about other pages, and any number of rows. Because DB2 is column oriented and uses variable-size columns, the actual data rows will be in different locations within the page, and the length may or may not be the same for each row. The BACKUP, RECOVERY, AND LOGGING function is based upon a page, not a row. When a change occurs to any data on a page, the WHOLE PAGE is written to the log (this includes ANY update, insert, or delete of a row onto that page). The BACKUP COPY utility makes copies of each page to the image copy file. The RECOVERY utility recovers full pages not rows. As a result, using the logs or image copies to recover individual rows or particular columns is very difficult and, in some cases, impossible.

Need for update/delete control. The primary need is to control and archive ALL updates and deletes in certain tables. Inserts themselves are not a consideration because they can be recovered using the normal DB2 recovery process. The concern lies in what happens after the data is inserted, and it becomes necessary to recover a previously updated data item or row that has been deleted. This archive ability must apply to access from ALL users and programs, including SPUFI and application code, as well as any Dynamic SQL code.

Application Archive Functional Requirements

Following is a list of the functional requirements and structure required for an effective application ARCHIVE facility:

* Restrict update/delete ability
* Archive updated/deleted rows
* Generic design
* Easy upgrade/addition of new tables
* Off-load of archived data
* Access to archived data

Application Archive Design Proposal

Following is a proposed archive design to satisfy the functional requirements.

System flow diagram.

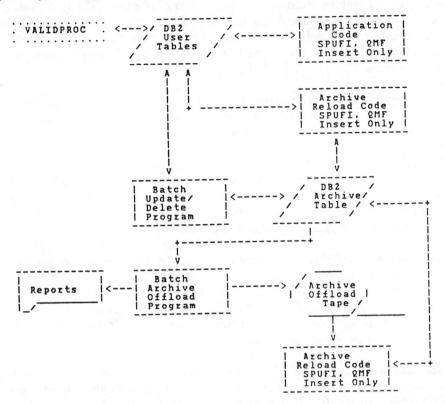

Restrict update/delete ability.   The key to the success of the archiving function is the restriction and control over the update and delete capability. The way to guarantee that no one can accidentally or otherwise delete and/or update any data from any particular table is to add a DB2 VALIDPROC procedure to the tables that need this type of protection, which does not allow ANY updating or deleting by any method except a specified procedure that is run nightly. All application code will be allowed only to update a status column in any affected table from a blank to a U for update and a D for delete. Then, in the case of an update, a new row will be inserted with a new date-time stamp and a status code of blank.

Archive updated/deleted rows.   At night, or whenever it is determined to be necessary, a batch DB2 job will be run which will archive all rows marked U and D and will delete those rows from the appropriate tables. This batch job will be the only application allowed to actually perform the delete and row update.

Generic design. The design of the system will be composed of a master routine that calls subroutines and a single generic DB2 table which will contain all of the archived data. Each row in this archive table will contain the table name or code from which the data came and the data that was necessary to be archived. Included should be the date-time stamp that shows the last insert/ update date.

Easy upgrade/addition of new tables. The subroutines and VALIDPROCs will all be similar in structure and will each be basically identical except for the columns and rows that are processed.

Off-load of archived data. At some determined time, another batch job will be run that will off-load all archived data based upon some factor such as time and date from the online DB2 archive tables to tape. These tapes can be created as separate tapes, or as continually modified daily tapes with separate weekly, monthly, or quarterly copies made.

Access to archived data. Archived data can be accessed using application code that can be written, or through systems such as SPUFI and/or the IBM Query Management Facility (QMF). The new release of QMF has a greatly improved interface to ISPF so that applications can be created quickly using this function. In addition, the report-writing facility would allow quick development of various requested reports.

Reloading archived data. Reloading of archived data can be done through online application programs that will insert the reloaded data into the appropriate table directly. If it is determined that this is not possible, SQL can be developed to manipulate the data so that it can be reloaded in the appropriate format. This SQL could be developed through the use of application code or through the usage of QMF, which would enable these special requirements to be met quickly and easily without the requirement of writing extensive application code. The Procedure feature of QMF allows extensive combinations of queries and temporary files to be created, which eliminate the need for extensive and complex application code development in many cases.

Access to off-loaded data. Off-loaded data can be accessed through programs that can ask for the necessary tapes to be loaded so that the requested off-loaded archive data can be reloaded into the online archive table. Then, by using the applications defined in reloading archived data, the data can be reloaded to the appropriate table.

Off-loaded data management. Whenever the OFFLOAD process is run, a report and/or file will be generated that will show the keys of the off-loaded data, the tables it came from, and the date the off-load occurred. This can be combined to give a complete report of all off-loaded data, or the individual listings can be kept.

DB2 APPLICATION UPDATE LOCKING MECHANISM

Locking Requirements Definition

The requirement for update locking is based on the assumption that the data needs to be locked to prevent an interim update from taking place while that data is being updated in an off-line mode, such as in a personal computer, or in a different process than that which is controlled by a Database Management System (DBMS) which, in this case, is Database2 (DB2).

The DBMS itself would take care of this process for online-type processing, but this is not always possible. Yet the need for data integrity and the guarantee of a certain level of data still exists.

As a result, a need exists for locking certain rows and/or column values within a particular DB2 table. This requirement can be satisfied to varying degrees of completeness, using parts of or all of the following procedures and/or processes.

Prerequisites. For implementation of any parts of the following solutions, the following is necessary:

> USERID column must be added for each column or row of each DB2 table to support the locking mechanism. This USERID column will be a character field of eight to correspond with MVS-based USERID.

Possible solutions.

- Use DB2 column-level update grant authority
- Use DB2 view definitions and user
- Use DB2 VALIDPROC
- Use application code

DB2 Column-Level Update Grant Authority

Solution description. The column-level update grant authority within DB2 could be used if it is known exactly who will be allowed to do updates to particular columns. This would allow only those who are authorized to update that column to actually do it. This would keep out all possible updates (except for the System Administrator or DBA personnel).

Limitations. This solution will NOT lock out interim updates unless only ONE person is allowed to do the update to the column. If more than one person is granted authority to update that column, interim updates can occur.

DB2 View Definitions and User

Solution description. Using a combination of DB2 view definitions with the addition of any column defined as USERID on each affected table is the easiest way to implement a locking mechanism. The view would be a DB2-defined view that would allow update of the particular column only if the USERID column matched the USERID of the person executing the DB2 update request. Initially, the person who has the intent of doing the update to the particular column would set the USERID column in the table to his ID, using a view that allows the update only if the USERID column on the table is blank. The update would then occur. Then, after the data has been edited, it will be up-loaded using a different view that allows an update only if the USERIDs match, as described earlier. In the meantime, if any other update is attempted by any other USERID, it will not be allowed, and an SQL return code of $+100$ or a -160 will be returned. Further locking can be done in that a Select view can also be generated allowing a Select Only if the USERID field is blank.

Assumptions. The assumptions are that each view will describe only some or all of the columns of a SINGLE DB2 table. Multiple tables cannot be updated in a single view. Also, cursors cannot be used in the view definition either, so the assumption is that either the row being updated is being accessed through a unique key, or ALL of the rows being accessed will ALWAYS be updated.

Limitations. The limitation of this solution is that it will have no effect on any calls that do not use the specified views and that use direct table access calls (either Dynamic or Static SQL). However, access can be checked through viewing the DB2 catalog for static calls; dynamic calls (such as SPUFI) cannot be checked.

DB2 VALIDPROC

Solution description. The use of DB2 VALIDPROCs would guarantee that only certain plans could update certain columns within a specified DB2 table, and that certain requirements would have to be met before the update would be allowed in any case, no matter whether it is Dynamic or Static SQL (SPUFI included), or the System Admininstrator or DBA personnel. DB2 VALIDPROCs are routines which are called by DB2 EVERY time the table specified is being updated, deleted, or inserted by any SQL call. The procedure listed above in using views could be implemented within the VALIDPROC with greater certainty than with views.

Assumptions. The assumptions are based on the fact that updates are based upon a single table. Whenever the VALIDPROC refuses to allow the insert, update, or delete, an SQL return code of -652 will be returned.

Limitations.   The limitations of the solution are that the VALIDPROCs must be written in Assembler, and only one VALIDPROC can be written and used on a single table.

Application Code

Solution description.   The application code will perform the checking of the USERID field within its own processing as defined in the view solution described above. The code will first check for a blank USERID field and, if it is not blank, will check for a matching USERID field with the user executing the application if an update is being attempted. If no update is being attempted and the USERID field is not blank, a message should be sent to the user executing the program explaining that this row and/or column is being updated off-line; the USERID who is doing it should also be passed along. If the user executing the program is going to off-load the row(s) for update and the USERID field is blank, the USERID of the person executing this code should be placed into the USERID column for that row, and an update should take place.

Assumptions.   The prime assumption is that these procedures will be written and implemented as required into the appropriate code.

Limitations.   There are no guarantees against other programs doing the update, and much now depends upon the application personnel in implementing and coding the appropriate code correctly. Use of Include modules could be incorporated, but with the lack of a standard coding methodology, the incorporation of a standard Include module could be very difficult and time-consuming.

DB2 COMMANDS AND HOW TO USE THEM

Types of commands

DB2 commands can be issued from the following attached subsystems:

- TSO/ISPF (DB2I)
- CICS
- IMS
- Batch

The format of the commands varies depending upon which subsystem the command is being issued from. Following is a breakdown by subsystem attachment type:

TSO Commands.   DB2 commands can be issued from TSO/ISPF through the COMMANDS option on the DB2 Interactive (DB2I) system under ISPF. To use these commands, the USERIDs executing them must have had the appropriate authorization granted to them. If the authorization has not been granted, the user will not be able to execute the command.

- DISPLAY XXXXXXXX
  Displays the current status of the following:
  DATABASE
  Depending upon which suboption is selected, specific tablespaces or all tablespaces will be shown with their read/write status and the locking status for tables and tablespaces (see *DB2 Reference Manual* for more detail).
  THREAD
  Shows all currently active DB2 threads that are attached to this particular DB2 subsystem.
  TRACE
  Shows the traces that are currently active.
  UTILITY
  Shows any DB2 utilities that are currently running, or are in some type of abended status.
- —STOP DB2
  Begins the shutdown of DB2.
- —STOP DATABASE
  Stops further access to the specified database(s) and/or tablespace(s).
- —STOP TRACE (type)
  Stops specified trace.
- —STOP RLIMIT
  Stops current Resource Limit Facilities
- —START TRACE (type)
  Starts the specified traces. Care must be used in the type of traces that are started and where the trace results will be sent.
- —START RLIMIT ID = XX
  Starts up the selected Resource Limit Facility Table
- —START DB2
  Starts up the DB2 subsystem. It can only be issued through the system console.
- —START DATABASE
  Starts up any database and/or tablespace that has been stopped.

CICS Commands. The commands that can be issued from CICS are listed below. These commands are issued through the DSNC CICS transaction.

- DSNC—DISPLAY xxxxxxxx
  The following subcommands are the same as described in the previous section, 'TSO Commands.'

    – DATABASE
    – THREAD
    – TRACE
    – UTILITY

The following commands are unique to the CICS ATTACHMENT facility and can only be executed in a CICS region with the ATTACHMENT facility installed.

- DSNC DISCONNECT planname
  Disconnects active threads for 'planname' plan.
- DSNC DISPLAY xxxxxxxxx
  Displays the following information depending upon which option is chosen.
  - PLAN planname
    Displays information on all plans defined in CICS Resource Control Table (RCT).
  - TRANSACTION transaction-id
    Displays information on all transactions defined in CICS RCT.
  - STATISTICS
    Displays statistical counters associated with each entry defined in the RCT.
- DSNC STRT
  Starts up ATTACHMENT facility to DB2 if it has not been started.
- DSNC STOP
  Stops ATTACHMENT facility to DB2.

IMS/DC Commands. The commands that can be issued from IMS/DC are listed below. These are commands by Master Terminal Operators. The same DB2 Commands that can be issued by both TSO and CICS can be issued, but must be preceded by /SSR.

- /SSR—DISPLAY xxxxxxxxx
  The following subcommands are the same as described in the section 'TSO Commands.'
  - DATABASE
  - THREAD
  - TRACE
  - UTILITY

The following commands are unique to the IMS/DC ATTACHMENT facility and can only be executed in an IMS region with the ATTACHMENT facility installed.

- /CHANGE SUBSYS subsystem-name
  Resets an indoubt unit of recovery.
- /DISPLAY SUBSYS subsystem-name
  Displays the status of the connection between IMS and DB2.
- /START
  Starts up ATTACHMENT facility to DB2 if it has not been started.
- /STOP
  Stops ATTACHMENT facility to DB2.

INTERNAL ARCHITECTURE

The internal architecture of DB2 is made up of the following parts:

- DB2 Applications
  The applications or interactive user systems contain the code and the ATTACHMENT facilities to the DB2 system. They pass to DB2 the requests for data that is in the DB2 tables.
- DB2 Relational Data System
  The DB2 Relational Data System (RDS) acts as the interface to the applications and is where the following type of work occurs. DB2 work that occurs in this area to satisfy data access requests is more costly in terms of CPU utilization than access requests that are satisfied in the Internal Data Manager. This includes the following:
  —Multiple-table sort
  —Non-sargable predicate application
- DB2 Internal Data Manager
  The Internal Data Manager applies sargable predicates to the data access requests.
- DB2 Buffer Manager
  The DB2 Buffer Manager does the following:
  —Manages data-buffering between DASD and Virtual Memory (CVM)
  —Transfers data in 4K or 32K blocks
  —Performs file OPEN/CLOSE functions
- VSAM Media Manager
  The VSAM Media Manager handles the actual I/O and provides device independence for the DB2 code itself.
- DB2 Databases
  VSAM files that contain the actual DB2 data.

The DB2 internal architecture is structured as shown below:

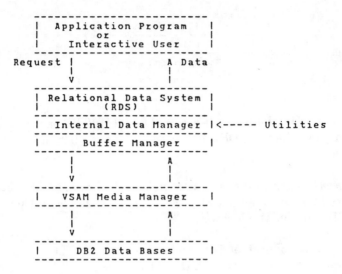

Buffer Manager Diagram

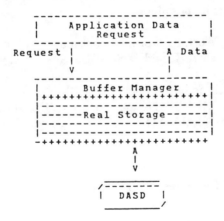

Recommendations.

- The Buffer Manager is critical in reducing transaction I/O.
- Avoid BP32.
- Use one large buffer pool. Let DB2 manage.
- Monitor buffer pool expansions.

DB Services Memory Map

```
-------------------------------
I       Buffer  Pools          I
-------------------------------
I          EDM  Pool           I
-------------------------------
I      Working  Storage        I
-------------------------------
I          VSAM  OPEN          I
-------------------------------
```

Buffer Pools.   DB2 buffer pools are used for all DB2 I/O operations. The more that is available, the more DB2 objects that will stay in memory, thus increasing performance.

Environment descriptors manager pool (EDM pool).   The Environment Descriptors Manager Pool (EDM pool) is the most important part of storage manager. It contains the following:

- 4K chunks of each active application plan (SKCT).
- Cursor Table (CT) for each thread.
- Database Descriptor (DBD) for each application plan.
- DSNZPARM option sets size.
- Degradation increases I/O for SCT01 and DBD01.
- Make as large as possible.

Working storage.   Working storage is not a specifiable parameter. Each active QMF user will use 76K, and each SQL transaction will need 24K.

VSAM OPEN.   Each open data set uses 2.3K of storage. The CREATE TABLESPACE has CLOSE YES/NO option. Use YES unless tablespace is frequently opened; then specify NO.

Tablespaces

The structure of a tablespace is as follows:

```
TABLESPACE Page
    ******************************************************************
    x  Space      +                                                 x
    x  Directory  +  ---------------------------                    x
    x++++++++++++++ I        Table Row           I                  x
    x               ---------------------------                     x
    x                                                               x
    x            ---------------------------                        x
    x            I       Table Row          I                       x
    x            ---------------------------                        x
    x                                                               x
    x                 ---------------------------                   x
    x                 I        Table Row        I                   x
    x                 ---------------------------                   x
    x                                             ................. x
    x                                             .  Page Row     x
    x                                             .  Directory    x
    ******************************************************************
```

Row Storage

The structure of a row is as follows:

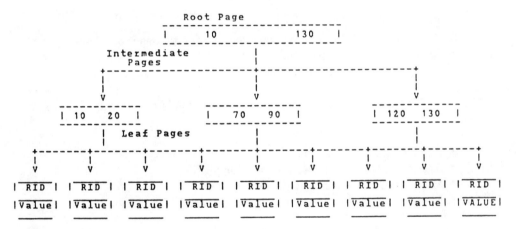

```
         *************************************************************
ROW      *  Table Name  |               |               |          *
         *  Delete Flag | Field One     | Field Two     | ...      *
         *  Row Length  |               |               |          *
         *************************************************************


         *************************************************************
FIELD    *  Field Length | NULL Flag    |     DATA                  *
         *************************************************************
```

Indexes

The structure of an index is as follows:

```
                          Root Page
               ----------------------------------
               |      10              130    |
               ----------------------------------
         Intermediate            |
            Pages                |
         +---------------------+---------------------------+
         |                     |                           |
         v                     v                           v
      ----------          --------------          --------------
      | 10    20 |        |  70    90  |          | 120   130  |
      ----------          --------------          --------------
         |  Leaf Pages       |                        |
         |                   |                        |
      +-------+-------+   +-------+--------+     +-------+-------+
      |       |       |   |       |        |     |       |       |
      v       v       v   v       v        v     v       v       v
   | RID | | RID | | RID | | RID | | RID | | RID | | RID | | RID | | RID |
   |Value| |Value| |Value| |Value| |Value| |Value| |Value| |Value| |VALUE|
```

DB2 CAPACITY PLANNING

The area of capacity planning for DB2 is going to be very difficult to manage, at least initially. This is primarily because of the ad hoc capability that is going to be demanded by the end user which, when he gets it, will release a very high level of unknown demand for usage and services. Most companies to date have failed miserably in their projections and have found themselves very far behind on the demand curve. As a result, the complaint level increases on levels of magnitude, along with the resource utilization level of the CPU. As a result, capacity planning using DB2 must be done on a very short-term basis, with resultant short-term projection and hardware purchase cycles.

Capacity Planning Factors for DB2

Capacity planning for DB2 will involve the following processes:

- Characterization of the workload
- Sizing of transactions
- Analytical modeling
- Modification analysis
- DB2 benchmarks

Each of the previously mentioned processes will be described in some detail in the following paragraphs. These processes are standard capacity planning processes, and there will be no attempt to completely train the reader on how to be a capacity planner. This is just an attempt to guide you in the right direction.

Characterization of the workload. Characterization of the workload determines the following:

- Size of workload for planning purposes
- Selection of level of detail: workload versus transaction sizing
- Existing characteristics versus future
- Using 'canned' transaction sizes

EXISTING WORKLOADS. Using existing workloads allows the following to occur:

- Existing data is available.
- Assume future workload has similar profile.
- Measure CPU and I/O requirements.
- Measure at performance group level or DB2 transaction level.

WORKLOAD MEASUREMENTS. Workload measurements for DB2 should be as follows:

- DB2 as CPU time should be less than 10 percent of total DB2 CPU.
- Apportion CPU time in proportion to CPU time used by DB2 users.
- DB2 disk volumes access should be ONLY DB2.
- Volumes can be further dedicated by following DB2 workloads.
  - DB2 storage groups
  - QMF storage groups
  - CICS access
  - Non-QMF TSO/ISPF access
  - IMS/DC access
  - DB2 logs
  - DB2 catalogs
- Distribute workloads by numbers of I/Os using SMF accounting.

Sizing of transactions. To perform transaction-level sizing, do the following:

- Use DB2 accounting reports from DB2PM.
- Directly measure CPU utilization (RMF, SMF, etc.).
- Calculate I/O or use I/O trace.
- Use reporting groups in DB2PM to group transactions into workloads.

Tracking read/write I/Os. To calculate I/Os attributable to DB2, do the following:

- Track logical and physical I/Os from SMF.
- Use BP1 for tablespaces and BP2 for indexes.
- Use BP0 for catalog.
- Catalog, tablespaces, and indexes will be separated.
- Apportion log I/Os using page updates in accounting reports against log I/Os reported in System Services Report using DB2PM.

Standard DB2 transactions. The usage of standard DB2 transactions instead of workload data or transaction sizing is necessary in the following situation:

- No existing measurement data
- Little to no information on applications

If this is the situation, then this will provide a starting point. In this process, two types of standard DB2 transaction environments are assumed:

- Query environment
- Transaction environment

In these environments, the following assumptions will be made:

QUERY ENVIRONMENT. The query environment assumes the following:

- QMF end users
- A standard transaction size
- Table sizes between 10 and 10,000 physical pages
- 80% inquiry-only
- 20% update

The average query is composed of the following:

- Average CPU path length—10 MIPS (Million Instructions Per Second).
- DB2 physical read I/Os—120.

- DB2 physical write I/Os—2.
- DB2 physical log I/Os—3.
- Average transaction on a 3081K uses 1.4 seconds of CPU time.*
- Average transaction on a 3084Q uses .75 seconds of CPU time.
- Average transaction on a 3090-200 uses .7 seconds of CPU time.
- Average transaction on a 3090-400 uses .37 seconds of CPU time.
- Average transaction on a 3090-600 uses .2 seconds of CPU time.
- Average I/O time on a 3380 is 2.8 seconds for 3380s.

*Transaction times are based upon 10 MIPS per transaction and estimated MIPS of the associated CPU.

TRANSACTION ENVIRONMENT. The transaction environment assumes the following:

- IMS, CICS, or TSO as front end
- Transactions highly optimized
- Table sizes between 10 and 10,000 physical pages
- 80% inquiry-only
- 20% update

The average transaction is composed of the following:

- Average CPU path length—600 thousand instructions.
- DB2 physical read I/Os—7.
- DB2 physical write I/Os—.3.
- DB2 physical log I/Os—.5.
- Average transaction on a 3081K uses .1 seconds of CPU time.*
- Average transaction on a 3084Q uses .05 seconds of CPU time.
- Average transaction on a 3090-200 uses .04 seconds of CPU time.
- Average transaction on a 3090-400 uses .02 seconds of CPU time.
- Average transaction on a 3090-600 uses .01 seconds of CPU time.
- Average I/O time on a 3380 is .17 seconds for 3380s.

*Transaction times are based upon 600 thousand instructions per second for each transaction and estimated MIPS of the associated CPU.

STANDARD TRANSACTION CAVEATS. Standard transactions should be used only as a rough first cut. Actual transaction sizes will vary greatly in size and content. You need to make sure that true measurements are acquired at the earliest possible time.

QUERY VS. TRANSACTION. As is shown, the use of Static SQL and the correct optimization of plans in a transaction processing environment is worth a considerable amount of savings as far as hardware utilization is concerned.

Analytical modeling. The input to the analytical model used in capacity planning for DB2 will be the following:

- Workload characterization
- Standard transactions (if no measurement data)
- Data reduction for performance group workload level modeling
- Created transaction level models from SMF Accounting Reports

Modification analysis. In doing modification analysis, the following factors should be included:

- Memory is KEY DB2 resource.
- Lack of memory affects transaction size.
- EDM pool shortage increases I/O.
- Buffer pool limits decrease logical to physical I/O ratio, thus increasing number of I/Os.
- Difficult to predict memory constraint effect.
- How applications access data affects Buffer Manager.
- Varies from application to application.
- Track Buffer Manager success of high and low periods.

What-if analysis. What-if analysis concerns the following:

- Transaction volume increases
- I/O configuration changes
- CPU upgrades
- Workload-balancing between machines

Perform same process used in modification analysis.

DB2 benchmarks. As DB2 is a relatively new product, in many cases DB2 benchmarks that have been run by IBM can prove to be very helpful in the capacity-planning effort.

Benchmark #1, which has been run by IBM, has the following characteristics:

- Transaction workload
- Measured of two machines
  - IBM 4381-2
  - IBM 3090-200
- CICS attach with 12 SQL calls per transaction
- Five transaction types

The results by machine are as follows:

IBM 4381-2

* Maximum four transactions/second
  - Response time—4 seconds
  - NO THREAD REUSE
* Maximum five transactions/second
  - Response time—.9 seconds
  - THREAD REUSE
* CICS 1.7
* 16M memory

IBM 3090-2

* Response time—.5 seconds
* THREAD REUSE
* 64M + 64M memory
* 24M buffer pool
* 47 transactions per second

This benchmark, as stated by IBM, was run in a standalone, dedicated environment.

DB2 PERFORMANCE MANAGEMENT

The area of performance management as it applies to DB2 spans many areas and software products because of the multitude of ways in which DB2 can be used and accessed. The factors that need to be considered include DB2 table access paths, DB2 internal performance factors, external subsystem performance (TSO/ISPF, CICS, IMS/DC), and the MVS operating system itself.

DB2 Access Path Selection

The access paths to the DB2 table data are created by the DB2 'optimizer.' This optimizer is a part of DB2 which creates the access path for the application plan at bind time. The information used in the process is a combination of the following processes:

1. Access catalog statistics.
2. Compute numbers of rows for each predicate.
3. Choose set of reasonable paths.
4. Calculate access path cost (includes I/Os and CPU).

5. Add required Sort cost.

6. Select least cost path.

Catalog statistics used. In access path selection, the following DB2 system catalog columns are used:

- SYSINDEXES columns
  - FULLKEYCARD
  - FIRSTKEYCARD
  - NLEAF
  - NLEVELS
  - CLUSTERED
- SYSTABLES columns
  - NPAGES
  - PCTPAGES
  - CARD
- SYSTABLESPACE columns
  - NACTIVE
- SYSCOLUMNS columns
  - COLCARD
  - HIGH2KEY
  - LOW2KEY

RUNSTATS updates these columns when it is run.

Use of RUNSTATS for performance. As is shown above, the catalog statistics are important factors in access path selection. As such, it is necessary to make sure those statistics are as up to date as possible. This is done through the execution of the RUNSTATS utility. For the best results overall, you should run RUNSTATS just after the data has been loaded and before the BIND is done, or if this is a REBIND on plans using data which has a heavy amount of insert, delete, and/or update activity, the RUNSTATS should be run before the REBIND.

Using indexes for performance. Creating the right index can have very large performance implications because of the changes to the access path selection process that can occur.

Access path selection. Three major factors influence the cost of the access path that is selected. These are:

- The Filter Factor
- Sargability
- Matching indexability

If predicate combinations have the above features, they will be much more efficient than other access path selection combinations. Otherwise, access path selection will be based on other considerations.

FILTER FACTOR. The filter factor represents a fraction based upon an assumption of the rows that will be selected to satisfy a given predicate. This factor is based upon the assumptions that there is a uniform distribution of values over a given range and that you have columns value independence.

This factor is not very accurate or helpful in reality, but if the above mentioned factors do exist, you have a better probability of selecting the best access path.

In any case, a default filter factor is used in the following situations:

- Queries against DB2 system catalogs.
- Column selected is NOT first column of index.
- No RUNSTATS have been executed.
- Host variables are used in range expression.

SARGABILITY. An SQL statement is considered sargable when the Internal Data Manager can process the request. When the Internal Data Manager can process the request, CPU time is reduced considerably. If the Internal Data Manager cannot process the request, then the Relational Data Manager must process the request, thus increasing CPU.

Current sargable predicates are as follows:

- COLUMN1 = value1
- COLUMN1 = COLUMN2 (different tables)
- COLUMN1 >, > =, −< value1
- COLUMN1 range-operator COLUMN2 (different tables)
- COLUMN1 BETWEEN (value1, value2)
- COLUMN1 IS NULL (if COLUMN1 defined as nullable)
- COLUMN1 IS NOT NULL (if COLUMN1 defined as nullable)
- COLUMN1 = (subquery)
- COLUMN1 >, < (subquery)
- COLUMN1 IN (list)
- COLUMN1 −IN (list)
- COLUMN1 LIKE 'CHAR'
- COLUMN1 −LIKE 'CHAR'
- COLUMN1 LIKE '%CHAR'
- COLUMN1 LIKE '_CHAR'
- COLUMN1 LIKE :host-variable

- COLUMN1 –BETWEEN (value1, value2)
- COLUMN1 > value1 OR COLUMN1 < value1
- COLUMN1 = value1 OR COLUMN2 = value2
- NOT basic predicate
- NOT COLUMN1 > value1
- NOT COLUMN1 like 'CHAR'
- NOT COLUMN1 IN (list)
- NOT COLUMN1 BETWEEN (value1, value2)

Other predicate combinations will be non-sargable and thus have to be processed by the Relational Data Manager.

As is obvious, most times you will get the default because of the column limitation.

MATCHING INDEXABILITY. The first point to be made in this case is that the predicates used must be sargable before they can have matching indexability. However, just because a predicate is sargable does not mean that it also has matching indexability. You have matching indexability when a predicate matches an index access path, is sargable, and when the columns defined in the predicate are an initial substring of the set defined in an index key that will be used.

Current matching indexability predicates are as follows:

- COLUMN1 = value1
- COLUMN1 = COLUMN2 (different tables)
- COLUMN1 >, >=, –< value1
- COLUMN1 range-operator COLUMN2 (different tables)
- COLUMN1 BETWEEN (value1, value2)
- COLUMN1 = (subquery)
- COLUMN1 >, < (subquery)
- COLUMN1 IN (list)
- COLUMN1 LIKE 'CHAR'
- COLUMN1 –LIKE 'CHAR'
- NOT basic predicate—(sometimes)
- NOT COLUMN1 > value1

ACCESS PATH EFFICIENCY. The preferred access paths in order of efficiency are as follows:

1. Match UNIQUE INDEX with Equal (=) Predicate—No data access
2. Non-matching INDEX—No data access
3. Match UNIQUE INDEX with Equal (=) Predicate—With data access
4. Match on clustering index
5. Match on non-clustered index
6. Non-matching clustered index

7. Non-matching index—With data access
8. Tablespace scan

The resultant scan that is chosen performs the following functions:

MATCHING INDEX SCAN—NO DATA ACCESS

* Reads index only
* Returns index values
* Does NOT access data rows

MATCHING INDEX SCAN—DATA ACCESS

* Reads index
* Selects subset data based on Select requirements
* Reads appropriate data rows
* Returns selected data

NON-MATCHING INDEX SCAN—NO DATA ACCESS

* Retrieves all index rows by processing leaf pages
* Returns index values
* Does NOT access data rows

NON-MATCHING INDEX SCAN—DATA ACCESS

* Retrieves all index rows by processing leaf pages
* Selects subset data based on Select requirements
* Reads appropriate data rows
* Returns selected data

TABLESPACE SCAN

* Retrieves data rows
* Selects subset data based on Select requirements
* Returns selected data
* DO NOT DO for large tables

DB2 Internal Performance Factors

Overall, there are not too many parameters that can be changed within DB2 that will affect performance. The factors that affect DB2 performance internally are as follows:

Application development. As in all DBMSs, bad application design and bad database design produces bad performance. This has not changed with

DB2. Bad SQL causes bad performance. Most of DB2's performance problems can be tracked back to design or lack of indexes. For severe problems, use DB2PM to determine the bottleneck, and then try to come up with a solution to the problem.

Items to analyze are the following:

- Logical design
- Physical design
- SQL optimization
- Database locking
- Referential Integrity Implementation

DB2 installation parameters. The following DB2 installation parameters can have an effect upon overall performance:

- Number of threads
- Memory allocation
- Buffer-pool sizing
- Logging subsystem

External Subsystem Performance

Other factors will influence the overall performance of DB2. The way the subsystems that attach to and use DB2 services are configured and managed will affect the user's overall response. Particular items to consider are as follows:

TSO/ISPF/QMF. The access to DB2 from TSO/ISPF can be bad because of the way the MVS dispatching priorities and performance groups are set up to handle certain classes of TSO commands. QMF and the various DB2I functions are very CPU-intensive. This will result in the MVS System Resource Manager quickly scheduling the DB2 transactions into very low-level performance groups. The solution to this is to set up a special performance group for TSO/ISPF/ QMF DB2 users to account for this situation by allowing initially higher re-source-utilization than is normally allowed for the average TSO user.

CICS. The access to DB2 from CICS will depend primarily upon the total utilization of the single CICS region and the number of threads created by that CICS region to DB2. The greater the number of CICS transactions that require DB2 resources, the greater the number of threads that should be created using the CICS RCT table.

IMS/DC. Connections to DB2 from IMS/DC are established from the Control Region and each dependent region that accesses DB2 resources. The Control Region connection takes care of DB2 commands issued from IMS, while each dependent region will take care of application requests. This reduces path length by eliminating Control Region overhead for DB2 calls. For performance, DLI-only regions should be created and separated from DB2 application regions. Then the two primary factors affecting performance will be thread creation and Logical Unit of Work Commit processing. Ways to control thread-processing include defining the DB2 applications as WFI (Wait For Input). You must be careful with LOCK problems then. And, as always, make sure your Commit processing and Logical Unit of Work is valid.

MVS Performance Parameters

As mentioned before, DB2 can be greatly affected by external system conditions that exist within MVS. Some of those that need to be addressed are as follows:

MVS/370 vs. MVS/XA.   DB2 is the first system put out by IBM that is designed to take great advantage of the MVS/XA software and appropriate hardware. It is designed to be run in the MVS/XA environment on the high-end hardware, primarily the 3090 Series. It can be run under MVS/370 on lower-end machines, but there will be substantial performance implications when any amount of volume through DB2 is attempted.

Memory size.   DB2 loves real memory and will take advantage of the extended storage that is available. The key as far as memory is concerned is to define as big an EDMPOOL as possible to use as much of the extended storage that you can add to your machine. The more the better.

DASD contention.   DASD contention will always be a problem. DB2 databases should be isolated from any other high-usage type data such as TSO/ISPF data sets, high-usage system data sets, etc. Isolation includes the analysis of head-of-string utilization, channel utilization (not so important with MVS/XA), unit utilization, spindle contention, etc. The sets of DB2 files that need to be watched are the logs and the system catalogs and directories. The logs especially must be watched, as they are written synchronously; the system catalogs and directories are what every user of DB2 must access for every execution of a DB2 transaction.

Machine size implications.   DB2 is not a small-machine system. The code that is generated for small to medium Dynamic SQL calls usually runs into the millions of instructions. Even the static calls will run into the hundreds of thousands of instructions. So, for high transaction rates, you will need the largest machines.

MVS/XA vs. MVS/ESA.   DB2 Version 2.1 is designed to take advantage of the latest version of the MVS Operating System which is known as MVS/ESA or MVS/Enterprise System Architecture. It is particularly structured to take advantage of the new 'Hiperspaces' within the extended storage facilities within MVS/ESA (MVS/Enterprise Systems Architecture).

DB2 PROBLEM DETERMINATION

Problem determination within DB2, in most cases, is much easier to deal with than with past IBM products. This is primarily because of the fact that the product itself was released at a higher level of quality than other products. Difficulty arises because of the many subsystems that interface and use DB2 services. Also, a high level of knowledge of the DB2 authorization scheme is needed, as most problems that do arise are authorization or procedurally oriented. A knowledge of what product that is using the interface (TSO, CICS, IMS, AS, APL2, Focus, etc.) is necessary in many cases to determine what the problem really is and how to fix it. As such, problem determination can be really difficult.

The diagnostic process to be followed for severe system problems can be found in the various DB2 diagnostic manuals listed in Appendix 1. In any case, with all problems, start with the DSN messages and/or SQL return codes that have been issued and check them in the *Messages and Codes Manual*. If you cannot find any messages, check the system log, and also run the DB2PM reports if the problem is application-related.

Authorization Problems

Authorization problems are the most common problems that will occur. Because of the highly involved authorization scheme within DB2, it is easy to forget to authorize a particular function or access to a user or system.

Application Problems

Many problems will occur in application code. It is necessary to make sure that all application code saves the full error message somewhere. The IBM-supplied module DSNTIAR (defined earlier), when properly used, will do this. Without the full error message, it is often impossible to find out what happened.

BIND Problems

Application plans for various reasons will occasionally become INVALID or INOPERATIVE, and thus execution of those plans will fail. Some of the reasons this occurs are as follows:

- Synonym, view, or table used in BIND was dropped
- BIND was not successful
- Mismatch between load module and plan

If a plan is invalid and still operative, a REBIND will resolve the problem. If the plan is invalid AND inoperative, a BIND REPLACE must be done.

Determining whether or not a plan is valid and/or operative is done by selecting the valid and operative columns from the SYSIBM.SYSPLAN table for the planname that you want to check. If the column values are both Y, everything is all right. If either is N, then you have to REBIND or BIND REPLACE.

Recovery Problems

Recovery scenarios are covered in great detail in this book and in the *DB2 Operations and Recovery Guide*.

DB2 Abend Problems

Problem determination procedures used in DB2 system abends start with the message that is issued by DB2 and checking it in the *Message and Codes Manual*. Then, depending upon the type of error that has occurred, appropriate action is suggested within the manual. The appropriate action may include using the diagnostic procedures defined in the appropriate DB2 diagnostics manual.

Subsystem Attach Problems

The usual problems that occur with the subsystem attach is that the attach is not started. Check first to make sure that DB2 itself is up and that you have the right default DB2 System ID specified for either TSO, TSO Batch, and/or ISPF. In the case of CICS, check to make sure that the CICS AT-TACHMENT facility has been started and that any necessary CICS RCT entries are included.

QMF Problems

A common problem with users trying to execute QMF for the first time is too small a TSO region-size. A minimum of 4096K is necessary to run QMF under TSO.

DB2 DATA SET MIGRATION PROCEDURES

There will be the necessity to migrate, move, or expand DB2 data sets or tables. The possible types of DB2 objects that may need to be moved are as follows:

- DB2 active log files
- DB2 bootstrap data sets
- DB2 directory/system tablespaces
- User tablespaces

Reasons for Migration

The reasons for migration of DB2 objects fall into the following areas:

- DB2 Backup and Recovery
  Certain data sets and tables within DB2 need to be positioned on separate disk volumes so that recovery can take place if a disk failure occurs. Some of these are as follows:
  1. DB2 dual log files. Separate from each other and other DB2 files.
  2. DB2 dual BSDS files. Separate from each other and other DB2 files.
  3. DB2 directory data sets.
  4. DB2 system catalog data sets.
- DB2 Performance
  For access performance, certain high-usage DB2 and user tables need to be on separate volumes, DASD units, and/or channels and strings.
- Hardware (DASD) Changes
  Certain hardware changes may require movement of DB2 objects to take advantage of new configurations, faster units, new technology, etc.

Procedures Used in Migration

The type of DB2 object that is being migrated will determine which migration procedure to use. The possible types of DB2 objects that can be migrated are as follows:

- DB2 Log Files
  The migration of a DB2 log file goes as follows:
  1. STOP DB2
  2. Use Access Method Services ALTER and DEFINE commands to rename the log to be migrated and to define the new log in its new location with the old name.
  3. Then use Access Method Services to verify the old log, and then REPRO the old log to the new log.
  4. Then restart DB2. If problems occur, -STOP DB2, rename the renamed log back to the original name, and recover the log as defined in other sections of this manual.
- DB2 BSDS Files
  The migration of a DB2 BSDS data set goes as follows:
  1. STOP DB2
  2. Use Access Method Services ALTER and DEFINE commands to rename the BSDS to be migrated and to define the new BSDS in its new location.
  3. Then use Access Method Services to verify the old BSDS, and then REPRO the old BSDS to the new BSDS with the old name.

4. Then restart DB2. If problems occur, -STOP DB2, rename the original BSDS back to the current BSDS, and recover BSDS as defined in other sections of this manual.

• DB2 Directory Data Sets
  The migration of a DB2 directory data set goes as follows:

  1. Perform full image copy of affected directory tablespaces.
  2. STOP DB2.
  3. Use Access Method Services ALTER and DEFINE commands to rename the directory tablespace to be migrated and to define the new directory tablespace in its new location.
  4. Then use the DSN1COPY utility to copy the old directory tablespace to the new data set.
  5. Then restart DB2. If problems occur, -STOP DB2, rename the renamed directory tablespace back to the original name, and restart DB2. Recover the tablespaces as defined in other sections of this document if problems continue.

• DB2 System Catalog Data Sets
  The migration of a DB2 system catalog data set goes as follows:

  1. Perform full image copy of affected system catalog tablespaces.
  2. STOP DB2.
  3. Use Access Method Services ALTER and DEFINE commands to rename the system catalog tablespaces to be migrated and define the new system catalog tablespace in its new location.
  4. Then use the DSN1COPY utility to copy the renamed system catalog tablespace to the new data set.
  5. Then restart DB2. If problems occur, -STOP DB2, rename the renamed system catalog tablespace back to the original name and restart DB2. Recover the tablespaces as defined in other sections of this document if problems continue. DB2 recovery can be used for the migration instead of DSN1COPY utility if so chosen after the affected DB2 tablespace data sets are successfully redefined.

• DB2 User Table Data Sets
  The migration of a DB2 user tablespace data set goes as follows:

  1. Perform full image copy of affected user tablespace data sets.
  2. STOP affected tablespaces (you do NOT have to stop DB2).
  3. Use Access Method Services ALTER and DEFINE commands to rename the user tablespace data sets to be migrated and to define the new user tablespace data set in its new location.
  4. Then use the DSN1COPY utility to copy the renamed user tablespace data set to the new data set.
  5. Then restart the affected tablespaces. If problems occur, you can -STOP the affected tablespaces and use Access Method Services to rename the renamed user tablespace back to the original data set name and then restart the affected tablespaces. Recover the

tablespaces as defined in other sections of this document if problems continue. Standard DB2 recovery can be used for the migration instead of the DSN1COPY utility if so chosen, and also to resolve problems after the new data sets are redefined.

DB2 Traces

Tracing of activities and functions within DB2 is done through the Instrumentation Facility Component (IFC). This facility creates Trace records which can be analyzed and reported against. DB2PM uses these records as input to its program processes for creating its reports. You can use other facilities and/or 'Roll Your Own' systems to format, print, and interpret DB2 Trace output.

DB2 TRACE records the following types of data:

1. **Statistics**
   This provides usage information for the DB2 System Services and Database Services Areas—used to tune entire DB2 set of programs. Can be automatically started.
2. **Accounting**
   This provides data regarding what resources individual application programs are using—used for Billing and program-related tuning. Can be automatically started.
3. **Audit**
   Used to create Audit Records—see next section.
4. **Performance**
   This provides data related to various Subsystem events—used for fine-tuning of DB2 programs and resources for individual users. Cannot be automatically started.
5. **Monitor**
   This records data to be used for online monitoring with user-written programs. It has three Classes of data.
6. **Global**
   This provides records on entries to and from functions and modules within DB2 and is primarily intended for Problem Determination within DB2.

Four different definitions for the resultant data can be defined. These are as follows.

1. SMF—System Management Facility
2. GTF—Generalized Trace Facility
3. SRV—Serviceability Routine
4. OPn—Identifies location belonging to specific Application Program

The default destination for Accounting, Statistics, Audit, and Performance data is SMF. For Monitor data it is OPX. Any of the types can be sent to either SMF, GTF, SRV, or OPn. SRV is reserved for IBM personnel.

Daily Monitoring data of low volume can be sent to SMF. Large quantities and special request Trace data should probably be sent to GTF. When using GTF follow the following procedure:

1. Start GTF
2. Start required DB2 Trace class(es)
3. Trace as needed
4. Stop GTF-base Trace
5. Stop GTF
6. Create desired report

Each of the above traces except for the GLOBAL trace has multiple Trace Classes which can be turned On or Off depending upon what is required. Care should be taken because of the tremendous amount of overhead that can be incurred in turning on certain traces, especially the performance traces.

If the automatic Accounting, Statistics and Audit traces are turned on, the default classes are Class 1 for each. These usually do not dramatically affect the system overall.

As stated previously, use care in using Traces and only trace what you need.

DB2 Audit Capability

Previous to Version 2 of DB2, if an audit capability was desired, it either had to be done by the programs or by using the logs. With Version 2, an audit capability is available internally on a selective basis. There are now two types of AUDIT. The first AUDIT capability is an AUDIT TRACE which is used to turn on the AUDIT capability based upon classes as follows:

Class 1 Access Attempts denied in DB2 for inadequate authorization.
Class 2 Results of explicit GRANT and REVOKE
Class 3 Results of CREATE, ALTER, and DROP operations affecting AUDITed Tables
Class 4 Changes to AUDITed Tables
Class 5 Read Accesses to Read AUDIT defined Tables
Class 6 BIND of Static and Dynamic SQL Statements for AUDITed Tables
Class 7 Assignment or Change of an Authorization ID
Class 8 Start of any UTILITY and the end of each Phase

To turn on the AUDIT capability for specific tables, the AUDIT TRACE for the desired class must be turned on and the AUDIT capability for the desired tables must be turned on. Desired tables can now be audited by specifying AUDIT on either the CREATE TABLE or ALTER TABLE statement.

AUDIT can be turned on for any particular PLAN and/or Primary Authorization ID combination. This includes SYSADM.

Selected AUDITs can be automatically started whenever DB2 starts by making the desired choices at installation time. Otherwise the desired AUDIT TRACE can be started and stopped using the -START TRACE (AUDIT) or -STOP TRACE (AUDIT) commands.

For detailed information on Auditing, read the manual:

GE20-0783 *Control and Audit in the DATABASE 2 Environment*

DB2 Resource Limit Facility (Governor)

DB2 Version 2.1 provided the capability to limit the resources used by any DYNAMIC SQL call that is issued. The limit is based upon exceeding some present CPU SERVICE UNIT LIMIT. Limits can be set for the entire site or limits can be set for individual users and/or application plans. Violations of the set limits result in the issuance of a -905 return code. The limits themselves are defined in Resource Limit Specification Tables, one of which can be invoked using the -START RLIMIT command. The execution of the command can be set online by someone with SYSADM or SYSOPR Authority.

The Resource Limit Specification Tables themselves are created as follows and rows can be INSERTed, UPDATEed, and/or DELETEd by anyone with the necessary authority for the created table, even when the selected table is the current Resource Limit Specification Table.

```
CREATE DATABASE DSNRLST;
CREATE TABLE authid.DSNRLSTxx

    (AUTHID      CHAR(8)     NOT NULL WITH DEFAULT,
     PLANNAME    CHAR(8)     NOT NULL WITH DEFAULT,
     ASUTIME     INTEGER)
    IN DATABASE DSNRLIST ;
CREATE UNIQUE INDEX authid.DSNARLxx
    ON aithid.DSNRLSTxx
     (AUTHID, PLANNAME)
      CLUSTER ;
```

AUTHID is the Authorization-ID of the executing SQL. Blank means ALL Authorization ID's.

PLANNAME is the name of the PLAN which is executing. Blank means ALL Plan names.

ASUTIME is the number of CPU SERVICE UNITS that will be permitted by a single dynamic SQL Statement execution for the selection AUTHID/PLANNAME combination. A Null value implies NO LIMIT and a value of Zero implies that no dynamic SQL statements are permitted.

An order of precedence is established by the index definition. Combinations and defaults can be defined for AUTHID and PLANNAME, certain AU-

THID's, certain PLANNAMES, and blank for both as the ultimate default for all Dynamic Calls. The table will be searched for matches to both the AUTHID and/or PLANNAME combination. If a match is found, or default match occurs, the defined Service Unit Limit will be imposed.

DB2 Futures and Interfaces

9

Since the general availability of DB2 in 1985, many changes have occurred to it and the environment in which it has entered. After an initially slow start coupled with a lot of skepticism and doubt, the acceptance and ordering of it began to skyrocket with the announcement and delivery of Version 2.1 with Referential Integrity in 1988. The performance of the product as well went through magnitudes of improvement from the initial Version 1.1 released in 1985. No other single product has had the impact or caused the controversy that DB2 has in its short life.

But the full impact is yet to be seen. The short- and long-term future holds many new and exciting things in addition to the features and interfaces that are already available.

Future factors to consider as well as interfaces to consider are the following:

1. DB2 and Systems Application Architecture (SAA)
2. DB2 and Computer-Aided Software Engineering (CASE)
3. DB2 and MVS/ESA
4. DB2 and the Personal Computer
5. DB2 and SQL/DS Comparisons
6. DB2 and Distributed Database
7. DB2 and the IBM Repository

DB2 and Systems Application Architecture (SAA)

As has been presented by IBM, DB2 and SQL-based products are the cornerstone of data access across the entire IBM definition of the Systems Application Architecture. The announcements do not specify any other method of accessing data between the personal computers (PS/2), mid-range (AS/400), or large systems (Enterprise Systems Architecture/370) machines and software. There is no mention of IMS/DB, VSAM, etc.

DB2 is the SQL Access system for the ESA/370 Systems using MVS and is the cornerstone of the entire structure. DB2 will have the first implementation of Distributed Database within this architecture with the full distributed interface between the PS/2-based OS/2 Extended Edition Database Manager and DB2 being the next piece of the picture to be completed.

Staying with DB2 or jumping on the bandwagon will keep you in synch with the IBM Systems Applications Architecture from the large-systems perspective in any case.

DB2 and Computer-Aided Software Engineering (CASE)

Besides relational database technology, the current 'hot' technology is Computer-Aided Software Engineering or CASE. There is currently a great deal of controversy and questions about CASE as well as a current low level of acceptance of it. The primary reasons for this are that there are no defined standards and no single product or even group of products to provide what is really needed. There are many data modeling products, enterprise modeling tools, application generators, and other products, but they do not provide a true fully integrated environment and in almost all cases are composed of theories and technologies that are obsolete and ineffective in the relational environment.

The reason that most of these products are ineffective for the relational environment is that the relational environment, to be effective, requires a data-driven methodology and structure. Almost every current product is based upon the entity-relationship structure which does NOT provide the capability to access data by element, only by the entity. The entity is equivalent to a primary key with all of its associated descriptive fields. Now this structure works fine with non-element structures such as IMS/DB, VSAM, IDMS, Total, etc. These record/segment-based structures require access to all of the elements defined in a record because of the inability to define and access specific elements.

The structure of a relational database such as DB2, however, requires you to access all elements explicitly by column. This is also how all data in ALL SYSTEMS is actually processed by the code. Very few programs actually process every data element define as part of an entity or record. Very few business processes process ALL elements at any point in time. Programs and business processes use various elements at any point in time. As a result you need to define business processes the same way.

Programs and Business Processes need specific elements NOT ENTITIES!

As a result, most CASE products DO NOT provide the methodology necessary for the Relational Environment. There are many products that claim to assist in DB2 development but they do not take advantage of the data-element structure of DB2. There are many CASE products on personal computers that produce nice pictures and diagrams, but then what? Many of these same products require degrees in data modeling to use and understand. Then there are the mainframe products. They cost tremendous amounts of money, take months to learn, suffer very low levels of acceptance, and then do NOT take advantage of the data-driven structure either.

A CASE product, to be usable for the DB2 or any relational environment, must have a data-element Definition Structure based upon a data-driven methodology. Any other structure cannot provide the flexibility and support for not only the programming environment but the ad-hoc access needs of the business user.

After all, the business user defines his needs by the individual data that he needs, not by the records and segments or entities that have been defined. Shouldn't the systems he needs provide the same capability and structure? After all, he does pay the bills.

DB2 and MVS/ESA

As stated earlier, DB2 will be taking advantage of the new MVS Enterprise Systems Architecture, and in fact, MVS/ESA has been developed primarily to promote DB2 and to increase its performance. To fully realize the improvements in performance using DB2 Version 2 and later requires that MVS/ESA is installed. The hook to all of this is that MVS/ESA requires the 3090 or 4381 E or greater Class machines, so that anyone without this class Machine must either upgrade or buy a new machine to get the benefit.

This will continue to be the case, and the interface between the software and hardware for the support of DB2 will become tighter and tighter.

DB2 and the Personal Computer

DB2 Data can be accessed from personal computers from a series of different methods. This includes using various SQL-based software and hardware products residing on the personal computers with associated mainframe software, to using various IBM and third-party-provided products which provide upload and download of DB2 data.

IBM provides the capability to download data from DB2 to the OS/2 Extended Edition Database Manager on the PS/2 personal computer using a very DB2-like database and query structure existing within the OS/2 software. As stated earlier, the intention is to link this product with DB2 in a distributed database environment within the next two years.

Other products are continually being announced which permit the Relational database Management Software products sitting on personal computers and minicomputers to upload and download data between themselves and DB2 and other SQL-based products.

DB2 and SQL/DS

IBM first announced and created SQL/DS for the IBM VM operating system environment before DB2 for the MVS operating system environment. SQL/DS and DB2, when initially announced, each had some major differences. Today there is almost 100% compatibility between the systems. Each is also part of the announced Systems Application Architecture (SAA), and SQL/DS now also runs under DOS/VSE.

Code written for one can usually be ported to the other. The primary differences remain in the Authorization and BIND support and implementation within each. Under SQL/DS only a single program can be bound into a single plan (which is an access module), while in DB2 multiple programs can be bound into a single PLAN.

DB2 and Distributed Database

It is IBM's intention to have a fully developed Distributed Database Functionality. The announcement of DB2 Version 2.2 and various position papers and statements of direction support this. Full and complete Distributed database Capability is a few years in the future because of the complexity and overhead involved in implementing this. The IBM repository will be an integral part of this as well and it will not be available for a couple of years either. Interfaces to OS/2 Extended Edition and the AS/400 are also not available and they are integral parts of the full distributed database scenario, at least in IBM's framework.

Version 2.2 of DB2, which will be available late 1989, will give the capability to retrieve data from one DB2 while in another DB2. There is also a limited Distributed Update Capability from the TSO environment. These are the first steps for distributed database between Separate DB2's. The OS/2 Extended Edition will be connecting up to DB2 sometime in 1990/91 in a full distributed mode. This will be the beginning of the full distributed capability that IBM is heading for.

True distributed database functionality will be forthcoming in pieces over the next two to seven years, but it will be here and DB2 will be an integral part of it.

DB2 and the IBM Repository

The often-mentioned IBM Repository will be announced soon and will contain many things. It will NOT be just another DB2. Separate groups are involved with the development of DB2 and the Repository and their goals are different. The Repository will contain all of the information about an ENTIRE ENTERPRISE. This includes data about data, data about software and hardware configurations, and will provide the central control point for the complete business enterprise. This will provide the capability to generate systems definition for networks, new hardware additions, etc. without impacting on the current environment. It will also include a structure for the base definitions and relationships within an entire enterprise such as the Enterprise Model, Data Repository, etc. But what it primarily will be is the point of control for the distributed data environment and the systems application architecture in all of its many forms.

DB2 will be included in this by way of the data repository support of the various DB2 subsystems and associated distributed database support between DB2 and the other SQL-based access methods such as SQL/DS on VM, the Database Manager in OS/2 Extended Edition, and the AS/SQL for the AS/400.

The repository is going to have a large cost, however. Think of a single control point for a system containing multitudes of central processing units, mid-range processors, personal computers, and other devices tied together using innumerable terminals, phone lines, networks, and other access ports, trying to access data from anywhere. Think about that. You are looking at probably a top-of-line large mainframe just to support this.

Very few of the current IBM customer base will run to jump on this bandwagon initially. At the beginning it will be just the very few with large networks, multi-site systems, and LARGE budgets.

Glossary

ABEND Abnormal End of Task. Termination of a task, job, or a subsystem caused by an error that cannot be resolved by the terminated task, job, or subsystem.

ABEND Reason Code A code that is returned by an abended task, job, or subsystem that uniquely identifies a problem. With DB2, these codes are identified and explained in the *IBM Database 2 Messages and Codes Manual.*

ACCESS PATH The path that DB2 will use to resolve the SQL statements used to request data.

ACTIVE LOG The log that is currently active and accepting DB2 log records.

APPLICATION A program or set of programs that perform a specific, defined function.

APPLICATION-EMBEDDED SQL SQL statements that are embedded in an application program.

APPLICATION PLAN The structure used by DB2 that controls access to data and specifies the path to be followed in accessing the data. It is produced in the DB2 BIND process.

ARCHIVE LOG Log records that have been moved from the active log because the log has become full.

ATTACHMENT FACILITY The facility through which TSO, CICS, and IMS/VS interface to DB2.

ATTRIBUTE A database design term that refers to the characteristics of an entity.

BACKWARD LOG RECOVERY Final phase of DB2 RESTART processing in which DB2 scans the log in a backward direction in order to complete the processing of changes that had been aborted.

BIND The DB2 process that takes input from the DB2 PRECOMPILE process and converts it to an application plan. Access paths are created and authorization checking is done in this process.

BOOTSTRAP DATA SET (BSDS) A VSAM data set that contains the information about active and archived log data sets, passwords, and conditional restart and checkpoint records.

BUFFER POOL Main storage reserved to satisfy buffering requirements for DB2 tablespaces and/or indexes.

CHECKPOINT The point at which DB2 records internal status information on the DB2 log.

CICS ATTACHMENT FACILITY DB2 subcomponent that uses the MVS Subsystem Interface (SSI) and cross-memory linkage to control and manage the interface between CICS and DB2.

CLAUSE Distinct part of an SQL statement, such as SELECT or WHERE.

CLUSTERING INDEX An index that forces a physical order to rows in a tablespace.

COLD START Restarting of a subsystem without processing log and/or recovery records.

COLUMN Basic component of a table-element name.

COMMAND A DB2 operator or TSO command; not an SQL statement.

COMMAND RECOGNITION CHARACTER (CRC) The character that precedes DB2 operator commands that tell MVS which DB2 system this command refers to.

COMMIT Process in which all processing (UPDATE, DELETE, INSERT) from the last COMMIT point is allowed to be accessed by other users. Everything done to this point can be recovered.

CONCURRENCY The shared use of DB2 resources by multiple users.

CONNECTION ID An identifier created by the ATTACHMENT facility that is associated with a particular address space connection.

CORRELATED SUBQUERY A subquery associated with a particular outer Select statement.

CORRELATION ID An identifier associated with a specific thread.

CORRELATION NAME The identifier of a specific table, view, or individual row within a table or view defined within a single SQL statement.

CURSOR A structure within DB2 used by application programs to point to a specific row.

CURSOR STABILITY An isolation level within DB2 that provides maximum concurrency.

DATABASE A collection of tablespaces and indexspaces.

DATABASE ADMINISTRATOR (DBA) Person responsible for designing, implementation of, and maintenance of an operational database.

DATABASE DESCRIPTOR (DBD) A control block within DB2 that describes the tables and indexes defined in a database.

DATABASE REQUEST MODULE (DBRM) A data set member created by the DB2 precompiler containing information about SQL statements. The DBRMs are the input to the BIND process.

DATA TYPE Attributes of columns, literals, and host variables.

DBA See Database Administrator.

DBADM Database administration-level authority over a DB2 database.

DBCS See Double Byte Character Set.

DBD See Database Descriptor.

DBRM See Database Request Module.

DB2 CATALOG DB2-maintained tables that contain information about all DB2 entities and objects.

DB2 DIRECTORY DB2 system database that contains internal definitions of DB2 objects such as Database Descriptors (DBDs) and Skeleton Cursor Tables (SKCTs). Also contains information necessary to install DB2.

DB2 Interactive The ISPF-based DB2 facility that provides the execution of SQL commands, DB2 commands, DB2 program preparation, and utility creation.

DEADLOCK Unresolved contention for the same resource.

DECLARATIONS GENERATOR (DCLGEN) A subcomponent of DB2 that creates SQL Declare table statements and PL/1 and/or COBOL table structures.

DEFAULT VALUE A predetermined value, attribute, or option that is assumed if no value is specified.

DIRECTORY See DB2 Directory.

DOUBLE BYTE CHARACTER SET (DBCS) A set of characters that has more than 256 characters. Each character is two bytes in length.

DSN Has three meanings:

1. Default DB2 subsystem prefix
2. DB2 TSO command processor
3. First three characters of DB2 modules and macros.

DSN COMMAND PROCESSOR TSO command processor that processes the DB2 DSN subcommands.

DYNAMIC SQL SQL statements that are created and executed while a program is executing.

EMBEDDED SQL SQL statements that are embedded within a program and are prepared before the program executes through the BIND process.

EXIT ROUTINE A program written by an installation or supplied by IBM as a default which, in the case of DB2, receives control from DB2 to allow processing of specific functions or specialized procedures.

FREE The DSN subcommand used to delete an application plan from DB2, as well as all related dependencies. The plan will then be available for use in a new BIND ADD process.

HOST PROGRAM A program written in a host language such as COBOL or PL1 that contains embedded SQL statements.

HOST STRUCTURE A structure reference in a host program by embedded SQL statements.

HOST VARIABLE A variable in a host program referenced by embedded SQL statements.

IMAGE COPY An exact copy of all or part of a DB2 tablespace. Contains copies of all pages in the case of a full image copy and contains copies of all changed pages in the case of an incremental image copy. Used to recover damaged tablespaces.

IMS/VS ATTACHMENT FACILITY A subcomponent of DB2 that uses the MVS Subsystem Interface (SSI) to process requests from IMS/VS to DB2.

IMS/VS RESOURCE LOCK MANAGER (IRLM) A program product used by DB2 to control database-locking within DB2 and IMS/VS.

IN ABORT Disposition of a unit of recovery when DB2 fails before entering abort processing. All changes so marked will be backed out upon successful recovery.

IN COMMIT Disposition of a unit of recovery that is applicable when DB2 fails after beginning Phase 2 recovery. Changes so marked will be made during recovery.

INDEX A set of pointers that are ordered by the values of a specified key or keys. In the case of DB2, indexes provide quick access to data and can also be used to enforce uniqueness of key or sets of keys, values.

INDEX KEY The set of columns used to define the index.

INDEXSPACE A pageset that contains the entries of a single index.

INDOUBT Disposition of a unit of recovery that fails after Phase 1 commit processing and before beginning Phase 2. DB2 must obtain information from coordinator before deciding what to do about units of recovery that are so marked.

INFLIGHT Disposition of a unit of recovery that fails before Phase 1 commit processing has finished. DB2 will back out all updates on units of recovery that are so marked.

ISOLATION LEVEL Degree to which a unit of work is isolated from other units of work. See Cursor Stability and Repeatable Read.

INSTALLATION SYSADM One of two USERIDs defined at installation time as having Install SYSADM authority. These USERIDs are not defined in the DB2 directory and have complete authority over DB2.

JOIN A relational operation that retrieves data from more than one table.

LOCK Mechanism used to serialize events or access to data within DB2. This is controlled by the IRLM.

LOCK ATTRIBUTES The characteristics of a lock and include object, size, mode, and duration of the lock.

LOCK DURATION Specifies how long a tablespace is locked.

LOCK ESCALATION The process in which a page lock is promoted to a full tablespace lock because the number of page locks exceeds the preset number of page locks allowed for a particular tablespace.

LOCKING The process in which DB2 ensures the integrity of the data. Locking prevents concurrent users from accessing and changing data that is in the process or potential process of being changed.

LOCK MODE Specifies the type of access that will be allowed by concurrently running programs towards the same data. This can be either shared or exclusive, or in a variant of each depending upon requirements of the accessing programs.

LOCK OBJECT Defines type of DB2 object to be locked, such as tablespaces, pages, and indexes.

LOCK PROMOTION The process of changing the size or mode lock attributes, or both. DB2 will promote attributes when concurrent access requests have conflicting attributes or the number of page locks exceeds preset limits (lock escalation).

LOG A collection of records that records DB2 events and the update, addition, or deletion of rows within DB2 pages.

LOG INITIALIZATION The first phase of restart processing during which DB2 locates the current end of the active log.

LOG TRUNCATION The process that establishes the explicit starting RBA from which the next byte of log data will be written.

NULL Indicates that no data value exists for this column in this row.

OBJECT Anything within DB2 that can be created or manipulated using SQL—databases, tables, views, or indexes.

PAGE Base unit of data storage within a tablespace (which can be either 4K or 32K) or indexspace (4K).

PAGESET Data sets used by DB2 to store data objects such as tables and indexes.

PARTITION A portion of a pageset (table or index) that can contain one, two, or four gigabytes of data.

PARTITIONED TABLESPACE A tablespace that is subdivided into parts which are based upon a key range and which can each be reorganized independently of the others.

PLAN See Application Plan.

PLAN NAME The name of an application plan.

PRECOMPILATION Processing of DB2 application programs that occurs before compilation. Creates modified source code for the compiler/assembler and the DBRM statements for the BIND process.

PREDICATE An element of a search condition which results in a comparison operation during the selection of rows of data.

PROGRAM PREPARATION Process by which programs using SQL are prepared for execution. See Precompilation, Bind.

REBIND The process by which a new application plan is created for a program that has previously been bound. It is used instead of the BIND REPLACE process when the program code or tables/views within the program have not changed but an index has been added or RUNSTATS has been run.

RECORD The storage representation of a DB2 row.

RECOVERY The process by which databases are rebuilt after a system failure or damage to those databases.

RECOVERY LOG See Log.

REPEATABLE READ (RR) The isolation level that provides maximum protection and locking of rows of selected data. A program that uses repeatable read locks all selected rows from update by all other programs whether or not the rows are actually updated or deleted.

RESULTS TABLE Set of rows selected by DB2 for the executed SQL.

ROLLBACK Restores data changed by SQL execution to the last commit point.

ROW Contains a set of single values for each column of a table.

SEARCH CONDITION Criteria used in selecting rows of data from DB2 tables. A search condition contains one or more predicates.

SPUFI SQL processor using File Input (SPUFI) is a facility of the TSO attachment facility that enables the DB2I user to execute SQL statements without the need for them to be embedded in an application program.

SQL Structured Query Language (SQL) is the language that is used to access and create DB2 resources and to control access to those resources.

SQLCA SQL Communication Area (SQLCA) is the collection of variables used by DB2 to provide the information to an application program about the

SQL that it has executed. It is a mandatory part of all programs using DB2.

SQLDA SQL Descriptor Area (SQLDA) is used by programs executing certain Dynamic SQL statements.

STATIC SQL SQL statements that are embedded within a program and are prepared by use of the program preparation process.

STORAGE GROUP A named set of Direct Access Storage Device (DASD) volumes on which DB2 data sets containing user data are created and stored.

SUBPAGE The unit into which an index page can be subdivided, which allows greater concurrent usage of indexes.

SUBSYSTEM RECOGNITION CHARACTER (SRC) A character that is used by MVS to identify the correct DB2 subsystem for the routing of DB2 commands and requests. This character prefixes all DB2 commands.

SUPER SYSADM See Installation SYSADM.

SYNC POINT See 'commit point' under Commit.

SYNONYM An alternative name for a DB2 table or view. It is defined at the USERID level and only for that USERID.

SYSADM See System Administrator.

SYSTEM ADMINISTRATOR Highest level of authority within a DB2 sub-system. People with these responsibilities manage and control the entire DB2 subsystem and have the required access capability to perform the functions necessary for that responsibility.

TABLE A DB2 object that contains a specific number of columns and some number of unordered rows.

TABLESPACE A pageset used to store the records contained in one or more tables.

THREAD The DB2 structure that describes, controls, and manages an application's connection to DB2 and structures its access to DB2 resources and services.

TRACE A DB2 tool that provides the capability to monitor and collect DB2 performance, accounting, statistics, and serviceability data.

TSO ATTACHMENT FACILITY A DB2 facility that consists of the DSN command processor and DB2I, and runs only through applications that run using TSO.

UNION A SQL operation that combines the results of two separate select operations.

UNIQUE INDEX A specific index that guarantees the uniqueness of the values of a key or set of keys in a table.

UNIT OF RECOVERY The data control information needed to recover or back out an application's changes to recoverable resources since the last commit point.

UNLOCK Release a system resource or function that was previously locked.

VALUE Data stored in a column in a row.

VIEW An alternative representation of the data in one or more tables and/or other views. These views can include some or all of the columns in the assigned tables/views and can contain certain SQL functions and specific WHERE criteria.

APPENDICES

APPENDICES

New Release Analysis

In mid-1987, IBM announced and began shipment of new Releases of DB2 and the related products Query Management Facility (QMF) and Data Extract (DXT). These were DB2 1.3, QMF 2.2, and DXT 2.2.

DB2 RELEASE 1.3

The changes and improvements of DB2 Release 1.3 were as follows:

- New data types

New data types were added. These were DATE (in various formats), TIME, TIME-STAMP, and FLOAT. Also included was a new function that enables you to calculate the duration between DATEs and/or TIMEs. The FLOAT(n) allows the scientific and engineering community another option for data representation.

- Additional performance improvements

New improvements in performance were gained from DB2 1.3 using the expanded storage capabilities of the 3090 and MVS/XA features, such as allowing a much larger buffer-pool size, using Sequential Prefetch, and better handling of the utilities Buffering and Query Sorts. In addition, the SQL optimization process was enhanced through the use of more efficient JOINs for subqueries, greater avoidance of SORTs for GROUP BY and ORDER BY, and greater optimization for uncorrelated subqueries.

- Operational improvements

The primary improvement of Release 1.3 was an increase in the maximum size of the Data Base Descriptors (DBDs) up from 64K. Also, samples of the CALL ATTACH programs were included in the Sample Library. Other items were announcement of IMS and DB2 batch capability, additional data type conversions (integer to decimal, etc.), and new substring and concatenation functions.

- SQL changes and improvements

Further progress towards the ANSI SQL Standard x3.135-1986 were implemented. The following changes were also incorporated:

Both single and double precision floating point representation

New synonyms

UNION ALL allowing duplicate rows

Certain VIEW restrictions removed, involving DISTINCT, GROUP BY, or HAVING

UNION enhancements for greater column compatibility

Additional use of long character strings in operations

Default field-lengths for CHAR, GRAPHIC, and DECIMAL fields

- Utility improvements

In the DB2 utility area, improvements were made in the RECOVER INDEX, LOAD REPLACE, and RUNSTATS utilities. The RECOVER INDEX now has the additional options of recovering a single index in a tablespace, recovering a list of indexes, recovering ALL indexes, and doing all of this in a single tablespace scan that will greatly improve performance. On the LOAD REPLACE, you can now do a single partition OR the whole tablespace across multiple partitions. RUNSTATS can now be run against catalog tablespaces, is more accurate, and you can now CHANGE the default statistics.

- Other enhancements and changes

Other changes include improved numeric error-handling for Select Conversion errors and enhanced DISPLAY THREAD Command. Also, DB2 dumps will contain the active SQL statement at the time the dump occurred.

- CICS considerations

Considerations for Customer Information Control System (CICS) are the fact that CICS 1.7 supports the eight-character USERID. Also, it seems that the testing for DB2 1.3 was primarily on CICS 1.7. So it is strongly advised by all that you only use DB2 1.3 with CICS 1.7 or greater. You need the eight-character-ID support to solve various security problems, anyway.

DB2 RELEASE 2.2

The announcement by IBM of DB2 Version 2 Release 2 of DB2 with availability planned for third quarter of 1989 begins the evolution to full Distributed Data Base processing by IBM. A DB2 user or application program connected to one DB2 subsystem will be able to access data in another DB2 subsystem. This will be accomplished by using the Virtual Telecommunication Access Method (VTAM) Logical Unit 6.2 (LU6.2) for communications between the DB2 subsystems. The access will be through an interactive query or Structured Query Language (SQL) request from an application. Specific capabilities will be as follows:

1. Initial unit-of-work capability will be as follows:

   a. Read will be supported from multiple sites under TSO, Batch, IMS/DC and CICS.

2. Update support will be supported for a *single* local *or* remote site from TSO and Batch, while IMS/DC and CICS will be permitted only the *local* site.

3. Access to any remote site will be done by only a *single* SQL request in a unit-of-work.

4. Local autonomy will be supported by each DB2 site defining its own local and remote authorization levels.

5. VTAM Logical Unit (LU) 6.2 programming support is provided.

6. DB2 Resource Limit Facility (RLF) will be extended.

7. A new address space, the Distributed Data Facility (DDF) will be added to the DB2 subsystem to support the distributed capability.

The distributed function support of this release will simplify the control and reporting between multiple sites using DB2 as well as supplying the capability to distribute data using DB2 data bases and supply for the first time a distributed processing environment with a centralized reporting capability.

Migration.   DB2 Version 2 Release 2 is upwardly compatible from DB2 2.1 and migratable from either DB2 1.3 or 2.1.

Performance and resource utilization.   DB2 Version 2 Release 2 will require more virtual storage and additional resource usage for the additional address space and network utilization during the distributed processing of DB2.

QMF RELEASE 2.2

The improvements and enhancements in QMF Release 2.2 were primarily in the areas of supporting the new DB2 data types and functions related to those data types. Additional changes and improvements were made in the forms and reports areas, as well as the capability to support the new Integration Exchange Format (IXF), which allows the transfer of data into and out of QMF from and to other products such as DXT, Query DLI Application System (AS), CMS and TSO Files, and others.

QMF RELEASE 2.3

The new features included in QMF Release 2.3 are as follows:

Prompted query .   Prompted Query provides the QMF user to be prompted step by step while building a query.

Report enhancements. Enhancements to the report mechanism of QMF are Column Reordering, Fixed Columns, Form and Data Independence, Form Modification, Calculations, and Detail Text addition.

Query conversion. Prompted, QBE, and SQL queries can be converted into standard SQL.

Show command. Allows navigation among object panels and displays the SQL equivalent of a Prompted Query.

DXT RELEASE 2.2

The improvements and enhancements in DXT Release 2.2 were like those of QMF, primarily in the areas of supporting the new DB2 data types. Additional changes and improvements were made in supplying full Boolean support for the non-relational extract part of DXT and providing a bridge to the other products, and through the use of the TSO CLIST execution capability.

DXT RELEASE 2.3

The improvements and enhancements in DXT Release 2.3 were as follows:

Generic data interface (GDI). The Generic Data Interface allows exits to be written which allow DXT to access various relational and nonrelational MVS data sources and non-IBM data sources as well as join diverse files and data bases, and perform two-stage extractions from DB2 Data Bases.

Variable length support. DXT can now extract data from variable-length fields, records, repeating groups and DB2 variable-length graphic (VG), variable-length character (VC) and one byte binary (B) fields.

References and Manuals APPENDIX **2**

Licensed Documentation

DB2 Version 1.

- *IBM DATABASE 2 Diagnosis Guide*, LY26-3850
  This publication describes how to diagnose and describe DB2 problems.
- *IBM DATABASE 2 Diagnosis Reference Volume 1*, LY26-3862
  This publication contains functional descriptions of each DB2 subcomponent, a CSECT (control section) directory that relates CSECTs to descriptions of the functions that contain them, an overview of data area linkages, and a description of service aids.
- *IBM DATABASE 2 Diagnosis Reference Volume 2: Data Area Descriptions*, LY26-3863
  This publication contains descriptions of the externalized data areas used by DB2.
- *IBM DATABASE 2 Diagnosis Reference Volume 3: Advanced Techniques*, LY26-3952
  This publication describes internal DB2 physical data structures and provides procedures to resolve inconsistent data problems.

DB2 Version 2.

- *IBM DATABASE 2 Diagnosis Guide and Reference*, LY27-9536
  This publication provides detailed information on the internal structure and format of DB2. Includes Keyword Descriptions, Functional Descriptions, Data Management, Diagnostic Aids and Techniques, Physical Formats and Diagrams, Data Areas, and Trace Messages and Codes.

QMF and DXT.

- *Query Management Facility: Diagnosis Guide for MVS*, LY26-3999
  This publication describes how to diagnose, describe, and solve Query Management Facility (QMF) problems.
- *Query Management Facility: Diagnosis Reference*, LY27-9501
  This publication describes how to diagnose, describe, and solve QMF problems.
- *Data Extract Version 2: Base Product Diagnosis*, LY27-9504

This publication describes how to diagnose, describe, and solve DXT base product problems.
* *Data Extract Version 2: Features Diagnosis Guide*, LY27-9502
This publication describes how to diagnose, describe, and solve DXT feature problems.

Unlicensed Documentation

DB2 Version 1.

* *IBM DATABASE 2 System Planning and Administration Guide*, SC26-4085
This publication describes how to plan for DB2 installation or migration, how to monitor and tune the subsystem, how to establish subsystem security, and how to modify the configuration of an installed or migrated subsystem.
* *IBM DATABASE 2 Installation*, SC26-4084
This publication describes how to install and migrate DB2, the DB2 ATTACHMENT facilities for TSO, IMS/VS and CICS/OS/VS, and the IMS/VS Resource Lock Manager (IRLM). It also explains how to verify that you have installed or migrated DB2 correctly.
* *IBM DATABASE 2 Sample Application Guide*, SC26-4086
This publication describes the sample applications that are shipped with DB2.
* *IBM DATABASE 2 Messages and Codes*, SC26-4113
This publication explains all messages and codes that DB2 issues.
* *IBM DATABASE 2 Guide to Publications*, GC26-4111
This publication describes the contents and the structure of the other DB2 publications and provides a master index to their contents.
* *IBM DATABASE 2 Licensed Program Specifications*, GC26-4108
This publication describes DB2 features and identifies the machine and programming requirements for operating DB2.
* *IBM DATABASE 2 General Information*, GC26-4073
This publication describes what DB2 is, what benefits it provides for the database user, an overview of how to use it, what training its users require, what hardware and software it requires, and what tasks must be performed to install, maintain, and operate it.
* *IBM DATABASE 2 Introduction to SQL*, GC26-4082
This publication contains an introduction to the Structured Query Language (SQL).
* *IBM DATABASE 2 Application Programming Guide for CICS/OS/VS Users*, SC26-4080
* *IBM DATABASE 2 Application Programming Guide for IMS/VS Users*, SC26-4079
* *IBM DATABASE 2 Application Programming Guide for TSO and Batch Users*, SC26-4081

The application programming guide describes how to design and write an application program, prepare it, and put it into production for each of the DB2 environments.

- *IBM DATABASE 2 Data Base Planning and Administration Guide*, SC26-4077
  This publication describes how to design DB2 databases, how to use SQL data definition language statements, DB2 Interactive (DB2I), and DB2 utilities to define, tune, and maintain DB2 databases. It also describes how to establish security and how to monitor the performance of the database.
- *IBM DATABASE 2 Operation and Recovery Guide*, SC26-4083
  This publication describes how to design operating and recovery procedures for DB2.
- *IBM DATABASE 2 Reference*, SC26-4078
  This publication describes the tools used for application program development, database and system administration recovery, and operation in a DB2 environment. It describes the syntax and use of SQL statements, DB2 commands, TSO commands and subcommands, relevant IMS/VS and CICS/OS/VS commands, and DB2 utility statements.
- *IBM DATABASE 2 Reference Summary*, SX26-3740
  This publication contains concise reference information on DB2 commands, DB2 utilities, DSN subcommands, IMS/VS and CICS/OS/VS commands, SQL return codes, and syntax for SQL statements.
- *IBM DATABASE 2 Call Attachment Facility User's Guide and Reference*, GC26-4220
  This publication describes how to use the DB2 call attachment facility.

DB2 Version 2.

- *IBM DATABASE 2 General Information*, GC26-4373
  This publication provides general information about DB2 Version 2.
- *IBM DATABASE 2 System and Database Administration Guide*, SC26-4374
  This publication provides the information for the Systems and Database Administration of DB2. It includes Planning and Installing DB2, Designing a Database, Security and Auditing, Operation and Recovery, and Performance Monitoring and Tuning.
- *IBM DATABASE 2 Programming Guide*, SC26-4374
  This publication provides the information for the personnel involved in programming using DB2. It includes SQL and the Program, Preparing and testing the program, and Interface information.
- *IBM DATABASE 2 SQL Reference*, SC26-4380
  This publication provides the information for the personnel involved in using SQL in DB2. It includes Language Elements, Functions, Queries, and Statements.
- *IBM DATABASE 2 Command and Utility Reference*, SC26-4378

This publication provides the information for the personnel involved in using DB2 Utilities and Commands. It includes Structure and Usage information on Commands and Utilities.

- *IBM DATABASE 2 Reference Summary*, SC26-3771
  This publication provides summary information for the personnel involved in using DB2 SQL, Utilities, and Commands. It includes SQL Reference Summary, and the Command and Utility Reference Summary.
- *IBM DATABASE 2 Messages and Codes*, SC26-4379
  This publication provides detailed information on DB2 and SQL Codes and Messages. This includes SQL Return Codes, DB2 Messages, DB2 Codes, and IRLM Messages and Codes.

QMF — Query Management Facility Version 2.

- *Query Management Facility Licensed Program Specifications* (LPS), GC26-4095
- *Query Management Facility: Planning and Administration Guide for MVS3*, SC26-4237
- *Query Management Facility: User's Guide and Reference*, SC26-4232
- *Query Management Facility: Learner's Guide*, SC26-4231
- *Query Management Facility: Application Development Guide for MVS*, SC26-4237
- *Query Management Facility: Installation Guide for MVS*, SC26-4245

DXT — Data Extract Version 2.

- *Data Extract Version 2: Base Product Planning and Administration Guide*, SC26-4243
- *Data Extract Version 2: Features Planning and User's Guide*, SC26-4315
- *Data Extract Version 2: General Information*, GC26-4241
- *Data Extract Version 2: Learner's Guide*, SC26-4242
- *Data Extract Version 2: Messages and Codes*, SC26-4251
- *Data Extract Version 2: Reference*, SC26-4248
- *Data Extract Version 2: Master Index*, SC26-4249

DB2PM — Database 2 Performance Monitor.

- *IBM Database 2 Performance Monitor: General Information*, GH20-6856
- *IBM Database 2 Performance Monitor: Installation and Maintenance*, SH20-6859
- *IBM Database 2 Performance Monitor: User's Guide*, SH20-6857
- *IBM Database 2 Performance Monitor: Report Reference*, SH20-6858
- *IBM Database 2 Performance Monitor: Command Reference*, SH20-6860

DBMAUI — Database Migration Aid Utility.

- *Database Migration Aid Utility User's Guide*, SH20-9232

DBEDIT — Database Edit Facility.

- *Data Base Edit Facility for MVS/TSO Program Description/Operations Manual*, SH20-0076
  This manual is for the use of personnel responsible for the installation, administration, and maintenance of DBEDIT. It contains an overall description of the DBEDIT program and the installation procedures.
- *Data Base Edit Facility User's Guide*, SH20-6522
  This manual gives a complete tutorial and reference information on using DBEDIT. DBEDIT messages are also in this manual.
- *Database Edit Facility Quick User's Guide to PQUERY*, SH20-6523
  This manual gives an introductory tutorial and reference information on using DBEDIT. It is meant for clerical personnel with NO data processing experience.

DBRAD—Database Relational Application Directory.

- *IBM Data Base Relational Application Directory for MVS—Program Description/Operations Manual*, SH20-9250
  This publication describes the DBRAD product and how to install and support it.
- *IBM Data Base Relational Application Directory for MVS—Guide and Reference*, SH20-9249
  This publication describes the features of the DBRAD product and how to use them.
- *IBM Data Base Relational Application Directory for MVS—Usage Guide*, GG24-3189
  This publication provides guidelines on the usage of DBRAD and is intended to be used by Systems and Data Base Administrators and application developers.

Development guides.

- *Development Guide—Relational Applications*, SC26-4130

MVS-related manuals.

- *System Modification Program (SMP) System Programmer's Guide*, GC28-0673
  This publication describes the Release 4 System Modification Program (SMP) program and the control statements required by the various SMP functions.

- *System Modification Program (SMP) Messages and Codes*, GC38-1047
  This publication describes Release 4 SMP return codes and messages and includes information on Release 4 SMP diagnostic techniques.
- *System Modification Program Extended (SMP/E) Users Guide*, SC28-1302
  This publication describes SMP Extended program and the control statements required by the various SMP functions.
- *System Modification Program Extended (SMP/E) Messages and Codes*, GC28-1108
  This publication describes SMP Extended return codes and messages and includes information on SMP Extended diagnostic techniques.
- *OS/VS2 MVS/370 Utilities*, GC26-3092
  This publication describes the use of OS/VS2 utilities and control statements for those utilities.
- *MVS/Extended Architecture Utilities*, GC26-4018
  This publication describes the use of MVS/Extended Architecture (MVS/XA) utilities and control statements for those utilities.
- *OS/VS2 MVS/370 JCL*, GC28-1300
  This publication describes OS/VS2 operating system services that can be requested by including various parameters on JCL statements and gives coding conventions for OS/VS2 MVS JCL.
- *MVS/Extended Architecture JCL*, GC28-1148
  This publication describes MVS/XA operating system services that can be requested by including various parameters on JCL statements and gives coding conventions for MVS/XA JCL.
- *OS/VS2 MVS System Programming Library: Initialization and Tuning*, GC28-0681
  This publication describes the PARMLIB entries updated during installation.
- *MVS/Extended Architecture System Programming Library: Initialization and Tuning*, GC28-1149
  This publication describes the PARMLIB entries updated during installation.
- *OS/VS2 MVS System Programming Library: Service Aids*, GC28-0674
  This publication discusses the service aids that are used in providing supporting documentation for DB2 problems.
- *MVS/Extended Architecture System Programming Library: Service Aids*, GC28-1159
  This publication discusses the service aids that are used in providing supporting documentation for DB2 problems.
- *OS/VS2 System Programming Library: Job Management*, GC28-1303
  This publication contains information about assigning special program properties.
- *MVS/Extended Architecture System Programming Library: System Modifications*, GC28-1152

This publication contains information about assigning special program properties.
- *OS/VS2 System Programming Library: TSO*, GC28-0629
  This publication discusses log-on procedures and the installation exit for the SUBMIT command.
- *MVS/Extended Architecture System Programming Library: TSO*, GC28-1173
  This publication discusses log-on procedures and the installation exit for the SUBMIT command.
- *MVS/370 Access Method Services: Integrated Catalog Facility*, SC26-4051
  This publication describes VSAM as used in the installation of DB2 and related products.
- *MVS/Extended Architecture: Access Method Services Reference for the Integrated Catalog Facility*, GC26-4019
  This publication describes VSAM as used in the installation of DB2 and related products.
- *System Programming Library: Resource Access Control Facility (RACF)*, SC28-1343
  This publication contains information about providing protection for user resources.
- *Interactive System Productivity Facility Version 2 Installation and Customization*, SC34-2139
  This publication discusses Interactive System Productivity Facility (ISPF) usage of the primary option panels used in establishing ISPF applications.
- *TSO Extensions User's Guide*, SC28-1333
  This publication provides usage information on the TSO/E products which is a prerequisite for DB2.
- *TSO Extensions Command Language Reference*, SC28-1307
  This publication provides usage information on the TSO/E Command Language which comprises the base of the DB2I system and DB2 Installation process.
- *Interactive System Productivity Guide—Dialog Manager Services*, SC34-4021
  This publication provides usage information on using Dialog Manager and developing ISPF-based applications.
- *Interactive System Productivity Guide—Reference*, SC34-4024
  This publication provides usage information on using the ISPF Functions and Facilities.
- *Interactive System Productivity Guide—Services*, SC34-4023
  This publication provides usage information on using the ISPF Services.
- *Systems Application Architecture—An Overview*, GC26-4341
  Overall base-level description of IBM Systems Application Architecture (SAA).

- *SQL/Data System—Concepts and Facilities for VSE*, GH09-8031
  Describes Concepts and Facilities of the VSE version of SQL/DS.
- *SQL/Data System—Concepts and Facilities for VM/SP*, GH09-8044
  Describes concepts and facilities of the VM/SP version of SQL/DS.

Online Information

DB2 online information consists of ISPF Help panels and TSO Help files which assist the online user in performing installation, administration, programming, and operation tasks.

DB2 Application Description —Part 1

```
                                              PAGE ___ of ___

APPLICATION NAME/CODE: _____  __        DATE:_____

REQUESTOR: _____

Attach Application Design/Flow Diagram

DESCRIPTION:
_____
_____
_____
_____
_____
_____
_____
_____
_____
_____
_____
_____
_____
_____
_____
_____
_____
_____
_____
_____
_____
_____



DATE NEEDED: _____  DATE COMPLETED: _____  INITIALS: ____

DATE ENTERED INTO DATA DICTIONARY: _____
```

```
                                                           PAGE ___ of ___

   APPLICATION NAME/CODE: _____  __            DATE: _____

   REQUESTOR: _____

   ON-LINE Statistics

      # OF ACTIVE QMF USERS:
         TOTAL AUTHORIZED:
         AVERAGE ACTIVE:     _____
         PEAK ACTIVE:        _____

      # OF OTHER DYNAMIC SQL USERS:
         TOTAL AUTHORIZED:   _____
         AVERAGE ACTIVE:     _____
         PEAK ACTIVE:        _____

      QUERY RATE (per hour) - Dynamic SQL
         AVERAGE:            _____
         PEAK:               _____

      TRANSACTION RATE (per minute) - Static SQL
         AVERAGE:            _____
         PEAK:               _____

   BATCH/UTILITIES

      PROCESSING WINDOW:
      _____
      _____
      _____
      _____


      PROCESSING REQUIREMENTS:
      _____
      _____
      _____
      _____
      _____

   DATE NEEDED: _____  DATE COMPLETED: _____  INITIALS: ____

   DATE ENTERED INTO DATA DICTIONARY: _____
```

DB2 Change Request Completion Notice

APPENDIX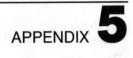

```
                                              PAGE ___ of ___

APPLICATION NAME/CODE: _____  __     DATE:_____

REQUESTOR: _____

TYPE OF CHANGE REQUEST:_____  SYSTEM-ID: _____

The following Requests Made by you have been completed:

__   Database Add

__   Table/Tablespace Add
       Database Name: _____
       Creator ID: _____
       Tablespace Name: _____
       Table Name: _____

__   Drop/Recreate Table/Tablespace/Views
       Database Name: _____
       Creator ID: _____
       Tablespace Name: _____
       Table Name: _____
       View Name: _____

__   Create New Bind
       Plan Name: _____

__   Production Table Backup Procedures
       Table Name: _____
       Tablespace Name: _____

__   System Migration
       System Name: _____
       System Type: _____

__   Column Add to Existing Table
       Table Name: _____
       Tablespace Name: _____
       Column Name(s): _____
       _____
       _____

DATE NEEDED: _____  DATE COMPLETED: _____  INITIALS: ____
```

DB2 Change Request Checklist

 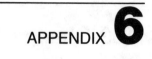

```
                                                    PAGE ___ of ___
APPLICATION NAME/CODE: _____ __          DATE:_____

REQUESTOR: _____        SYSTEM-ID: _____

DESCRIPTION:_____
_____
_____

    __  Database Add                        Edit Source
                                            Create Database       __
                                            Grant Authority       __

    __  Table/Tablespace Add/Migration      Edit Table Source     __
        Database Name: _____      Create Tables         __
        Creator ID: _____       Edit Synonyms         __
        Tablespace Name: _____      Create Synonyms       __
        Table Name: _____       Bind Plans            __
                                            Create Indexes        __
                                            Grant Authority       __

    __  Drop/Recreate Table/Tablespace/Views  List Authorities    __
        Database Name: _____        Check Source        __
        Creator ID: _____         Edit Source         __
        Tablespace Name: _____        Unload Table        __
        Table Name: _____         Drop Table          __
        View Name: _____         Recreate Table      __
                                              Recreate Indexes    __
                                              Load Table          __
                                              Regrant Authorities__

    __  Create New Bind                     Perform Bindadd       __
        Plan Name: _____       Grant Authority       __

    __  Production Table Backup Procedures  Create Tables         __
        Table Name: _____       Create Backup JCL     __
        Tablespace Name: _____      Load Data             __
        Creator ID: _____       Run Image Copy        __

DATE NEEDED: _____  DATE COMPLETED: _____ INITIALS: ____

DATE ENTERED INTO DATA DICTIONARY: _____

COMPLETION SIGNATURE: _____ NAME: _____
```

DB2 Report Request

```
                                              PAGE ___ of ___

APPLICATION NAME/CODE: _____ __      DATE:_____

REQUESTOR: _____

DESCRIPTION:_____
_____

TYPE OF REPORT:                    SYSTEM-ID: _____

    __   Table/Column Cross Reference
             Table Name: _____
             Database Name: _____
             Creator ID: _____

    __   Index/Column Cross Reference
             Index Name: _____
             Database Name: _____
             Creator ID: _____
             Table Name: _____

    __   View/Column Cross Reference
             View Name: _____
             Database Name: _____
             Creator ID: _____

    __   Column Only Report
             Column Name: _____

    __   Tablespace/Table Cross Reference
             Table Name: _____
             Database Name: _____
             Creator ID: _____

    __   Data Dictionary Listing
             Creator ID: _____
             Application: _____
             Database Name: _____

DATE NEEDED: _____   DATE COMPLETED: _____  INITIALS: ____

DATE ENTERED INTO DATA DICTIONARY: _____

AUTHORIZATION SIGNATURE: _____  NAME: _____
```

DB2 Table Change Request   APPENDIX **8**

```
                                                    PAGE ___ of ___
APPLICATION NAME/CODE: _____  __        DATE: _____

TABLE NAME: _____        CREATOR-ID: _____

REQUESTOR: _____        SYSTEM-ID: _____

DESCRIPTION: _____
_____
_____
_____
_____
_____

TYPE OF CHANGE:

                        Column Changes

    1. Change Existing Column: __   Column Name: _____
          New Size: _____   New Type: _____

    2. Add New Column: __             Column Name: _____
          New Size: _____   New Type: _____

    3. Delete Columns: __             Column Name: _____

                        Table Changes

    1. Recreate Table: __

    2. Copy Table: __       Copy Creator Qualifier: _____

    3. Drop Table: __

DATE NEEDED: _____  DATE COMPLETED: _____  INITIALS: ____

DATE ENTERED INTO DATA DICTIONARY: _____

AUTHORIZATION SIGNATURE: _____  NAME: _____
```

DB2 Table Narrative

```
                                                  PAGE ___ of ___
APPLICATION NAME/CODE: _____  __       DATE:_____

TABLE NAME: _____

TABLE TITLE: _____

REQUESTOR: _____

DESCRIPTION:_____
_____
_____
_____
_____
_____
_____
_____

DATA ELEMENTS IN TABLE (COLUMNS):
_____   _____   _____   _____
_____   _____   _____   _____
_____   _____   _____   _____
_____   _____   _____   _____
_____   _____   _____   _____
_____   _____   _____   _____
_____   _____   _____   _____
_____   _____   _____   _____
_____   _____   _____   _____
_____   _____   _____   _____
_____   _____   _____   _____

DATE NEEDED: _____  DATE COMPLETED: _____ INITIALS: ____

DATE ENTERED INTO DATA DICTIONARY: _____

AUTHORIZATION SIGNATURE: _____ NAME: _____
```

DB2 View Creation Request   APPENDIX 10

```
                                              PAGE ___ of ___
APPLICATION NAME/CODE: _____ __     DATE: _____

VIEW NAME: _____        CREATOR-ID: _____

VIEW TITLE: _____

REQUESTOR: _____            SYSTEM: _____

DESCRIPTION: _____
_____
_____
_____

DATA ELEMENTS IN VIEW (COLUMNS)
    TABLE NAME        COLUMN         TABLE NAME        COLUMN
_____    _____    _____    _____
_____    _____    _____    _____
_____    _____    _____    _____
_____    _____    _____    _____
_____    _____    _____    _____
_____    _____    _____    _____
_____    _____    _____    _____
_____    _____    _____    _____
_____    _____    _____    _____

SELECT REQUIREMENTS: _____
_____
_____
_____
_____
_____
_____

DATE NEEDED: _____  DATE COMPLETED: _____  INITIALS: ____

DATE ENTERED INTO DATA DICTIONARY: _____

AUTHORIZATION SIGNATURE: _____  NAME: _____
```

Data Element Definition APPENDIX **11**

```
                                              PAGE ___ of ___

APPLICATION NAME/CODE: _____ __           DATE:_____

DATA ELEMENT NAME: _____

REQUESTOR: _____

DESCRIPTION:_____
_____
_____
_____

TYPE FIELD: _____    FIELD SIZE: _____
DEFAULT:_____

LOGICAL RELATIONSHIPS:

DATA ELEMENT     RELATIONSHIP     DATA ELEMENT     RELATIONSHIP
   NAME             TYPE             NAME             TYPE

_____      _____      _____      _____
_____      _____      _____      _____
_____      _____      _____      _____
_____      _____      _____      _____
_____      _____      _____      _____
_____      _____      _____      _____
_____      _____      _____      _____
_____      _____      _____      _____
_____      _____      _____      _____
_____      _____      _____      _____
_____      _____      _____      _____
_____      _____      _____      _____

DATE NEEDED: _____    DATE COMPLETED: _____  INITIALS: ____

DATE ENTERED INTO DATA DICTIONARY: _____

AUTHORIZATION SIGNATURE: _____  NAME: _____
```

DB2 Storage Group Creation Request

```
                                                    PAGE ___ of ___
APPLICATION NAME/CODE: _____ __        DATE:_____

STORAGE GROUP NAME: _____

REQUESTOR: _____                    SYSTEM:_____

DESCRIPTION:_____
_____
_____
_____
_____

VOLUMES ASSIGNED:  _____  _____  _____
                   _____  _____  _____

DEFAULT BUFFERPOOL: _____

VCAT CATALOG NAME:  _____

USE AUTHORIZATION:

    USERID    ACCESS    USERID    ACCESS    USERID    ACCESS

   _____  _____  _____  _____  _____  _____
   _____  _____  _____  _____  _____  _____
   _____  _____  _____  _____  _____  _____
   _____  _____  _____  _____  _____  _____

DATE NEEDED: _____  DATE COMPLETED: _____  INITIALS: ____

DATE ENTERED INTO DATA DICTIONARY: _____

AUTHORIZATION SIGNATURE: _____  NAME: _____
```

DB2 Entity Creation Request

```
                                              PAGE ___ of ___

APPLICATION NAME/CODE: _____ __       DATE:_____

REQUESTOR: _____              SYSTEM:_____

DESCRIPTION: _____
_____

REQUEST TYPE:

1.  Table   __  Table Name _____  DSN _____

2.  Column  __  Column Name _____  Table Name _____
        ADD __  Type _____  Size _____  Default _____

3.  Plan    __  Plan Name _____  DBRM Name _____
                DBRMLIB DSN _____

4.  Grant Authority
        Type of Grant          DB2 Entity          Userid
        _____      _____      _____
        _____      _____      _____
        _____      _____      _____
        _____      _____      _____
        _____      _____      _____
        _____      _____      _____

DATE NEEDED: _____  DATE COMPLETED: _____  INITIALS: ____

DATE ENTERED INTO DATA DICTIONARY: _____

AUTHORIZATION SIGNATURE:_____  NAME:_____
```

DB2 Initial Development Checklist

```
                                              PAGE ___ of ___
APPLICATION NAME/CODE: _____ __       DATE:_____

REQUESTOR: _____                    SYSTEM:_____

DESCRIPTION:_____
_____
_____
_____

     1. __ Logical Data Design Complete
     2. __ Tables Generated
     3. __ DCLGEN's Completed
     4. __ SYNONYM Definitions Generated
     5. __ View Analysis Completed
     6. __ Initial BIND's Generated
     7. __ Index Evaluations Completed

DATE NEEDED: _____  DATE COMPLETED: _____ INITIALS: ____

DATE ENTERED INTO DATA DICTIONARY: _____

AUTHORIZATION SIGNATURE:_____  NAME:_____
```

DB2 Index Creation Request

```
                                          PAGE ___ of ___
APPLICATION NAME/CODE: _____ __      DATE:_____

INDEX NAME:_____      CREATOR-ID: _____

REQUESTOR: _____           SYSTEM:_____

TABLE NAME:_____    TABLE CREATOR-ID: _____

DESCRIPTION:_____
_____
_____
_____
_____
_____

   UNIQUE: _____   SORT ORDER: _____   CLUSTERED: _____

COLUMNS TO BE INDEXED:

  Column Name        Key Order     Column Name        Key Order
  _____    ____         _____     ____
  _____    ____         _____     ____
  _____    ____         _____     ____

DATE NEEDED: _____   DATE COMPLETED: _____ INITIALS: ____

DATE ENTERED INTO DATA DICTIONARY: _____

AUTHORIZATION SIGNATURE:_____ NAME:_____
```

DB2 Database Creation Request

APPENDIX **16**

```
                                                          PAGE ___ of ___
  APPLICATION NAME/CODE: _____  __            DATE:_____
  DATABASE NAME: _____
  REQUESTOR: _____                         SYSTEM:_____
  DBADM AUTHORITY USERID: _____
  DESCRIPTION:_____
  _____
  _____
  _____
  _____
  _____
  _____
  _____
  _____
  _____
  _____
  _____
  _____

  TOTAL # OF TABLESPACES: _____

  TOTAL # OF TABLES: _____

  TOTAL # OF INDEXES: _____

  TOTAL # OF VIEWS: _____

  DATE NEEDED: _____  DATE COMPLETED: _____  INITIALS: ____

  DATE ENTERED INTO DATA DICTIONARY: _____

  AUTHORIZATION SIGNATURE:_____  NAME:_____
```

DB2 Tablespace Creation Request

```
                                              PAGE ___ of ___

APPLICATION NAME/CODE: _____ __       DATE:_____

TABLESPACE NAME: _____

REQUESTOR: _____           SYSTEM:_____

DESCRIPTION:_____
_____
_____
_____
_____
_____
_____
_____


DATABASE NAME: _____

BUFFER POOL TO BE USED: _____

TOTAL STORAGE ESTIMATE (In Kilobytes) :_____

DATE NEEDED: _____  DATE COMPLETED: _____ INITIALS: ____

DATE ENTERED INTO DATA DICTIONARY: _____

AUTHORIZATION SIGNATURE:_____ NAME:_____
```

DB2 Backup/Recovery Requirements

```
                                                    PAGE ___ of ___
APPLICATION NAME/CODE: _____ __        DATE:_____

REQUESTOR: _____                      SYSTEM: _____

TABLESPACE/TABLE NAMES:
     _____/_____    _____/_____
     _____/_____    _____/_____
     _____/_____    _____/_____

DESCRIPTION:_____
_____
_____
_____
_____

BACKUP FREQUENCY: _____

RETENTION CYCLE:_____

RECOVERY PROCESS:_____
_____
_____
_____

    JOB NAMES (JCL JOBCARD NAME)          JOB DESCRIPTION

    _____       _____
    _____       _____
    _____       _____
    _____       _____

DATE NEEDED: _____   DATE COMPLETED: _____ INITIALS: ____

DATE ENTERED INTO DATA DICTIONARY: _____

AUTHORIZATION SIGNATURE: _____  NAME: _____
```

DB2 Plan Creation Request   APPENDIX **19**

```
                                              PAGE ___ of ___
APPLICATION NAME/CODE: _____ __      DATE:_____

PLAN NAME: _____

REQUESTOR: _____               SYSTEM:_____

DESCRIPTION:_____
_____
_____

PROGRAM NAME(S): _____  _____  _____
                 _____  _____  _____

DBRM LIBRARY(S):_____
_____

DBRM LIST: _____  _____  _____
           _____  _____  _____

SYNONYM LIBRARY: _____

SYNONYM  TABLE/VIEW    SYNONYM  TABLE/VIEW    SYNONYM  TABLE/VIEW

_____  _____    _____  _____    _____  _____
_____  _____    _____  _____    _____  _____

GRANT ACCESS:
   USERID    ACCESS     USERID    ACCESS     USERID    ACCESS

   _____   _____    _____   _____    _____   _____
   _____   _____    _____   _____    _____   _____
   _____   _____    _____   _____    _____   _____
   _____   _____    _____   _____    _____   _____

DATE NEEDED: _____   DATE COMPLETED: _____  INITIALS: ____

DATE ENTERED INTO DATA DICTIONARY: _____

AUTHORIZATION SIGNATURE: _____  NAME: _____
```

DB2 Migration Request— Batch

```
                                              PAGE ___ of ___
APPLICATION NAME/CODE: _____ __      DATE:_____
REQUESTOR: _____          TO  SYSTEM:_____
                                      FROM SYSTEM:_____
DESCRIPTION:_____
_____
HIGH-LEVEL QUALIFIER (CREATOR) OF 'TO' SYSTEM:_____
SYNONYM LIBRARY DSN AND MEMBER(S):_____
TABLE CREATE LIBRARY DSN:_____
TABLE NAMES:
_____    _____    _____    _____
_____    _____    _____    _____
DBRM LIBRARY DSN:_____
  PLAN NAMES        PROGRAM NAME              DBRM NAMES
_____  *  _____ / _____    _____
_____  *  _____ / _____    _____
_____  *  _____ / _____    _____
_____  *  _____ / _____    _____
_____  *  _____ / _____    _____
_____  *  _____ / _____    _____
_____  *  _____ / _____    _____
  BATCH JOBNAME   /   EXECUTION ID   / PLAN CROSS REFERENCE:
                /               /
_____  /  _____ / _____
_____  /  _____ / _____
_____  /  _____ / _____

DATE NEEDED: _____ DATE COMPLETED: _____ INITIALS: ____
DATE ENTERED INTO DATA DICTIONARY: _____
AUTHORIZATION SIGNATURE:_____ NAME:_____
```

272

DB2 Migration Request— CICS

```
                                              PAGE ___ of ___

APPLICATION NAME/CODE: _____ __      DATE:_____

REQUESTOR: _____            TO   SYSTEM:_____
                                          FROM SYSTEM:_____

DESCRIPTION:_____
_____

HIGH-LEVEL QUALIFIER (CREATOR) OF 'TO' SYSTEM:_____

SYNONYM LIBRARY DSN AND MEMBER(S):_____

TABLE CREATE LIBRARY DSN:_____

TABLE NAMES:
_____  _____  _____  _____
_____  _____  _____  _____

DBRM LIBRARY DSN:_____

  PLAN NAMES       PROGRAM NAME              DBRM NAMES
                *             /
_____ * _____ / _____  _____
_____ * _____ / _____  _____
_____ * _____ / _____  _____
_____ * _____ / _____  _____
_____ * _____ / _____  _____
_____ * _____ / _____  _____

CICS TRANSACTION/PLAN CROSS REFERENCE:   CICS REGION: _____

_____/_____  _____/_____
_____/_____  _____/_____
_____/_____  _____/_____
_____/_____  _____/_____

DATE NEEDED: _____  DATE COMPLETED: _____  INITIALS: ____

DATE ENTERED INTO DATA DICTIONARY: _____

AUTHORIZATION SIGNATURE:_____  NAME:_____
```

```
                                              PAGE ___ of ___

APPLICATION NAME/CODE: _____ __      DATE:_____

REQUESTOR: _____              TO   SYSTEM:_____
                                           FROM SYSTEM:_____

DESCRIPTION:_____
_____

HIGH-LEVEL QUALIFIER (CREATOR) OF 'TO' SYSTEM:_____

SYNONYM LIBRARY DSN AND MEMBER(S):_____

TABLE CREATE LIBRARY DSN:_____

TABLE NAMES:
_____    _____    _____    _____
_____    _____    _____    _____

DBRM LIBRARY DSN:_____

   PLAN NAMES        PROGRAM NAME              DBRM NAMES
_____ *  _____ / _____  _____
_____ *  _____ / _____  _____
_____ *  _____ / _____  _____
_____ *  _____ / _____  _____
_____ *  _____ / _____  _____
_____ *  _____ / _____  _____
_____ *  _____ / _____  _____

CICS TRANSACTION/PLAN CROSS REFERENCE:   CICS REGION: _____

_____/_____     _____/_____
_____/_____     _____/_____
_____/_____     _____/_____
_____/_____     _____/_____

DATE NEEDED: _____  DATE COMPLETED: _____ INITIALS: ____

DATE ENTERED INTO DATA DICTIONARY: _____

AUTHORIZATION SIGNATURE:_____ NAME:_____
```

DB2 Migration Request— QMF

APPENDIX **23**

```
                                              PAGE ___ of ___

APPLICATION NAME/CODE: _____ __    DATE: _____

REQUESTOR: _____           TO   SYSTEM:_____
                                        FROM SYSTEM:_____

DESCRIPTION:_____
_____
_____
_____

HIGH-LEVEL QUALIFIER (CREATOR) OF 'TO' SYSTEM:_____

   PROCEDURE  NAME      QUERY NAME(S)        FORM NAME(S)
                     *                    /
_____ * _____ / _____
_____ * _____ / _____
_____ * _____ / _____
_____ * _____ / _____
_____ * _____ / _____
_____ * _____ / _____

   PROCEDURE  NAME           TABLE(S) ACCESSED
                     *
_____ * _____   _____
_____ * _____   _____
_____ * _____   _____
_____ * _____   _____
_____ * _____   _____

   Attach List of Procedure

DATE NEEDED: _____ DATE COMPLETED: _____ INITIALS: ____

DATE ENTERED INTO DATA DICTIONARY: _____

AUTHORIZATION SIGNATURE:_____ NAME:_____
```

275

DB2 Security Authorization Request

```
                                              PAGE ___ of ___

APPLICATION NAME/CODE: _____ __      DATE:_____

REQUESTOR: _____               SYSTEM:_____

DESCRIPTION:_____
_____
_____
_____

    DB2 ENTITY              ENTITY              AUTHORIZATION
      NAME                   TYPE                  LEVEL

_____ / _____ / _____ _____
                                / _____ _____
                                / _____ _____

                    AUTHORIZATION ID's

     ID           TYPE          ID              TYPE
_____   *  _____   _____   *  _____
_____   *  _____   _____   *  _____
_____   *  _____   _____   *  _____
_____   *  _____   _____   *  _____
_____   *  _____   _____   *  _____
_____   *  _____   _____   *  _____
_____   *  _____   _____   *  _____
_____   *  _____   _____   *  _____
_____   *  _____   _____   *  _____
_____   *  _____   _____   *  _____


DATE NEEDED: _____ DATE COMPLETED: _____ INITIALS: ____

DATE ENTERED INTO DATA DICTIONARY: _____

AUTHORIZATION SIGNATURE:_____ NAME:_____
```

DB2 Migration Checklist   APPENDIX **25**

```
                                              PAGE ___ of ___

APPLICATION NAME/CODE: _____  __    DATE:_____

REQUESTOR: _____              SYSTEM:_____


DESCRIPTION:_____
_____
_____
_____
_____


       1. __   Tables Created (if necessary)
       2. __   Source Code Moved
       3. __   DCLGEN's Generated (if necessary)
       4. __   Source Pre-compiled and Compiled
       5. __   Production Control Completed
       6. __   Synonyms Generated
       7. __   Plans Bound
       8. __   DBEDIT Data EXPORTED/IMPORTED
       9. __   Data Unloaded/Loaded (if necessary)
      10. __   CICS RCT Updated (if necessary)
      11. __   Security Authorizations Completed (CICS and DB2)
               (Tables and Plans)

DATE NEEDED: _____  DATE COMPLETED: _____ INITIALS: ____

DATE ENTERED INTO DATA DICTIONARY: _____

AUTHORIZATION SIGNATURE:_____  NAME:_____
```

DB2 Performance Impact Analysis

APPENDIX **26**

```
                                                    PAGE ___ of ___

APPLICATION NAME/CODE: _____  __        DATE: _____

PLAN NAME: _____  TYPE: _____  (TSO, BATCH,  ICS)

REQUESTOR: _____                      SYSTEM: _____

                      PLAN EXPLAIN INFORMATION
                                                 REAL   INT.   TS
QUERY   QB    PLAN  METHOD  TABLE    TB   AC   M   INDEX   SORT   SORT  LOCK
  #      #      #            NAMES    #         #   NAME    UJOG   UJOG  MODE
```

QUERY #	QB #	PLAN #	METHOD	TABLE NAMES	TB #	AC	M #	INDEX NAME	REAL SORT UJOG	INT. SORT UJOG	TS LOCK MODE
___	___	___	___	_____	___	___	___	_____	_____	_____	___
___	___	___	___	_____	___	___	___	_____	_____	_____	___
___	___	___	___	_____	___	___	___	_____	_____	_____	___
___	___	___	___	_____	___	___	___	_____	_____	_____	___
___	___	___	___	_____	___	___	___	_____	_____	_____	___
___	___	___	___	_____	___	___	___	_____	_____	_____	___
___	___	___	___	_____	___	___	___	_____	_____	_____	___
___	___	___	___	_____	___	___	___	_____	_____	_____	___

```
                       EXECUTION INFORMATION

QUERY #     QUERY      ESTIMATED     # OF EXECUTIONS OF SQL STATEMENTS
            TYPE       # OF ROWS     9AM - 5PM   5PM - 1AM   1AM - 9AM
```

QUERY #	QUERY TYPE	ESTIMATED # OF ROWS	9AM - 5PM	5PM - 1AM	1AM - 9AM
___	_____	_____	_____	_____	_____
___	_____	_____	_____	_____	_____
___	_____	_____	_____	_____	_____
___	_____	_____	_____	_____	_____
___	_____	_____	_____	_____	_____
___	_____	_____	_____	_____	_____
___	_____	_____	_____	_____	_____
___	_____	_____	_____	_____	_____
___	_____	_____	_____	_____	_____

```
DATE NEEDED: _____   DATE COMPLETED: _____  INITIALS: ____

AUTHORIZATION SIGNATURE:_____  NAME:_____
```

DB2 Capacity Impact Analysis

```
                                                  PAGE ___ of ___

APPLICATION NAME/CODE: _____ __          DATE:_____

TABLESPACE NAME: _____

REQUESTOR: _____               SYSTEM:_____

DESCRIPTION:_____
_____
_____
_____

DATABASE NAME: _____

BUFFER POOL TO BE USED: _____

INITIAL STORAGE ESTIMATE (In Kilobytes) : _____

GROWTH STORAGE ESTIMATE (In Kilobytes Per Month) : _____

MAXIMUM STORAGE ESTIMATE (In Kilobytes) : _____

                        ACCESS INFORMATION

      ACCESS     ESTIMATED     # OF ACCESSES OF TABLESPACE DATA
       TYPE      # OF ROWS     9AM - 5PM    5PM - 1AM    1AM - 9AM

     _____    _____     _____    _____    _____
     _____    _____     _____    _____    _____
     _____    _____     _____    _____    _____
     _____    _____     _____    _____    _____
     _____    _____     _____    _____    _____
     _____    _____     _____    _____    _____
     _____    _____     _____    _____    _____
     _____    _____     _____    _____    _____
     _____    _____     _____    _____    _____

DATE NEEDED: _____  DATE COMPLETED: _____  INITIALS: ____

DATE ENTERED INTO DATA DICTIONARY: _____

AUTHORIZATION SIGNATURE:_____ NAME:_____
```

DB2 Utility/DXT Usage APPENDIX **28**

```
                                                    PAGE ___ of ___
  APPLICATION NAME/CODE: _____ __     DATE: _____

  REQUESTOR: _____              SYSTEM: _____

  DESCRIPTION: _____
  _____
  _____

  LOAD:    How Many: _____   When: _____

  REORG:   How Many: _____   When: _____

  RUNSTATS: How Many: _____   When/Frequency: _____

  DXT USAGE:

  SOURCE FORMAT: _____   DSN: _____

  DESCRIPTION:
               _____
               _____
               _____
               _____

  RESTRUCTURING DESCRIPTION (If Necessary):
               _____
               _____
               _____
               _____

   TABLES TO BE LOADED:

      Table Name          Extract Rate        Update/Refresh
      _____     _____     _____
      _____     _____     _____
      _____     _____     _____

  DATE NEEDED: _____  DATE COMPLETED: _____ INITIALS: ____

  DATE ENTERED INTO DATA DICTIONARY: _____

  AUTHORIZATION SIGNATURE: _____  NAME: _____
```

QMF Procedure Processing   APPENDIX 29

```
                                              PAGE ___ of ___
APPLICATION NAME/CODE: _____ __        DATE:_____
REQUESTOR: _____                     SYSTEM:_____
QMF PROCEDURE NAME: _____
QMF PROCEDURE TITLE: _____
DESCRIPTION:_____
_____
_____

EXECUTION RATE/HOUR: _____  # OF AUTHORIZED USERS: _____
RESPONSE TIME REQUIREMENT: _____
AUXILIARY TABLES CREATED BY THIS PROCEDURE:
      TABLE NAME              SIZE              DURATION
   _____     _____    _____
   _____     _____    _____

PROCEDURE LISTING:   (Include QUERIES and FORMS Used)




DATE NEEDED:  _____   DATE COMPLETED:  _____   INITIALS: ____
DATE ENTERED INTO DATA DICTIONARY:  _____
AUTHORIZATION SIGNATURE:_____  NAME:_____
```

DB2 SQL Statement Processing

```
                                              PAGE ___ of ___
APPLICATION NAME/CODE: _____  __    DATE:_____

REQUESTOR: _____               SYSTEM:_____

DESCRIPTION:_____
_____
_____

EXECUTION RATE/HOUR: _____  # OF USERS AUTHORIZED: _____

TABLES USED BY THIS SQL STATEMENT:

     TABLE NAME                NUMBER OF ROWS
                        Retrieved  Updated  Inserted  Deleted

     _____    _____  _____  _____  _____
     _____    _____  _____  _____  _____
     _____    _____  _____  _____  _____
     _____    _____  _____  _____  _____

SQL STATEMENT LISTING:




OUTPUT:    # Of ROWS Returned: _____
      (Provide Sample Listing)

DATE NEEDED: _____  DATE COMPLETED: _____  INITIALS: ____

DATE ENTERED INTO DATA DICTIONARY: _____

AUTHORIZATION SIGNATURE:_____  NAME:_____
```

DB2 QMF Query Processing APPENDIX **31**

```
                                          PAGE ___ of ___

                                          DATE:_____
APPLICATION NAME/CODE: _____ __
                                          SYSTEM:_____
REQUESTOR: _____

QMF QUERY NAME: _____

QMF QUERY TITLE: _____
_____
DESCRIPTION:_____
_____
_____

Attach DB2 SQL STATEMENT PROCESSING FORM

QMF QUERY:
     Save Data After Query: _____   Save Data In New Table: _____
     Print Without Scrolling: _____

     FORM Specifications:
      (Provide Sample Listing)




DATE NEEDED: _____  DATE COMPLETED: _____ INITIALS: ____

DATE ENTERED INTO DATA DICTIONARY: _____

AUTHORIZATION SIGNATURE:_____ NAME:_____
```

Production Control Migration APPENDIX **32**
Request for DB2 Applications

```
                                              PAGE ___ of ___

  APPLICATION NAME/CODE: _____  __   DATE:_____

  REQUESTOR: _____                   SYSTEM:_____

  DESCRIPTION:_____
  _____
  _____
  _____

  PROGRAM TYPE:    CICS _____    BATCH _____    ISPF _____
  PROGRAM LANGUAGE:  COBOL _____   ASSEMBLER _____  OTHER _____
  DEVELOPMENT SOURCE FILE DSN: _____
  PRODUCTION SOURCE FILE DSN: _____
  PRODUCTION DBRM LIBRARY DSN: _____
  PRODUCTION DCLGEN LIBRARY DSN: _____
  PRODUCTION DB2 LOAD LIBRARY DSN: _____

  DCLGENS TO BE CREATED:

       _____    _____    _____
       _____    _____    _____

  SYNONYMS TO BE CREATED:

       _____    _____    _____
       _____    _____    _____

    SOURCE NAME     DBRM NAME      SOURCE NAME      DBRM NAME
  _____ / _____   _____ / _____
  _____ / _____   _____ / _____

  PLAN NAME            DBRM MEMBER NAMES
  _____ / _____   _____   _____
  _____ / _____   _____   _____
  _____ / _____   _____   _____
  _____ / _____   _____   _____

  DATE NEEDED: _____  DATE COMPLETED: _____ INITIALS: ____

  AUTHORIZATION SIGNATURE:_____ NAME:_____
```

Production Control Checklist APPENDIX 33
for DB2 Applications

```
                                          PAGE ___ of ___

APPLICATION NAME/CODE: _____ __     DATE:_____

REQUESTOR: _____                 SYSTEM:_____

DESCRIPTION:_____
_____
_____
_____
_____

PROGRAM TYPE:    CICS _____    BATCH _____    ISPF _____

PROGRAM LANGUAGE:  COBOL _____  ASSEMBLER _____  OTHER _____


                        CHECKLIST

     1. Check With DB2 SYSADM/DBADM
            Are Necessary DB2 Tables Generated? _____
            What are High-Level Qualifiers?     _____
     2. Create SYNONYMS                         _____
     3. Create DCLGENS If Needed                _____
     4. Precompile and Compile Source           _____
            Into Production Libraries
     5. Notify SYSADM/DBADM Upon Completion     _____
     6. Send This Completed Form to SYSADM      _____
     7. Schedule Batch Programs                 _____
     8. Schedule Necessary Backups              _____
     9. Implement Online Systems                _____
    10. Notify Development                      _____


DATE NEEDED: _____  DATE COMPLETED: _____  INITIALS: ____

AUTHORIZATION SIGNATURE:_____  NAME:_____
```

DB2 Migration Request— DBEDIT

```
                                              PAGE ___ of ___

APPLICATION NAME/CODE: _____ __     DATE:_____

REQUESTOR: _____              SYSTEM TO:_____
                                           SYSTEM FROM:_____

DESCRIPTION:_____
_____
_____
_____


PANELS TO BE MIGRATED:

        _____    _____    _____
        _____    _____    _____



DATE NEEDED: _____  DATE COMPLETED: _____ INITIALS: ____

DATE ENTERED INTO DATA DICTIONARY: _____

AUTHORIZATION SIGNATURE:_____ NAME:_____
```

```
//DB2DBA JOB (DB2U),DBA,MSGLEVEL=(1,1),REGION=4096K,
//       MSGCLASS=X,CLASS=X,NOTIFY=DB2DBA
//*
//* ************************************************************ */
//*                                                             */
//*      CHECK UTILITY JCL                                      */
//*                                                             */
//* ************************************************************ */
//*
//UTIL EXEC DSNUPROC,SYSTEM=DSN,UID='CHECKLV',UTPROC=
//*
//DSNUPROC.SORTWK01 DD DSN=1&SORTWK01,
//   DISP=(MOD,DELETE),
//   SPACE=(4000,(20,20),,,ROUND),
//   UNIT=SYSDA
//DSNUPROC.SORTWK02 DD DSN=1&SORTWK02,
//   DISP=(MOD,DELETE),
//   SPACE=(4000,(20,20),,,ROUND),
//   UNIT=SYSDA
//DSNUPROC.SORTWK03 DD DSN=1&SORTWK03,
//   DISP=(MOD,DELETE),
//   SPACE=(4000,(20,20),,,ROUND),
//   UNIT=SYSDA
//DSNUPROC.SORTWK04 DD DSN=1&SORTWK04,
//   DISP=(MOD,DELETE),
//   SPACE=(4000,(20,20),,,ROUND),
//   UNIT=SYSDA
//DSNUPROC.SYSUT1 DD DSN=1&SYSUT1,
//   DISP=(MOD,DELETE),
//   SPACE=(4000,(20,20),,,ROUND),
//   UNIT=SYSDA
//*
//*
//DSNUPROC.SYSIN DD   *
CHECK INDEX TABLESPACE DATABASE.STBLSPC1 SORTDEVT SYSDA SORTNUM 4
CHECK INDEX TABLESPACE DATABASE.STBLSPC2 SORTDEVT SYSDA SORTNUM 4
CHECK INDEX TABLESPACE DATABASE.STBLSPC3 SORTDEVT SYSDA SORTNUM 4
//
```

```
//DB2DBAI JOB (DB2U),DBA,MSGLEVEL=(1,1),REGION=4096K,
//      MSGCLASS=X,CLASS=X,NOTIFY=DB2DBA
//*
//* ************************************************************ */
//*                                                             */
//*      CREATE IMAGE COPIES OF ALL THE SYSTEM CATALOG TABLES   */
//*                                                             */
//*      DBUTIL   PROC        INVOKE DATA BASE UTILITY PROGRAM  */
//*      IMGCPY   STEP        CREATE IMAGE COPIES OF ALL TABLES */
//*                                                             */
//* ************************************************************ */
//DBUTIL PROC
//* ************************************************************ */
//* SYSTEM CATALOG IMAGE COPY STEP                              */
//* ************************************************************ */
//DBUTIL EXEC PGM=DSNUTILB,PARM='DSN,SYSCPY'
//SYSCOPY1 DD UNIT=TAPE,DISP=(NEW,KEEP),
//          DSN=DB2DBA.IMAGCPYC.SYSCOPY,
//          LABEL=(1,SL,,,RETPD=30)
//SYSCOPY2 DD UNIT=AFF=SYSCOPY1,VOL=REF=*.SYSCOPY1,DISP=(NEW,KEEP),
//          DSN=DB2DBA.IMAGCPYC.SYSDBASE,
//          LABEL=(2,SL,,,RETPD=30)
//SYSCOPY3 DD UNIT=AFF=SYSCOPY1,VOL=REF=*.SYSCOPY1,DISP=(NEW,KEEP),
//          DSN=DB2DBA.IMAGCPYC.SYSDBAUT,
//          LABEL=(3,SL,,,RETPD=30)
//SYSCOPY4 DD UNIT=AFF=SYSCOPY1,VOL=REF=*.SYSCOPY1,DISP=(NEW,KEEP),
//          DSN=DB2DBA.IMAGCPYC.SYSGPAUT,
//          LABEL=(4,SL,,,RETPD=30)
//SYSCOPY5 DD UNIT=AFF=SYSCOPY1,VOL=REF=*.SYSCOPY1,DISP=(NEW,KEEP),
//          DSN=DB2DBA.IMAGCPYC.SYSGROUP,
//          LABEL=(5,SL,,,RETPD=30)
//SYSCOPY6 DD UNIT=AFF=SYSCOPY1,VOL=REF=*.SYSCOPY1,DISP=(NEW,KEEP),
//          DSN=DB2DBA.IMAGCPYC.SYSPLAN,
//          LABEL=(6,SL,,,RETPD=30)
//SYSCOPY7 DD UNIT=AFF=SYSCOPY1,VOL=REF=*.SYSCOPY1,DISP=(NEW,KEEP),
//          DSN=DB2DBA.IMAGCPYC.SYSUSER,
//          LABEL=(7,SL,,,RETPD=30)
//SYSCOPY8 DD UNIT=AFF=SYSCOPY1,VOL=REF=*.SYSCOPY1,DISP=(NEW,KEEP),
//          DSN=DB2DBA.IMAGCPYC.SYSVIEWS,
//          LABEL=(8,SL,,,RETPD=30)
//SYSPRINT DD SYSOUT=*
//SYSUDUMP DD SYSOUT=*
//DBUTIL PEND
```

```
//IMGCPY EXEC DBUTIL
//SYSIN DD  *
COPY TABLESPACE DSNDB06.SYSCOPY    COPYDDN SYSCOPY1   DEVT TAPE
COPY TABLESPACE DSNDB06.SYSDBASE   COPYDDN SYSCOPY2   DEVT TAPE
COPY TABLESPACE DSNDB06.SYSDBAUT   COPYDDN SYSCOPY3   DEVT TAPE
COPY TABLESPACE DSNDB06.SYSGPAUT   COPYDDN SYSCOPY4   DEVT TAPE
COPY TABLESPACE DSNDB06.SYSGROUP   COPYDDN SYSCOPY5   DEVT TAPE
COPY TABLESPACE DSNDB06.SYSPLAN    COPYDDN SYSCOPY6   DEVT TAPE
COPY TABLESPACE DSNDB06.SYSUSER    COPYDDN SYSCOPY7   DEVT TAPE
COPY TABLESPACE DSNDB06.SYSVIEWS   COPYDDN SYSCOPY8   DEVT TAPE
//*
```

```
//DB2DBAI JOB (DB2U),DBA,MSGLEVEL=(1,1),REGION=4096K,
//       MSGCLASS=X,CLASS=X,NOTIFY=DB2DBA
//*
//* ************************************************************ */
//*                                                              */
//*      CREATE IMAGE COPIES OF ALL THE DIRECTORY TABLESPACES    */
//*                                                              */
//*      DBUTIL    PROC      INVOKE DATA BASE UTILITY PROGRAM     */
//*      IMGCPY    STEP      CREATE IMAGE COPIES OF ALL TABLES    */
//*                                                              */
//* ************************************************************ */
//DBUTIL PROC
//* ************************************************************ */
//* DIRECTORY IMAGE COPY STEP                                    */
//* ************************************************************ */
//DBUTIL EXEC PGM=DSNUTILB,PARM='DSN,SYSCPY'
//SYSCOPY1 DD UNIT=TAPE,DISP=(NEW,KEEP),
//         DSN=DB2DBA.IMAGCPYC.DBD01,
//         LABEL=(1,SL,,,RETPD=30)
//SYSCOPY2 DD UNIT=AFF=SYSCOPY1,VOL=REF=*.SYSCOPY1,DISP=(NEW,KEEP),
//         DSN=DB2DBA.IMAGCPYC.SCT02,
//         LABEL=(2,SL,,,RETPD=30)
//SYSCOPY3 DD UNIT=AFF=SYSCOPY1,VOL=REF=*.SYSCOPY1,DISP=(NEW,KEEP),
//         DSN=DB2DBA.IMAGCPYC.SYSLGRNG,
//         LABEL=(3,SL,,,RETPD=30)
//SYSCOPY4 DD UNIT=AFF=SYSCOPY1,VOL=REF=*.SYSCOPY1,DISP=(NEW,KEEP),
//         DSN=DB2DBA.IMAGCPYC.SYSUTIL,
//         LABEL=(4,SL,,,RETPD=30)
//SYSPRINT DD SYSOUT=*
//SYSUDUMP DD SYSOUT=*
//DBUTIL PEND
//IMGCPY EXEC DBUTIL
//SYSIN DD   *
COPY TABLESPACE DSNDB01.DBD01       COPYDDN SYSCOPY1    DEVT TAPE
COPY TABLESPACE DSNDB01.SCT02       COPYDDN SYSCOPY2    DEVT TAPE
COPY TABLESPACE DSNDB01.SYSLGRNG    COPYDDN SYSCOPY3    DEVT TAPE
COPY TABLESPACE DSNDB01.SYSUTIL     COPYDDN SYSCOPY4    DEVT TAPE
//*
```

```
//DB2DBAR JOB (DB2U),DBA,MSGCLASS=X,REGION=2048K,NOTIFY=DB2DBA
//UTIL EXEC DSNUPROC,SYSTEM=DSN,UID='DB2DBA',UTPROC=''
//*
//*****************************************/
//*                                       */
//*   JCL FOR THE LOAD UTILITY            */
//*                                       */
//*****************************************/
//*
//DSNUPROC.SORTWK01 DD DSN=DB2DBA.SORTWK01,
//   DISP=(MOD,DELETE,CATLG),
//   SPACE=(4000,(20,20),,,ROUND),
//   UNIT=SYSDA
//DSNUPROC.SORTWK02 DD DSN=DB2DBA.SORTWK02,
//   DISP=(MOD,DELETE,CATLG),
//   SPACE=(4000,(20,20),,,ROUND),
//   UNIT=SYSDA
//DSNUPROC.SORTWK03 DD DSN=DB2DBA.SORTWK03,
//   DISP=(MOD,DELETE,CATLG),
//   SPACE=(4000,(20,20),,,ROUND),
//   UNIT=SYSDA
//DSNUPROC.SORTWK04 DD DSN=DB2DBA.SORTWK04,
//   DISP=(MOD,DELETE,CATLG),
//   SPACE=(4000,(20,20),,,ROUND),
//   UNIT=SYSDA
//DSNUPROC.SYSRECOO DD DSN=DB2DBA.UNLOAD.SYSRECOO,
//   DISP=(MOD,CATLG)
//DSNUPROC.SYSDISC DD DSN=DB2DBA.LOAD.DISCARD,
//   DISP=(MOD,CATLG),
//   SPACE=(4000,(20,20),,,ROUND),
//   UNIT=SYSDA
//DSNUPROC.SYSUT1 DD DSN=DB2DBA.SYSUT1,
//   DISP=(MOD,DELETE,CATLG),
//   SPACE=(4000,(20,20),,,ROUND),
//   UNIT=SYSDA
//DSNUPROC.SORTOUT DD DSN=DB2DBA.SORTOUT,
//   DISP=(MOD,DELETE,CATLG),
//   SPACE=(4000,(20,20),,,ROUND),
//   UNIT=SYSDA
//DSNUPROC.SYSIN DD    *
LOAD DATA INDDN SYSRECOO INTO TABLE
    CREATOR.TABLE1
 (
```

```
TBCOL1                 POSITION(        1        ) CHAR(        12),
TBCOL2                 POSITION(       13        ) SMALLINT       ,
TBCOL3                 POSITION(       15        ) SMALLINT       ,
TBCOL4                 POSITION(       17        ) INTEGER        ,
TBCOL5                 POSITION(       21        ) SMALLINT       ,
TBCOL6                 POSITION(       23        ) CHAR(         1),
TBCOL7                 POSITION(       24        ) INTEGER        ,
TBCOL8                 POSITION(       28        ) INTEGER        ,
TBCOL9                 POSITION(       32        ) CHAR(        12),
TBCOL10                POSITION(       44        ) CHAR(        12),
TBCOL11                POSITION(       56        ) CHAR(        48),
TBCOL12                POSITION(      104        ) CHAR(         1),
TBCOL13                POSITION(      105        ) SMALLINT       ,
TBCOL14                POSITION(      107        ) CHAR(        30)
)
//
```

```
//* *************************************************************** */
//*                                                                 */
//*                   RESTORE THE LOG DATA                          */
//*                                                                 */
//*      AMSPROC PROC        JCL PROCEDURE TO INVOKE AMS            */
//*      COPYPROC PROC       JCL PROCEDURE TO INVOKE DSN1COPY       */
//*      AMSRENM STEP        RENAMES DATA SETS TO BE RESTORED       */
//*      RESTALLC STEP       ALLOCATES NEW DATA SETS FOR RESTORE    */
//*      BSDSRPRO STEP       REPRO BSDS LOG DATA SETS               */
//*                                                                 */
//*                                                                 */
//* *************************************************************** */
//*
//JOBLIB DD DISP=SHR,
//          DSN=DSN.DB2.DSNLOAD
//*
//AMSPROC PROC
//AMSPROC EXEC PGM=IDCAMS,DYNAMNBR=50
//STEPCAT DD DISP=SHR,DSN=DSNCAT
//SYSPRINT DD SYSOUT=*
//SYSUDUMP DD SYSOUT=*
//AMSPROC PEND
//*
//COPYPROC PROC DBASE=DSNDBO1,TBLSPC=DBDO1
//* COPY VSAM TO VSAM AND CHECK PAGES
//RUNCOPY EXEC PGM=DSN1COPY,PARM='CHECK'
//STEPCAT DD DISP=SHR,DSN=DSNCAT
//SYSPRINT DD SYSOUT=*
//SYSUT1 DD DISP=SHR,
//          DSN=DSNCAT.DSNBKC.&DBASE..&TBLSPC..I0001.A001
//SYSUT2 DD DISP=SHR,
//          DSN=DSNCAT.DSNDBC.&DBASE..&TBLSPC..I0001.A001
//COPYPROC PEND
//DB2S1REN EXEC AMSPROC
//SYSIN DD   *

  ALTER                                                -
        DB2CAT.LOGCOPY1.DS01/XXXXXXXX -
        NEWNAME(DB2CAT.OLDLOG1.DS01)   -
        CATALOG(DB2CAT/XXXXXXXX)

IF LASTCC = 0                                          -
THEN                                                   -
  DO
```

```
ALTER                                           -
      DB2CAT.LOGCOPY1.DS01.DATA/XXXXXXXX -
      NEWNAME(DB2CAT.OLDLOG1.DS01.DATA)    -
      CATALOG(DB2CAT/XXXXXXXX)

ALTER                                      -
      DB2CAT.LOGCOPY1.DS02/XXXXXXXX -
      NEWNAME(DB2CAT.OLDLOG1.DS02)    -
      CATALOG(DB2CAT/XXXXXXXX)

ALTER                                      -
      DB2CAT.LOGCOPY1.DS02.DATA/XXXXXXXX -
      NEWNAME(DB2CAT.OLDLOG1.DS02.DATA)    -
      CATALOG(DB2CAT/XXXXXXXX)

ALTER                                      -
      DB2CAT.LOGCOPY1.DS03/XXXXXXXX -
      NEWNAME(DB2CAT.OLDLOG1.DS03)    -
      CATALOG(DB2CAT/XXXXXXXX)

ALTER                                      -
      DB2CAT.LOGCOPY1.DS03.DATA/XXXXXXXX -
      NEWNAME(DB2CAT.OLDLOG1.DS03.DATA)    -
      CATALOG(DB2CAT/XXXXXXXX)


   END
  ELSE
  SET MAXCC = 0
//RESTALLC EXEC AMSPROC,COND=(2,LT)
//SYSIN DD  *

   DEFINE CLUSTER                               -
      ( NAME(DB2CAT.LOGCOPY1.DS01) -
        READPW(XXXXXXXX)                      -
        VOLUMES(DSNV01)                       -
        REUSE                                 -
        RECORDS(1000)                         -
        RECORDSIZE(4089 4089)                 -
        CONTROLINTERVALSIZE(4096)             -
        NONINDEXED )                          -
      DATA                                     -
      ( NAME(DB2CAT.LOGCOPY1.DS01.DATA))     -
      CATALOG(DB2CAT/XXXXXXXX)

 IF LASTCC = 0                                  -
  THEN                                          -
   DO
```

```
DEFINE CLUSTER                                         -
   ( NAME(DB2CAT.LOGCOPY1.DS02) -
     READPW(XXXXXXXX)                                  -
     VOLUMES(DSNV01)                                   -
     REUSE                                             -
     RECORDS(1000)                                     -
     RECORDSIZE(4089 4089)                             -
     CONTROLINTERVALSIZE(4096)                         -
     NONINDEXED )                                      -
   DATA                                                -
   ( NAME(DB2CAT.LOGCOPY1.DS02.DATA))                  -
   CATALOG(DB2CAT/XXXXXXXX)
DEFINE CLUSTER                                         -
   ( NAME(DB2CAT.LOGCOPY1.DS03) -
     READPW(XXXXXXXX)                                  -
     VOLUMES(DSNV01)                                   -
     REUSE                                             -
     RECORDS(1000)                                     -
     RECORDSIZE(4089 4089)                             -
     CONTROLINTERVALSIZE(4096)                         -
     NONINDEXED )                                      -
   DATA                                                -
   ( NAME(DB2CAT.LOGCOPY1.DS03.DATA))                  -
   CATALOG(DB2CAT/XXXXXXXX)

DEFINE CLUSTER                                         -
   ( NAME(DB2CAT.LOGCOPY2.DS01) -
     READPW(XXXXXXXX)                                  -
     VOLUMES(DSNV01)                                   -
     REUSE                                             -
     RECORDS(1000)                                     -
     RECORDSIZE(4089 4089)                             -
     CONTROLINTERVALSIZE(4096)                         -
     NONINDEXED )                                      -
   DATA                                                -
   ( NAME(DB2CAT.LOGCOPY2.DS01.DATA))                  -
   CATALOG(DB2CAT/XXXXXXXX)

DEFINE CLUSTER                                         -
   ( NAME(DB2CAT.LOGCOPY2.DS02) -
     READPW(XXXXXXXX)                                  -
     VOLUMES(DSNV01)                                   -
     REUSE                                             -
     RECORDS(1000)                                     -
     RECORDSIZE(4089 4089)                             -
     CONTROLINTERVALSIZE(4096)                         -
     NONINDEXED )                                      -
   DATA                                                -
   ( NAME(DB2CAT.LOGCOPY2.DS02.DATA))                  -
   CATALOG(DB2CAT/XXXXXXXX)
```

```
    DEFINE CLUSTER                                       -
    ( NAME(DB2CAT.LOGCOPY2.DS03) -
      READPW(XXXXXXXX)                                   -
      VOLUMES(DSNV01)                                    -
      REUSE                                              -
      RECORDS(1000)                                      -
      RECORDSIZE(4089 4089)                              -
      CONTROLINTERVALSIZE(4096)                          -
      NONINDEXED )                                       -
    DATA                                                 -
    ( NAME(DB2CAT.LOGCOPY2.DS03.DATA))   -
    CATALOG(DB2CAT/XXXXXXXX)


  END
ELSE                                                     -

  SET MAXCC = 0
//BSDSRPRO EXEC AMSPROC,COND=(2,LT)
//SYSIN DD   *

    VERIFY DATASET(DB2CAT.BKUP.LOGCOPY1.DS01/XXXXXXXX)

    REPRO   ODS(DB2CAT.LOGCOPY1.DS01/XXXXXXXX) -
            REUSE                                        -
            IDS(DB2CAT.BKUP.LOGCOPY1.DS01/XXXXXXXX)

    VERIFY DATASET(DB2CAT.BKUP.LOGCOPY2.DS01/XXXXXXXX)

    REPRO   ODS(DB2CAT.LOGCOPY2.DS01/XXXXXXXX) -
            REUSE                                        -
            IDS(DB2CAT.BKUP.LOGCOPY2.DS01/XXXXXXXX)

    VERIFY DATASET(DB2CAT.BKUP.LOGCOPY1.DS02/XXXXXXXX)

    REPRO   ODS(DB2CAT.LOGCOPY1.DS02/XXXXXXXX) -
            REUSE                                        -
            IDS(DB2CAT.BKUP.LOGCOPY1.DS02/XXXXXXXX)

    VERIFY DATASET(DB2CAT.BKUP.LOGCOPY2.DS02/XXXXXXXX)

    REPRO   ODS(DB2CAT.LOGCOPY2.DS02/XXXXXXXX) -
            REUSE                                        -
            IDS(DB2CAT.BKUP.LOGCOPY2.DS02/XXXXXXXX)

    VERIFY DATASET(DB2CAT.BKUP.LOGCOPY1.DS03/XXXXXXXX)

    REPRO   ODS(DB2CAT.LOGCOPY1.DS03/XXXXXXXX) -
            REUSE                                        -
            IDS(DB2CAT.BKUP.LOGCOPY1.DS03/XXXXXXXX)
```

```
VERIFY DATASET(DB2CAT.BKUP.LOGCOPY2.DS03/XXXXXXXX)

REPRO  ODS(DB2CAT.LOGCOPY2.DS03/XXXXXXXX) -
       REUSE                             -
       IDS(DB2CAT.BKUP.LOGCOPY2.DS03/XXXXXXXX)

//*
```

```
//*  ************************************************************  */
//*                                                                */
//*            MIGRATION JCL FOR DIRECTORY DATASETS                */
//*                                                                */
//*       AMSPROC PROC        JCL PROCEDURE TO INVOKE AMS          */
//*       COPYPROC PROC       JCL PROCEDURE TO INVOKE DSN1COPY     */
//*       AMSRENM STEP        RENAMES DATA SETS TO BE RESTORED     */
//*       RESTALLC STEP       ALLOCATES NEW DATA SETS FOR RESTORE  */
//*       DBDCOPY STEP        COPY DSNDBO1.DBDO1    DATA SET       */
//*       SYSUCOPY STEP       COPY DSNDBO1.SYSUTIL  DATA SET       */
//*       SYSLCOPY STEP       COPY DSNDBO1.SYSLGRNG DATA SET       */
//*                                                                */
//*                                                                */
//*  ************************************************************  */
//*
//JOBLIB DD DISP=SHR,
//          DSN=DSN.DB2.DSNLOAD
//*
//AMSPROC PROC
//AMSPROC EXEC PGM=IDCAMS,DYNAMNBR=50
//STEPCAT DD DISP=SHR,DSN=DSNCAT
//SYSPRINT DD SYSOUT=*
//SYSUDUMP DD SYSOUT=*
//AMSPROC PEND
//*
//COPYPROC PROC DBASE=DSNDBO1,TBLSPC=DBDO1
//* COPY VSAM TO VSAM AND CHECK PAGES
//RUNCOPY EXEC PGM=DSN1COPY,PARM='CHECK'
//STEPCAT DD DISP=SHR,DSN=DSNCAT
//SYSPRINT DD SYSOUT=*
//SYSUT1 DD DISP=SHR,
//          DSN=DSNCAT.DSNBKC.&DBASE..&TBLSPC..I0001.A001
//SYSUT2 DD DISP=SHR,
//          DSN=DSNCAT.DSNBC.&DBASE..&TBLSPC..I0001.A001
//COPYPROC PEND
//DB2S1REN EXEC AMSPROC
//SYSIN DD  *

ALTER                                                   -
     DB2CAT.DSNDBC.DSNDBO1.DBDO1.I0001.A001/XXXXXXXX -
     NEWNAME(DB2CAT.DSNDBC.OLD.DBDO1.I0001.A001) -
     CATALOG(DB2CAT/XXXXXXXX)
```

```
IF LASTCC = 0                                       -
 THEN                                               -
   DO

   ALTER                                            -
         DB2CAT.DSNDBD.DSNDB01.DBD01.I0001.A001/XXXXXXXX -
         NEWNAME(DB2CAT.DSNDBD.OLD.DBD01.I0001.A001)    -
         CATALOG(DB2CAT/XXXXXXXX)

   ALTER                                            -
         DB2CAT.DSNDBC.DSNDB01.SYSUTIL.I0001.A001/XXXXXXXX -
         NEWNAME(DB2CAT.DSNDBC.OLD.SYSUTIL.I0001.A001) -
         CATALOG(DB2CAT/XXXXXXXX)

   ALTER                                            -
         DB2CAT.DSNDBD.DSNDB01.SYSUTIL.I0001.A001/XXXXXXXX -
         NEWNAME(DB2CAT.DSNDBD.OLD.SYSUTIL.I0001.A001) -
         CATALOG(DB2CAT/XXXXXXXX)

   ALTER                                            -
         DB2CAT.DSNDBC.DSNDB01.SYSLGRNG.I0001.A001/XXXXXXXX -
         NEWNAME(DB2CAT.DSNDBC.OLD.SYSLGRNG.I0001.A001) -
         CATALOG(DB2CAT/XXXXXXXX)

   ALTER                                            -
         DB2CAT.DSNDBD.DSNDB01.SYSLGRNG.I0001.A001/XXXXXXXX -
         NEWNAME(DB2CAT.DSNDBD.OLD.SYSLGRNG.I0001.A001) -
         CATALOG(DB2CAT/XXXXXXXX)

   END
   ELSE
   SET MAXCC = 0
//RESTALLC EXEC AMSPROC,COND=(2,LT)
//SYSIN DD   *
       DEFINE CLUSTER                               -
       ( NAME(DB2CAT.DSNDBC.DSNDB01.DBD01.I0001.A001) -
         NONINDEXED                                 -
         REUSE                                      -
         CONTROLINTERVALSIZE(4096)                  -
         RECORDSIZE(4089 4089)                      -
         SHAREOPTIONS(3 3)                          -
         MASTERPW(XXXXXXXX)                         -
         CONTROLPW(XXXXXXXX)                        -
                                 )                  -
       DATA                                         -
       ( NAME(DB2CAT.DSNDBD.DSNDB01.DBD01.I0001.A001) -
         MASTERPW(XXXXXXXX)                         -
         CONTROLPW(XXXXXXXX)                        -
```

```
        RECORDS(114 30)                          -
        VOLUMES(DSNVO1) )                         -
     CATALOG(DB2CAT/XXXXXXXX)


  IF LASTCC = 0                                   -
   THEN                                           -
    DO
       DEFINE CLUSTER                             -
       ( NAME(DB2CAT.DSNDBC.DSNDBO1.SYSLGRNG.I0001.A001) -
         NONINDEXED                               -
         REUSE                                    -
         CONTROLINTERVALSIZE(4096)                -
         VOLUMES(DSNVO1)                          -
         MASTERPW(XXXXXXXX)                       -
         CONTROLPW(XXXXXXXX)                      -
         RECORDS(10 10)                           -
         RECORDSIZE(4089 4089)                    -
         SHAREOPTIONS(3 3) )                      -
       DATA                                       -
       ( NAME(DB2CAT.DSNDBD.DSNDBO1.SYSLGRNG.I0001.A001) -
         MASTERPW(XXXXXXXX)                       -
         CONTROLPW(XXXXXXXX)                      -
                            )                     -
       CATALOG(DB2CAT/XXXXXXXX)

     DEFINE CLUSTER                               -
       ( NAME(DB2CAT.DSNDBC.DSNDBO1.SYSUTIL.I0001.A001) -
         NONINDEXED                               -
         REUSE                                    -
         CONTROLINTERVALSIZE(4096)                -
         VOLUMES(DSNVO1)                          -
         MASTERPW(XXXXXXXX)                       -
         CONTROLPW(XXXXXXXX)                      -
         RECORDS(10 10)                           -
         RECORDSIZE(4089 4089)                    -
         SHAREOPTIONS(3 3) )                      -
       DATA                                       -
       ( NAME(DB2CAT.DSNDBD.DSNDBO1.SYSUTIL.I0001.A001) -
         MASTERPW(XXXXXXXX)                       -
         CONTROLPW(XXXXXXXX)                      -
                            )                     -
       CATALOG(DB2CAT/XXXXXXXX)

   END
   ELSE                                           -
   SET MAXCC = 0
//DBDCOPY EXEC COPYPROC,TBLSPC=DBDO1,COND=(2,LT)
//SYSUCOPY EXEC COPYPROC,TBLSPC=SYSUTIL,COND=(2,LT)
//SYSLCOPY EXEC COPYPROC,TBLSPC=SYSLGRNG,COND=(2,LT)
//*
```

```
//* ************************************************************ */
//*                                                              */
//*          MIGRATION JCL FOR SYSTEM CATALOG DATASETS           */
//*                                                              */
//*      AMSPROC PROC        JCL PROCEDURE TO INVOKE AMS         */
//*      COPYPROC PROC       JCL PROCEDURE TO INVOKE DSN1COPY    */
//*      AMSRENM STEP        RENAMES DATA SETS TO BE RESTORED    */
//*      RESTALLC STEP       ALLOCATES NEW DATA SETS FOR RESTORE */
//*      DBDCOPY STEP        COPY DSNDB06.DBD01    DATA SET      */
//*      SYSUCOPY STEP       COPY DSNDB06.SYSUTIL  DATA SET      */
//*      SYSLCOPY STEP       COPY DSNDB06.SYSLGRNG DATA SET      */
//*                                                              */
//*                                                              */
//* ************************************************************ */
//*
//JOBLIB DD DISP=SHR,
//          DSN=DSN.DB2.DSNLOAD
//*
//AMSPROC PROC
//AMSPROC EXEC PGM=IDCAMS,DYNAMNBR=50
//STEPCAT DD DISP=SHR,DSN=DSNCAT
//SYSPRINT DD SYSOUT=*
//SYSUDUMP DD SYSOUT=*
//AMSPROC PEND
//*
//COPYPROC PROC DBASE=DSNDB01,TBLSPC=DBD01
//* COPY VSAM TO VSAM AND CHECK PAGES
//RUNCOPY EXEC PGM=DSN1COPY,PARM='CHECK'
//STEPCAT DD DISP=SHR,DSN=DSNCAT
//SYSPRINT DD SYSOUT=*
//SYSUT1 DD DISP=SHR,
//          DSN=DSNCAT.DSNBKC.&DBASE..&TBLSPC..I0001.A001
//SYSUT2 DD DISP=SHR,
//          DSN=DSNCAT.DSNDBC.&DBASE..&TBLSPC..I0001.A001
//COPYPROC PEND
//DB2S1REN EXEC AMSPROC
//SYSIN DD   *

  ALTER                                      -
        DB2CAT.DSNDBC.DSNDB01.DBD01.I0001.A001/XXXXXXXX -
        NEWNAME(DB2CAT.DSNDBC.OLD.DBD01.I0001.A001) -
        CATALOG(DB2CAT/XXXXXXXX)
```

```
IF LASTCC = 0                                       -
 THEN                                               -
  DO

    ALTER                                           -
         DB2CAT.DSNDBD.DSNDBO1.DBD01.I0001.A001/XXXXXXXX -
         NEWNAME(DB2CAT.DSNDBD.OLD.DBD01.I0001.A001)    -
         CATALOG(DB2CAT/XXXXXXXX)

    ALTER                                           -
         DB2CAT.DSNDBC.DSNDBO1.SYSUTIL.I0001.A001/XXXXXXXX -
         NEWNAME(DB2CAT.DSNDBC.OLD.SYSUTIL.I0001.A001) -
         CATALOG(DB2CAT/XXXXXXXX)

    ALTER                                           -
         DB2CAT.DSNDBD.DSNDBO1.SYSUTIL.I0001.A001/XXXXXXXX -
         NEWNAME(DB2CAT.DSNDBD.OLD.SYSUTIL.I0001.A001) -
         CATALOG(DB2CAT/XXXXXXXX)

    ALTER                                           -
         DB2CAT.DSNDBC.DSNDBO1.SYSLGRNG.I0001.A001/XXXXXXXX -
         NEWNAME(DB2CAT.DSNDBC.OLD.SYSLGRNG.I0001.A001) -
         CATALOG(DB2CAT/XXXXXXXX)

    ALTER                                           -
         DB2CAT.DSNDBD.DSNDBO1.SYSLGRNG.I0001.A001/XXXXXXXX -
         NEWNAME(DB2CAT.DSNDBD.OLD.SYSLGRNG.I0001.A001) -
         CATALOG(DB2CAT/XXXXXXXX)

   END
   ELSE
   SET MAXCC = 0
//RESTALLC EXEC AMSPROC,COND=(2,LT)
//SYSIN DD   *
       DEFINE CLUSTER                               -
       ( NAME(DB2CAT.DSNDBC.DSNDBO1.DBD01.I0001.A001) -
         NONINDEXED                                 -
         REUSE                                      -
         CONTROLINTERVALSIZE(4096)                  -
         RECORDSIZE(4089 4089)                      -
         SHAREOPTIONS(3 3)                          -
         MASTERPW(XXXXXXXX)                         -
         CONTROLPW(XXXXXXXX)                        -
                                 )                  -
       DATA                                         -
       ( NAME(DB2CAT.DSNDBD.DSNDBO1.DBD01.I0001.A001) -
         MASTERPW(XXXXXXXX)                         -
         CONTROLPW(XXXXXXXX)                        -
         RECORDS(114 30)                            -
```

```
         VOLUMES(DSNV01) )                                    -
      CATALOG(DB2CAT/XXXXXXXX)


  IF LASTCC = 0                                               -
   THEN                                                       -
    DO
       DEFINE CLUSTER                                             -
       ( NAME(DB2CAT.DSNDBC.DSNDB01.SYSLGRNG.I0001.A001) -
         NONINDEXED                                          -
         REUSE                                               -
         CONTROLINTERVALSIZE(4096)                           -
         VOLUMES(DSNV01)                                     -
         MASTERPW(XXXXXXXX)                                  -
         CONTROLPW(XXXXXXXX)                                 -
         RECORDS(10 10)                                      -
         RECORDSIZE(4089 4089)                               -
         SHAREOPTIONS(3 3) )                                 -
       DATA                                                  -
       ( NAME(DB2CAT.DSNDBD.DSNDB01.SYSLGRNG.I0001.A001) -
         MASTERPW(XXXXXXXX)                                  -
         CONTROLPW(XXXXXXXX)                                 -
                         )                                   -
       CATALOG(DB2CAT/XXXXXXXX)

     DEFINE CLUSTER                                          -
       ( NAME(DB2CAT.DSNDBC.DSNDB01.SYSUTIL.I0001.A001) -
         NONINDEXED                                          -
         REUSE                                               -
         CONTROLINTERVALSIZE(4096)                           -
         VOLUMES(DSNV01)                                     -
         MASTERPW(XXXXXXXX)                                  -
         CONTROLPW(XXXXXXXX)                                 -
         RECORDS(10 10)                                      -
         RECORDSIZE(4089 4089)                               -
         SHAREOPTIONS(3 3) )                                 -
       DATA                                                  -
       ( NAME(DB2CAT.DSNDBD.DSNDB01.SYSUTIL.I0001.A001) -
         MASTERPW(XXXXXXXX)                                  -
         CONTROLPW(XXXXXXXX)                                 -
                         )                                   -
       CATALOG(DB2CAT/XXXXXXXX)

   END
   ELSE                                                      -
   SET MAXCC = 0
//DBDCOPY EXEC COPYPROC,TBLSPC=DBD01,COND=(2,LT)
//SYSUCOPY EXEC COPYPROC,TBLSPC=SYSUTIL,COND=(2,LT)
//SYSLCOPY EXEC COPYPROC,TBLSPC=SYSLGRNG,COND=(2,LT)
//*
```

```
//* ************************************************************ */
//*                                                              */
//*         MIGRATION JCL FOR USER TABLE DATASETS                */
//*                                                              */
//*     AMSPROC PROC        JCL PROCEDURE TO INVOKE AMS          */
//*     COPYPROC PROC       JCL PROCEDURE TO INVOKE DSN1COPY     */
//*     AMSRENM STEP        RENAMES DATA SETS TO BE RESTORED      */
//*     RESTALLC STEP       ALLOCATES NEW DATA SETS FOR RESTORE   */
//*     DBDCOPY STEP        COPY DSNDB06.DBD01   DATA SET        */
//*     SYSUCOPY STEP       COPY DSNDB06.SYSUTIL  DATA SET        */
//*     SYSLCOPY STEP       COPY DSNDB06.SYSLGRNG DATA SET        */
//*                                                              */
//*                                                              */
//* ************************************************************ */
//*
//JOBLIB DD DISP=SHR,
//          DSN=DSN.DB2.DSNLOAD
//*
//AMSPROC PROC
//AMSPROC EXEC PGM=IDCAMS,DYNAMNBR=50
//STEPCAT DD DISP=SHR,DSN=DSNCAT
//SYSPRINT DD SYSOUT=*
//SYSUDUMP DD SYSOUT=*
//AMSPROC PEND
//*
//COPYPROC PROC DBASE=DSNDB01,TBLSPC=DBD01
//* COPY VSAM TO VSAM AND CHECK PAGES
//RUNCOPY EXEC PGM=DSN1COPY,PARM='CHECK'
//STEPCAT DD DISP=SHR,DSN=DSNCAT
//SYSPRINT DD SYSOUT=*
//SYSUT1 DD DISP=SHR,
//          DSN=DSNCAT.DSNBKC.&DBASE..&TBLSPC..I0001.A001
//SYSUT2 DD DISP=SHR,
//          DSN=DSNCAT.DSNDBC.&DBASE..&TBLSPC..I0001.A001
//COPYPROC PEND
//DB2S1REN EXEC AMSPROC
//SYSIN DD  *

ALTER                                          -
      DB2CAT.DSNDBC.DSNDB01.DBD01.I0001.A001/XXXXXXXX -
      NEWNAME(DB2CAT.DSNDBC.OLD.DBD01.I0001.A001) -
      CATALOG(DB2CAT/XXXXXXXX)
```

```
IF LASTCC = 0                                    -
 THEN                                            -
  DO

   ALTER                                         -
         DB2CAT.DSNDBD.DSNDBO1.DBDO1.I0001.A001/XXXXXXXX -
         NEWNAME(DB2CAT.DSNDBD.OLD.DBDO1.I0001.A001)     -
         CATALOG(DB2CAT/XXXXXXXX)

   ALTER                                         -
         DB2CAT.DSNDBC.DSNDBO1.SYSUTIL.I0001.A001/XXXXXXXX -
         NEWNAME(DB2CAT.DSNDBC.OLD.SYSUTIL.I0001.A001) -
         CATALOG(DB2CAT/XXXXXXXX)

   ALTER                                         -
         DB2CAT.DSNDBD.DSNDBO1.SYSUTIL.I0001.A001/XXXXXXXX -
         NEWNAME(DB2CAT.DSNDBD.OLD.SYSUTIL.I0001.A001) -
         CATALOG(DB2CAT/XXXXXXXX)

   ALTER                                         -
         DB2CAT.DSNDBC.DSNDBO1.SYSLGRNG.I0001.A001/XXXXXXXX -
         NEWNAME(DB2CAT.DSNDBC.OLD.SYSLGRNG.I0001.A001) -
         CATALOG(DB2CAT/XXXXXXXX)

   ALTER                                         -
         DB2CAT.DSNDBD.DSNDBO1.SYSLGRNG.I0001.A001/XXXXXXXX -
         NEWNAME(DB2CAT.DSNDBD.OLD.SYSLGRNG.I0001.A001) -
         CATALOG(DB2CAT/XXXXXXXX)

   END
   ELSE
   SET MAXCC = 0
//RESTALLC EXEC AMSPROC,COND=(2,LT)
//SYSIN DD   *
       DEFINE CLUSTER                            -
       ( NAME(DB2CAT.DSNDBC.DSNDBO1.DBDO1.I0001.A001) -
         NONINDEXED                              -
         REUSE                                   -
         CONTROLINTERVALSIZE(4096)               -
         RECORDSIZE(4089 4089)                   -
         SHAREOPTIONS(3 3)                       -
         MASTERPW(XXXXXXXX)                      -
         CONTROLPW(XXXXXXXX)                     -
                              )                  -
       DATA                                      -
       ( NAME(DB2CAT.DSNDBD.DSNDBO1.DBDO1.I0001.A001) -
         MASTERPW(XXXXXXXX)                      -
         CONTROLPW(XXXXXXXX)                     -
         RECORDS(114 30)                         -
```

```
        VOLUMES(DSNV01) )                         -
     CATALOG(DB2CAT/XXXXXXXX)


 IF LASTCC = 0                                    -
   THEN                                           -
     DO
        DEFINE CLUSTER                                -
        ( NAME(DB2CAT.DSNDBC.DSNDB01.SYSLGRNG.I0001.A001) -
          NONINDEXED                              -
          REUSE                                   -
          CONTROLINTERVALSIZE(4096)               -
          VOLUMES(DSNV01)                         -
          MASTERPW(XXXXXXXX)                      -
          CONTROLPW(XXXXXXXX)                     -
          RECORDS(10 10)                          -
          RECORDSIZE(4089 4089)                   -
          SHAREOPTIONS(3 3) )                     -
        DATA                                      -
        ( NAME(DB2CAT.DSNDBD.DSNDB01.SYSLGRNG.I0001.A001) -
          MASTERPW(XXXXXXXX)                      -
          CONTROLPW(XXXXXXXX)                     -
                            )                     -
        CATALOG(DB2CAT/XXXXXXXX)

     DEFINE CLUSTER                               -
        ( NAME(DB2CAT.DSNDBC.DSNDB01.SYSUTIL.I0001.A001) -
          NONINDEXED                              -
          REUSE                                   -
          CONTROLINTERVALSIZE(4096)               -
          VOLUMES(DSNV01)                         -
          MASTERPW(XXXXXXXX)                      -
          CONTROLPW(XXXXXXXX)                     -
          RECORDS(10 10)                          -
          RECORDSIZE(4089 4089)                   -
          SHAREOPTIONS(3 3) )                     -
        DATA                                      -
        ( NAME(DB2CAT.DSNDBD.DSNDB01.SYSUTIL.I0001.A001) -
          MASTERPW(XXXXXXXX)                      -
          CONTROLPW(XXXXXXXX)                     -
                            )                     -
        CATALOG(DB2CAT/XXXXXXXX)

   END
   ELSE                                           -
   SET MAXCC = 0
//DBDCOPY EXEC COPYPROC,TBLSPC=DBD01,COND=(2,LT)
//SYSUCOPY EXEC COPYPROC,TBLSPC=SYSUTIL,COND=(2,LT)
//SYSLCOPY EXEC COPYPROC,TBLSPC=SYSLGRNG,COND=(2,LT)
//*
```

DB2 DSN1CHKR Service Aid Sample

APPENDIX  **43**

```
//DB2DBAC JOB (DB2U),DBA,MSGLEVEL=(1,1),REGION=4096K,
//       MSGCLASS=X,CLASS=X,NOTIFY=DB2DBA
//*
//*------------------------------------------------------------------
//* NOTE: THIS JOB RUNS THE DB2 DSN1CHKR SERVICE AID
//*------------------------------------------------------------------
//RUNCHKR EXEC PGM=DSN1CHKR,PARM='FORMAT'
//*
//*
//SYSPRINT DD SYSOUT=*
//SYSUT1 DD DSN=DSNSYS.DSNDBD.DB2DBASE.STABLE3.I0001.A001,DISP=SHR
```

JCL—DB2 PRINT Utility Sample (DSN1PRNT)

```
//DB2DBAL JOB (DB2U),DBA,MSGLEVEL=(1,1),REGION=4096K,
//         MSGCLASS=X,CLASS=X,NOTIFY=DB2DBA
//*
//*-------------------------------------------------------------
//* NOTE: THIS JOB RUNS THE DB2 PRINT UTILITY
//*-------------------------------------------------------------
//RUNPRNT EXEC PGM=DSN1PRNT,PARM='PRINT,FORMAT'
//*
//*
//SYSPRINT DD SYSOUT=*
//SYSUT1 DD DSN=DSNSYS.DSNDBD.DB2DBASE.STABLE4.I0001.A001,DISP=SHR
```

```
//DB2DBAH JOB (DB2U),DBA,MSGLEVEL=(1,1),REGION=4096K,
//       MSGCLASS=X,CLASS=X,NOTIFY=DB2DBA
//*
//*-------------------------------------------------------------------
//* NOTE: THIS JOB RUNS THE DB2 LOG PRINT UTILITY
//*-------------------------------------------------------------------
//LOGPRNT EXEC PGM=DSN1LOGP
//*
//*
//SYSABEND DD SYSOUT=*
//SYSPRINT DD SYSOUT=*
//SYSSUMRY DD SYSOUT=*
//BSDS    DD DSN=DSNCAT.BSDS01,DISP=SHR
//SYSIN  DD *
 RBASTART (00004FD793CE)   RBAEND (00004FFF58AB)
 DBID(0115)
 SUMMARY(YES)
 DATAONLY(YES)
/*
```

```
//DB2DBAB JOB (DB2U),DBA,MSGLEVEL=(1,1),REGION=4096K,
//       MSGCLASS=X,CLASS=A,NOTIFY=DB2DBA
//*
//* *************************************************************** */
//*                                                                 */
//*       RENAME, COPY AND MIGRATE BSDS DATA SETS                   */
//*                                                                 */
//*       AMSPROC PROC        JCL PROCEDURE TO INVOKE AMS           */
//*       AMSRENM STEP        RENAMES DATA SETS TO BE RESTORED      */
//*       RESTALLC STEP       ALLOCATES NEW DATA SETS FOR RESTORE   */
//*       BSDSRPRO STEP       REPRO BSDS DATA SETS                  */
//*                                                                 */
//*                                                                 */
//* *************************************************************** */
//*
//JOBLIB DD DISP=SHR,
//          DSN=DSN.DB2.DSNLOAD
//*
//AMSPROC PROC
//AMSPROC EXEC PGM=IDCAMS,DYNAMNBR=50
//STEPCAT DD DISP=SHR,DSN=DSNCAT
//SYSPRINT DD SYSOUT=*
//SYSUDUMP DD SYSOUT=*
//AMSPROC PEND
//*
//DB2S1REN EXEC AMSPROC
//SYSIN DD  *
    ALTER                                        -
          DB2CAT.BSDS01/XXXXXXXX                 -
          NEWNAME(DB2CAT.OLD.BSDS01)             -
          CATALOG(DB2CAT/XXXXXXXX)

 IF LASTCC = 0                                   -
  THEN                                           -
   DO
    ALTER                                        -
      DB2CAT.BSDS01.DATA/XXXXXXXX            -
      NEWNAME(DB2CAT.OLD.BSDS01.DATA)        -
      CATALOG(DB2CAT/XXXXXXXX)

    ALTER                                        -
      DB2CAT.BSDS01.INDEX/XXXXXXXX          -
      NEWNAME(DB2CAT.OLD.BSDS01.INDEX)      -
      CATALOG(DB2CAT/XXXXXXXX)
```

```
    ALTER                                         -
       DB2CAT.BSDS02/XXXXXXXX             -
       NEWNAME(DB2CAT.OLD.BSDS02)         -
       CATALOG(DB2CAT/XXXXXXXX)

    ALTER                                         -
       DB2CAT.BSDS02.DATA/XXXXXXXX          -
       NEWNAME(DB2CAT.OLD.BSDS02.DATA)      -
       CATALOG(DB2CAT/XXXXXXXX)

    ALTER                                    -
       DB2CAT.BSDS02.INDEX/XXXXXXXX            -
       NEWNAME(DB2CAT.OLD.BSDS02.INDEX)       -
       CATALOG(DB2CAT/XXXXXXXX)


    END
   ELSE
   SET MAXCC = 0
//RESTALLC EXEC AMSPROC,COND=(2,LT)
//SYSIN DD   *
    DEFINE CLUSTER                                -
       ( NAME(DB2CAT.BSDS01)      -
         READPW(XXXXXXXX)                   -
         VOLUMES(DSNV01)                    -
         REUSE                              -
         SHAREOPTIONS(2 3) )                -
       DATA                                       -
       ( NAME(DB2CAT.BSDS01.DATA)           -
         RECORDS(70 20)                     -
         RECORDSIZE(4089 4089)              -
         READPW(XXXXXXXX)                   -
         CONTROLINTERVALSIZE(4096)          -
         FREESPACE(0 20)                    -
         KEYS(4 0) )                        -
       INDEX                                   -
       ( NAME(DB2CAT.BSDS01.INDEX)          -
         RECORDS(5 5)                       -
         CONTROLINTERVALSIZE(1024) )        -
       CATALOG(DB2CAT/XXXXXXXX)

  IF LASTCC = 0                              -
   THEN                                      -
    DO
    DEFINE CLUSTER                                -
       ( NAME(DB2CAT.BSDS02)      -
         READPW(XXXXXXXX)                   -
         VOLUMES(DSNV01)                    -
         REUSE                              -
         SHAREOPTIONS(2 3) )                -
```

```
  DATA                                        -
    ( NAME(DB2CAT.BSDS02.DATA)                -
      RECORDS(70 20)                          -
      RECORDSIZE(4089 4089)                   -
      READPW(XXXXXXXX)                        -
      CONTROLINTERVALSIZE(4096)               -
      FREESPACE(0 20)                         -
      KEYS(4 0) )                             -
  INDEX                                       -
    ( NAME(DB2CAT.BSDS02.INDEX)               -
      RECORDS(5 5)                            -
      CONTROLINTERVALSIZE(1024) )             -
   END
   ELSE                                       -
   SET MAXCC = 0
//BSDSRPRO EXEC AMSPROC,COND=(2,LT)
//SYSIN DD  *

   VERIFY DATASET(DB2CAT.BKUP.BSDS01/XXXXXXXX)

   REPRO  ODS(DB2CAT.BSDS01/XXXXXXXX)    -
          REUSE                          -
          IDS(DB2CAT.BKUP.BSDS01/XXXXXXXX)

   VERIFY DATASET(DB2CAT.BKUP.BSDS02/XXXXXXXX)

   REPRO  ODS(DB2CAT.BSDS02/XXXXXXXX)    -
          REUSE                          -
          IDS(DB2CAT.BKUP.BSDS02/XXXXXXXX)


  //*
```

JCL—DB2 RUNSTATS Utility APPENDIX **47** Sample

```
//DB2DBAR JOB (DB2U),DBA,MSGCLASS=X,REGION=3072K,CLASS=A,
//          NOTIFY=DB2DBA
//UTIL EXEC DSNUPROC,SYSTEM=DSN,UID='DB2DBAU',UTPROC=''
//*
//*********************************************
//*
//* JCL FOR THE RUNSTATS UTILITY
//*
//*********************************************
//*
//DSNUPROC.SYSIN DD  *
RUNSTATS TABLESPACE DATABASE.STABLE5
RUNSTATS TABLESPACE DATABASE.STABLE6
RUNSTATS TABLESPACE DATABASE.STABLE7
RUNSTATS TABLESPACE DATABASE.STABLE8
//
```

```
//DB2DBAR JOB (DB2U),DBA,MSGCLASS=X,REGION=3072K,CLASS=A,
//         NOTIFY=DB2DBA
//UTIL EXEC DSNUPROC,SYSTEM=DSN,UID='DB2DBAU',UTPROC=''
//*
//*********************************************
//*
//* JCL FOR THE REPAIR UTILITY
//*
//*********************************************
//*
//DSNUPROC.SYSIN DD  *
REPAIR OBJECT -
    SET TABLESPACE DSNDB04.STABLE8 DSNUM 0 NOCOPYEND
REPAIR OBJECT -
    LOCATE TABLESPACE DSNDB04.STABLE8 PAGE X'000000'
        VERIFY OFFSET X'00000000' DATA X'00000000'
        REPLACE OFFSET X'00000000' DATA X'00000000'
        REPLACE RESET
        DELETE
        DUMP OFFSET X'00000000' LENGTH X'00000000' PAGES X'00000000'
    LOCATE INDEX XTABLE8 PAGE X'000000'
        VERIFY OFFSET X'00000000' DATA X'00000000'
        REPLACE OFFSET X'00000000' DATA X'00000000'
        REPLACE RESET
        DELETE
        DUMP OFFSET X'00000000' LENGTH X'00000000' PAGES X'00000000'
//
```

JCL—DB2 REORG Utility Sample

```
//DB2DBAR JOB (DB2U),DBA,MSGCLASS=X,REGION=3072K,CLASS=A,
//         NOTIFY=DB2DBA
//UTIL EXEC DSNUPROC,SYSTEM=DSN,UID='DB2DBA',UTPROC=''
//*
//********************************************
//*
//* REORGANIZATION JCL FOR TTABLE7/STABLE7
//*
//********************************************
//*
//DSNUPROC.SORTWK01 DD DSN=DB2DBA.SORTWK01,
//  DISP=(MOD,DELETE,CATLG),
//  SPACE=(4000,(20,20),,,ROUND),
//  UNIT=SYSDA
//DSNUPROC.SORTWK02 DD DSN=DB2DBA.SORTWK02,
//  DISP=(MOD,DELETE,CATLG),
//  SPACE=(4000,(20,20),,,ROUND),
//  UNIT=SYSDA
//DSNUPROC.SORTWK03 DD DSN=DB2DBA.SORTWK03,
//  DISP=(MOD,DELETE,CATLG),
//  SPACE=(4000,(20,20),,,ROUND),
//  UNIT=SYSDA
//DSNUPROC.SORTWK04 DD DSN=DB2DBA.SORTWK04,
//  DISP=(MOD,DELETE,CATLG),
//  SPACE=(4000,(20,20),,,ROUND),
//  UNIT=SYSDA
//DSNUPROC.SYSREC DD DSN=DB2DBA.REORG.STABLE7,
//  DISP=(MOD,CATLG),
//  SPACE=(4000,(20,20),,,ROUND),
//  UNIT=SYSDA
//DSNUPROC.SYSUT1 DD DSN=DB2DBA.SYSUT1,
//  DISP=(MOD,DELETE,CATLG),
//  SPACE=(4000,(20,20),,,ROUND),
//  UNIT=SYSDA
//DSNUPROC.SORTOUT DD DSN=DB2DBA.SORTOUT,
//  DISP=(MOD,DELETE,CATLG),
//  SPACE=(4000,(20,20),,,ROUND),
//  UNIT=SYSDA
//DSNUPROC.SYSIN DD  *
REORG TABLESPACE DATABASE.STABLE7
//
```

JCL—DB2 MODIFY Utility Sample

```
//DB2DBAMR JOB (DB2U),DBA,MSGCLASS=X,REGION=3072K,CLASS=A,
//          NOTIFY=DB2DBA
//UTIL EXEC DSNUPROC,SYSTEM=DSN,UID='MODIFY',UTPROC=''
//*
//*****************************************
//*
//* MODIFY/RECOVERY UTILITY
//*
//*****************************************
//*
//DSNUPROC.SYSIN DD  *
MODIFY RECOVERY TABLESPACE DATABASE.STABLE5 DELETE AGE(3)
//
```

DB2 DIAGNOSE Utility Sample

```
//DB2DBAD JOB (DB2U),DBA,MSGCLASS=X,REGION=3072K,CLASS=A,
//         NOTIFY=DB2DBA
//UTIL EXEC DSNUPROC,SYSTEM=DSN,UID='DIAGNOSE',UTPROC=''
//*
//*********************************************
//*
//* DIAGNOSE UTILITY
//*
//*********************************************
//*
//DSNUPROC.SYSIN DD  *
DIAGNOSE
   ALLDUMPS
   COPY TABLESPACE DSNDB06.SYSDBASE
DIAGNOSE END
//
```

```
//DB2DBAQ JOB (DB2U),DBA,MSGCLASS=X,REGION=3072K,CLASS=A,
//         NOTIFY=DB2DBA
//UTIL EXEC DSNUPROC,SYSTEM=DSN,UID='QUIESCE',UTPROC=''
//*
//*******************************************
//*
//* QUIESCE UTILITY
//*
//*******************************************
//*
//DSNUPROC.SYSIN DD  *
QUIESCE TABLESPACE DSNDB06.SYSDBASE
//
```

```
//DB2DBAR JOB (DB2U),DBA,MSGCLASS=X,REGION=3072K,CLASS=A,
//         NOTIFY=DB2DBA
//UTIL EXEC DSNUPROC,SYSTEM=DSN,UID='QUIESCE',UTPROC=''
//*
//*******************************************
//*
//* REPORT UTILITY
//*
//*******************************************
//*
//DSNUPROC.SYSIN DD   *
REPORT RECOVERY DSNUM ALL
//
```

JCL—DB2 DIRECTORY RECOVERY

```
//DB2DBAB JOB (DB2U),DBA,MSGCLASS=X,REGION=3072K,CLASS=A,
//         NOTIFY=DB2DBA
//UTIL EXEC DSNUPROC,SYSTEM=DSN,UID='DB2DBA',UTPROC=''
//*
//*********************************************
//*
//* DB2 RECOVERY JCL FOR TTABLE5/STABLE5
//*
//*********************************************
//*
//DSNUPROC.SYSIN DD   *
RECOVER TABLESPACE DATABASE.STABLE5
//
```

JCL—DB2 SYSTEM CATALOG RECOVERY

```
//DB2DBAB JOB (DB2U),DBA,MSGCLASS=X,REGION=3072K,CLASS=A,
//         NOTIFY=DB2DBA
//UTIL EXEC DSNUPROC,SYSTEM=DSN,UID='DB2DBA',UTPROC=''
//*
//*********************************************
//*
//* DB2 RECOVERY JCL FOR SYSTEM CATALOG TABLES
//*
//*********************************************
//*
//DSNUPROC.SYSIN DD   *
RECOVER TABLESPACE DSNDB01.SYSUTIL
RECOVER TABLESPACE DSNDB01.DBD01
RECOVER TABLESPACE DSNDB06.SYSCOPY
RECOVER TABLESPACE SYSIBM.DSNUCH01
RECOVER TABLESPACE DSNDB01.SYSLGRNG
RECOVER TABLESPACE DSNDB06.SYSDBAUT
RECOVER TABLESPACE DSNDB06.SYSUSER
RECOVER TABLESPACE DSNDB06.SYSDBASE
//
```

```
//DB2DBAB JOB (DB2U),DBA,MSGCLASS=X,REGION=3072K,CLASS=A,
//         NOTIFY=DB2DBA
//UTIL EXEC DSNUPROC,SYSTEM=DSN,UID='DB2DBA',UTPROC=''
//*
//*********************************************
//*
//* DB2 RECOVERY JCL FOR TTABLE5/STABLE5
//*
//*********************************************
//*
//DSNUPROC.SYSIN DD  *
RECOVER TABLESPACE DATABASE.STABLE5
//
```

JCL—DB2 USER TABLESPACE INCREMENTAL IMAGE COPY

```
//DB2DBAU JOB (DB2U),DBA,CLASS=A,MSGCLASS=X,NOTIFY=DB2DBA
//UTIL EXEC DSNUPROC,SYSTEM=DSN,UID=PRDCPY1,UTPROC=
//*
//*********************************************
//*
//* FOR INCREMENTAL COPY OF STABLE5
//*
//*********************************************
//*
//DSNUPROC.SYSCOPY DD DSN=DB2DBA.INCRCOPY.STABLE5,
//  DISP=(MOD,CATLG),
//  SPACE=(4000,(20,20),,,ROUND),
//  UNIT=SYSDA
//DSNUPROC.SYSIN DD  *
COPY TABLESPACE DATABASE.STABLE5 FULL=NO DEVT SYSDA
//
```

JCL—DB2 USER TABLESPACE FULL IMAGE COPY ON DISK

```
//DB2DBAU JOB (DB2U),DBA,CLASS=A,MSGCLASS=X,NOTIFY=DB2DBA
//UTIL EXEC DSNUPROC,SYSTEM=DSN,UID=PRDCPY1,UTPROC=
//*
//*********************************************
//*
//* FOR FULL IMAGE COPY OF STABLE5
//*
//*********************************************
//*
//DSNUPROC.SYSCOPY DD DSN=DB2DBA.IMAGCPYC.STABLE5,
//  DISP=(MOD,CATLG),
//  SPACE=(4000,(20,20),,,ROUND),
//  UNIT=SYSDA
//DSNUPROC.SYSIN DD   *
COPY TABLESPACE DATABASE.STABLE5 DEVT SYSDA
//
```

```
//DB2DBAQ JOB (DB2U),DBA,MSGLEVEL=(1,1),CLASS=X,MSGCLASS=X,
//        REGION=4096K,NOTIFY=DB2DBA
//*
//* ====================================================================*
//* D B 2 P M R E P O R T GENERATION                                    *
//* ====================================================================*
//*
//      EXEC PGM=DSNPM
//STEPLIB  DD DSN=DSNPM.V110.SDGOLMDO,DISP=SHR
//INPUTDD  DD DSN=SYS1.MAN1,DISP=SHR
//SYSPRINT DD SYSOUT=*,DCB=BLKSIZE=133
//JOBSUMDD DD SYSOUT=*,DCB=BLKSIZE=133
//SYSUDUMP DD DUMMY
//JSSRSDD  DD DUMMY
//DISTDD   DD DUMMY
//MSGRPTDD DD DUMMY
//ACRPTDD  DD SYSOUT=*,DCB=BLKSIZE=133
//ACTRCDD1 DD SYSOUT=*,DCB=BLKSIZE=133
//IORPTDD  DD SYSOUT=*,DCB=BLKSIZE=133
//LORPTDD  DD SYSOUT=*,DCB=BLKSIZE=133
//LOTRCDD1 DD SYSOUT=*,DCB=BLKSIZE=133
//RTTRCDD1 DD SYSOUT=*,DCB=BLKSIZE=133
//RTTRCDD2 DD SYSOUT=*,DCB=BLKSIZE=133
//SQTRCDD1 DD SYSOUT=*,DCB=BLKSIZE=133
//SQTRCDD2 DD SYSOUT=*,DCB=BLKSIZE=133
//SQTRCDD3 DD SYSOUT=*,DCB=BLKSIZE=133
//SQLINDX  DD SYSOUT=*,DCB=BLKSIZE=133
//STRPTDD  DD SYSOUT=*,DCB=BLKSIZE=133
//STTRCDD1 DD SYSOUT=*,DCB=BLKSIZE=133
//CORRELDD DD DUMMY
//DPMOUTDD DD DUMMY
//SYSIN DD  *
 PARM PLI,NOSTAE
*
*  DSNPM GROUP(AUTHID(PRODUCR(XYZ*)))
*  DSNPM GROUP(AUTHID(PRODUCR(XCF*)))
*
   DSNPM STATISTICS(REDUCE,
                    TRACE,
                    REPORT(LEVEL(SUMMARY)))
*
   DSNPM ACCOUNTING(REDUCE,
                    TRACE,
                    REPORT(LEVEL(DETAIL),ORDER(PLANNAME)))
```

```
*
    DSNPM LOCKING(REDUCE,
              REPORT(LEVEL(SUSPENSION),
                    ORDER(AUTH)))
*
    DSNPM IOACTIVITY(REDUCE,
                REPORT(LEVEL(SUMM,ACTLOG,ARCLOG,BUFFER,EDM),
                    ORDER(AUTH)))
*
    DSNPM SQLTRACE(TRACE(LEVEL(SUMMARY),
                    LIMIT(02)),
                TRACE(LEVEL(SHORT),
                    LIMIT(01)),
                TRACE(LEVEL(LONG),
                    LIMIT(01)))
*
DSNPM EXEC
```

JCL—STOSPACE Utility Sample

```
//DB2DBAS JOB (DB2U),DBA,MSGCLASS=X,NOTIFY=DB2DBA,REGION=2048K
//UTIL EXEC DSNUPROC,SYSTEM=DSN,UID='STOSPACE',UTPROC=
//*
//*******************************************
//*
//*   STOSPACE UTILITY
//*
//*******************************************
//*
//DSNUPROC.SYSIN DD  *
STOSPACE STOGROUP DSN8G000
STOSPACE STOGROUP DSN8G200
STOSPACE STOGROUP DBASTOGP
STOSPACE STOGROUP SYSDEFLT
//
```

```
//DB2DBAM JOB (DB2U),DBA,MSGCLASS=X,REGION=3072K,CLASS=A,
//         NOTIFY=DB2DBA
//UTIL EXEC DSNUPROC,SYSTEM=DSN,UID='DB2DBA',UTPROC=''
//*
//***********************************************************
//*
//* MERGECOPY JCL FOR TABLESPACE STABLE5
//*
//***********************************************************
//*
//DSNUPROC.SYSIN DD  *
MERGECOPY TABLESPACE DATABASE.STABLE5 NEWCOPY YES
//
```

```
//DB2DBAB JOB (DB2U),DBA,MSGCLASS=X,REGION=3072K,CLASS=A,
//         NOTIFY=DB2DBA
//UTIL EXEC DSNUPROC,SYSTEM=DSN,UID='DB2DBA',UTPROC=''
//*
//*****************************************************************
//*
//* DB2 RECOVERY JCL FOR TTABLE5/STABLE5 USING TORBA OPTION
//*
//*****************************************************************
//*
//DSNUPROC.SYSIN DD  *
RECOVER TABLESPACE DATABASE.STABLE5 TORBA '12345678'
//
```

```
//DB2DBAB JOB (DB2U),DBA,MSGCLASS=X,REGION=3072K,CLASS=A,
//         NOTIFY=DB2DBA
//UTIL EXEC DSNUPROC,SYSTEM=DSN,UID='DB2DBA',UTPROC=''
//*
//**********************************************************
//*
//* DB2 RECOVERY JCL FOR TTABLE5/STABLE5 USING TOCOPY OPTION
//*
//**********************************************************
//*
//DSNUPROC.SYSIN DD  *
RECOVER TABLESPACE DATABASE.STABLE5 TOCOPY    -
    DB2DBA.IMAGCPYA.STABLE5 TOVOLUME 123456
//
```

```
//DB2DBAI JOB (DB2U),DBA,MSGLEVEL=(1,1),REGION=4096K,
//       MSGCLASS=X,CLASS=X,NOTIFY=DB2DBA
//*
//* ************************************************************ */
//*                                                             */
//*      CREATE IMAGE COPIES USING TAPES                        */
//*                                                             */
//* ************************************************************ */
//DBUTIL EXEC PGM=DSNUTILB,PARM='DSN,SYSCPY'
//STABLE5 DD UNIT=TAPE,DISP=(NEW,KEEP),
//        DSN=DB2DBA.IMAGCPYC.STABLE5,
//          LABEL=(1,SL,,,RETPD=30)
//STABLE9 DD UNIT=AFF=STABLE5,VOL=REF=*.STABLE5,DISP=(NEW,KEEP),
//        DSN=DB2DBA.IMAGCPYC.STABLE9,
//          LABEL=(2,SL,,,RETPD=30)
//SYSPRINT DD SYSOUT=*
//SYSUDUMP DD SYSOUT=*
//SYSIN DD   *
COPY TABLESPACE DSNDB06.STABLE5    COPYDDN STABLE5    DEVT TAPE
COPY TABLESPACE DSNDB06.STABLE9    COPYDDN STABLE9    DEVT TAPE
//*
```

```
//DB2DBAB JOB (DB2U),DBA,MSGCLASS=X,REGION=3072K,CLASS=A,
//         NOTIFY=DB2DBA
//*
//************************************************************
//*
//* DB2 CHANGE LOG INVENTORY UTILITY (DSNUJ003)
//*
//************************************************************
//*
//RUNCOPY EXEC PGM=DSNJU003,PARM='CHECK'
//SYSPRINT DD SYSOUT=*
//SYSUT1 DD DISP=SHR,
//          DSN=DSNCAT.DSNBKC.&DBASE..&TBLSPC..I0001.A001
//SYSUT2 DD DISP=SHR,
//          DSN=DSNCAT.DSNDBC.&DBASE..&TBLSPC..I0001.A001
//COPYPROC PEND
//SYSLCOPY EXEC COPYPROC,TBLSPC=SYSLGRNG
```

JCL—DB2 Print Log Map Utility (DSNUJ004)

```
//DB2DBAB JOB (DB2U),DBA,MSGCLASS=X,REGION=3072K,CLASS=A,
//         NOTIFY=DB2DBA
//*
//*************************************************************
//*
//* DB2 PRINT LOG MAP UTILITY (DSNUJ004)
//*
//*************************************************************
//*
//RUNCOPY EXEC PGM=DSNJU004
//SYSPRINT DD SYSOUT=*
//SYSUT1 DD DISP=SHR,
//          DSN=DSNCAT.BSDS01
```

```
//DB2DBAB JOB (DB2U),DBA,MSGCLASS=X,REGION=3072K,CLASS=A,
//         NOTIFY=DB2DBA
//*
//***************************************************************
//*
//* DB2 DSN1COPY UTILITY JCL SAMPLE
//*
//***************************************************************
//*
//RUNCOPY EXEC PGM=DSN1COPY,PARM='CHECK'
//SYSPRINT DD SYSOUT=*
//SYSUT1 DD DISP=SHR,
//         DSN=DSNCAT.DSNBKC.&DBASE..&TBLSPC..I0001.A001
//SYSUT2 DD DISP=SHR,
//         DSN=DSNCAT.DSNDBC.&DBASE..&TBLSPC..I0001.A001
//COPYPROC PEND
//SYSLCOPY EXEC COPYPROC,TBLSPC=SYSLGRNG
```

```
//DB2DBAB JOB (DB2U),DBA,MSGCLASS=X,REGION=3072K,CLASS=A,
//         NOTIFY=DB2DBA
//UTIL EXEC DSNUPROC,SYSTEM=DSN,UID='DB2DBA',UTPROC=''
//*
//************************************************************
//*
//* DB2 RECOVERY JCL FOR INDEXSPACE RECOVERY
//*
//************************************************************
//*
//DSNUPROC.SYSIN DD   *
RECOVER INDEX index-name
//
```

```
//DB2DBAB JOB (DB2U),DBA,MSGCLASS=X,REGION=3072K,CLASS=A,
//         NOTIFY=DB2DBA
//*
//*      DSNHCOB2 - COMPILE AND LINKEDIT A COBOL PROGRAM
//*
//DSNHCOB2 PROC WSPC=500,MEM=TEMPNAME,USER=USER
//*
//*            PRECOMPILE THE COBOL PROGRAM
//*
//PC    EXEC PGM=DSNHPC,PARM='HOST(COBOL)'
//DBRMLIB DD DSN=&USER..DBRMLIB.DATA(&MEM),
//      DISP=SHR
//STEPLIB DD DISP=SHR,
//           DSN=DSN.V210.PS.DSNLOAD
//SYSCIN DD DSN=49&DSNHOUT,DISP=(MOD,PASS),UNIT=SYSDA,
//           SPACE=(800,(&WSPC,&WSPC))
//SYSLIB DD DSN=&USER..SRCLIB.DATA,
//      DISP=SHR
//SYSPRINT DD SYSOUT=*
//SYSTERM DD SYSOUT=*
//SYSUDUMP DD SYSOUT=*
//SYSUT1 DD SPACE=(800,(&WSPC,&WSPC),,,ROUND),UNIT=SYSDA
//SYSUT2 DD SPACE=(800,(&WSPC,&WSPC),,,ROUND),UNIT=SYSDA
//*
//*            COMPILE THE COBOL PROGRAM IF THE PRECOMPILE
//*            RETURN CODE IS 4 OR LESS
//*
//COB   EXEC PGM=IGYCRCTL,COND=(4,LT,PC)
//SYSIN DD   DSN=49&DSNHOUT,DISP=(OLD,DELETE)
//*SYSLIB DD DSN=CICS161.COBLIB,DISP=SHR
//SYSLIN DD DSN=49&LOADSET,DISP=(MOD,PASS),UNIT=SYSDA,
//           SPACE=(800,(&WSPC,&WSPC))
//SYSPRINT DD SYSOUT=*
//SYSUDUMP DD SYSOUT=*
//SYSUT1 DD SPACE=(800,(&WSPC,&WSPC),,,ROUND),UNIT=SYSDA
//SYSUT2 DD SPACE=(800,(&WSPC,&WSPC),,,ROUND),UNIT=SYSDA
//SYSUT3 DD SPACE=(800,(&WSPC,&WSPC),,,ROUND),UNIT=SYSDA
//SYSUT4 DD SPACE=(800,(&WSPC,&WSPC),,,ROUND),UNIT=SYSDA
//SYSUT5 DD SPACE=(800,(&WSPC,&WSPC),,,ROUND),UNIT=SYSDA
//*
//*            LINKEDIT IF THE PRECOMPILE AND COMPILE
//*            RETURN CODES ARE 4 OR LESS
//*
```

```
//LKED EXEC PGM=IEWL,PARM='XREF',
//           COND=((4,LT,COB),(4,LT,PC))
//SYSLIB DD DSN=SYS1.COB2LIB,DISP=SHR
//       DD  DISP=SHR,
//           DSN=DSN.V210.DSNLOAD
//*      DD  DISP=SHR,DSN=IMSVS.RESLIB
//*      DD  DISP=SHR,DSN=CICS161.LOADLIB
//SYSLIN DD DSN=49&LOADSET,DISP=(OLD,DELETE)
//       DD  DDNAME=SYSIN
//SYSLMOD DD DSN=&USER..RUNLIB.LOAD(&MEM),
//       DISP=SHR
//SYSPRINT DD SYSOUT=*
//SYSUDUMP DD SYSOUT=*
//SYSUT1 DD SPACE=(1024,(50,50)),UNIT=SYSDA
//DSNHCOB2 PEND
//DSNHCOB2 EXEC DSNHCOB2
```

```
//DB2DBAB JOB (DB2U),DBA,MSGCLASS=X,REGION=3072K,CLASS=A,
//         NOTIFY=DB2DBA
//*
//*     DSNHCOB - COMPILE AND LINKEDIT A COBOL PROGRAM
//*
//DSNHCOB PROC WSPC=500,MEM=TEMPNAME,USER=USER
//*
//*          PRECOMPILE THE COBOL PROGRAM
//*
//PC   EXEC PGM=DSNHPC,PARM='HOST(COBOL)'
//DBRMLIB DD DSN=&USER..DBRMLIB.DATA(&MEM),
//       DISP=SHR
//STEPLIB DD DISP=SHR,
//           DSN=DSN.V210.PS.DSNLOAD
//SYSCIN DD DSN=51&DSNHOUT,DISP=(MOD,PASS),UNIT=SYSDA,
//           SPACE=(800,(&WSPC,&WSPC))
//SYSLIB DD DSN=&USER..SRCLIB.DATA,
//       DISP=SHR
//SYSPRINT DD SYSOUT=*
//SYSTERM DD SYSOUT=*
//SYSUDUMP DD SYSOUT=*
//SYSUT1 DD SPACE=(800,(&WSPC,&WSPC),,,ROUND),UNIT=SYSDA
//SYSUT2 DD SPACE=(800,(&WSPC,&WSPC),,,ROUND),UNIT=SYSDA
//*
//*          COMPILE THE COBOL PROGRAM IF THE PRECOMPILE
//*          RETURN CODE IS 4 OR LESS
//*
//COB   EXEC PGM=IKFCBL00,COND=(4,LT,PC)
//SYSIN DD   DSN=51&DSNHOUT,DISP=(OLD,DELETE)
//*SYSLIB DD DSN=CICS161.COBLIB,DISP=SHR
//SYSLIN DD DSN=51&LOADSET,DISP=(MOD,PASS),UNIT=SYSDA,
//           SPACE=(800,(&WSPC,&WSPC))
//SYSPRINT DD SYSOUT=*
//SYSUDUMP DD SYSOUT=*
//SYSUT1 DD SPACE=(800,(&WSPC,&WSPC),,,ROUND),UNIT=SYSDA
//SYSUT2 DD SPACE=(800,(&WSPC,&WSPC),,,ROUND),UNIT=SYSDA
//SYSUT3 DD SPACE=(800,(&WSPC,&WSPC),,,ROUND),UNIT=SYSDA
//SYSUT4 DD SPACE=(800,(&WSPC,&WSPC),,,ROUND),UNIT=SYSDA
//*
//*          LINKEDIT IF THE PRECOMPILE AND COMPILE
//*          RETURN CODES ARE 4 OR LESS
//*
//LKED EXEC PGM=IEWL,PARM='XREF',
```

```
//             COND=((4,LT,COB),(4,LT,PC))
//SYSLIB DD DSN=SYS1.COBLIB,DISP=SHR
//        DD  DISP=SHR,
//            DSN=DSN.V210.PS.DSNLOAD
//*       DD  DISP=SHR,DSN=IMSVS.RESLIB
//*       DD  DISP=SHR,DSN=CICS161.LOADLIB
//SYSLIN DD DSN=51&LOADSET,DISP=(OLD,DELETE)
//        DD  DDNAME=SYSIN
//SYSLMOD DD DSN=&USER..RUNLIB.LOAD(&MEM),
//        DISP=SHR
//SYSPRINT DD SYSOUT=*
//SYSUDUMP DD SYSOUT=*
//SYSUT1 DD SPACE=(1024,(50,50)),UNIT=SYSDA
//DSNHCOB PEND
//DSNHCOB EXEC DSNHCOB
```

```
//DB2DBAB JOB (DB2U),DBA,MSGCLASS=X,REGION=3072K,CLASS=A,
//         NOTIFY=DB2DBA
//*
//*      DSNHPLI - COMPILE AND LINKEDIT A PL/I PROGRAM
//*
//DSNHPLI PROC WSPC=500,MEM=TEMPNAME,USER=USER
//*
//*          PROCESS PL/I MACROS
//*
//PPLI EXEC PGM=IELOAA,PARM='MACRO,NOSYNTAX,MDECK,NOINSOURCE'
//SYSLIB DD DISP=SHR,DSN=C1612A.PL1LIB
//SYSLIN DD DUMMY
//SYSPRINT DD SYSOUT=*,
//           DCB=(RECFM=VBA,LRECL=125,BLKSIZE=629)
//SYSPUNCH DD DSN=53&DSNHIN,DISP=(MOD,PASS),UNIT=SYSDA,
//           SPACE=(800,(250,100))
//SYSUDUMP DD SYSOUT=*
//SYSUT1 DD SPACE=(1024,(60,60),,CONTIG),UNIT=SYSDA,
//         DCB=BLKSIZE=1024
//*
//*          PRECOMPILE THE PL/I PROGRAM
//*
//PC   EXEC PGM=DSNHPC,PARM='HOST(PLI)',
//         COND=(8,LT,PPLI)
//DBRMLIB DD DSN=&USER..DBRMLIB.DATA(&MEM),
//      DISP=SHR
//STEPLIB DD DISP=SHR,
//           DSN=DSN.V210.PS.DSNLOAD
//SYSCIN DD DSN=53&DSNHOUT,DISP=(MOD,PASS),UNIT=SYSDA,
//           SPACE=(800,(&WSPC,&WSPC))
//SYSIN DD  DSN=53&DSNHIN,DISP=(OLD,DELETE)
//SYSLIB DD DSN=&USER..SRCLIB.DATA,
//      DISP=SHR
//SYSPRINT DD SYSOUT=*
//SYSTERM DD SYSOUT=*
//SYSUDUMP DD SYSOUT=*
//SYSUT1 DD SPACE=(800,(&WSPC,&WSPC),,,ROUND),UNIT=SYSDA
//*
//*          COMPILE THE PL/I PROGRAM IF THE PRECOMPILE
//*          RETURN CODE IS 4 OR LESS
//*
//PLI  EXEC PGM=IELOAA,PARM='OBJECT,NODECK',
//         COND=((4,LT,PC),(8,LT,PPLI))
```

```
//SYSIN DD   DSN=53&DSNHOUT,DISP=(OLD,DELETE)
//SYSLIB DD DISP=SHR,DSN=C1612A.PL1LIB
//SYSLIN DD DSN=53&LOADSET,DISP=(MOD,PASS),UNIT=SYSDA,
//           SPACE=(800,(&WSPC,&WSPC))
//SYSPRINT DD SYSOUT=*
//SYSUDUMP DD SYSOUT=*
//SYSUT1 DD SPACE=(800,(&WSPC,&WSPC),,,ROUND),UNIT=SYSDA
//SYSUT2 DD SPACE=(800,(&WSPC,&WSPC),,,ROUND),UNIT=SYSDA
//SYSUT3 DD SPACE=(800,(&WSPC,&WSPC),,,ROUND),UNIT=SYSDA
//SYSUT4 DD SPACE=(800,(&WSPC,&WSPC),,,ROUND),UNIT=SYSDA
//*
//*          LINKEDIT IF THE COMPILE RETURN CODE IS 8 OR
//*          LESS AND PRECOMPILE RETURN CODE IS 4 OR LESS
//*
//LKED EXEC PGM=IEWL,PARM='XREF,AMODE=31,RMODE=31',
//           COND=((8,LT,PLI),(4,LT,PC),(8,LT,PPLI))
//SYSLIB DD DISP=SHR,
//      DSN=LNKLST.R50.PLILINK,DCB=(BLKSIZE=32720)
//        DD  DISP=SHR,
//      DSN=LNKLST.R50.PLIBASE,DCB=(BLKSIZE=32720)
//        DD  DISP=SHR,
//           DSN=DSN.V210.PS.DSNLOAD
//*      DD  DISP=SHR,DSN=IMSVS.RESLIB
//*      DD  DISP=SHR,DSN=CICS161.LOADLIB
//SYSLIN DD DSN=54&LOADSET,DISP=(OLD,DELETE)
//        DD  DDNAME=SYSIN
//SYSLMOD DD DSN=&USER..RUNLIB.LOAD(&MEM),
//      DISP=SHR
//SYSPRINT DD SYSOUT=*
//SYSUDUMP DD SYSOUT=*
//SYSUT1 DD SPACE=(1024,(50,50)),UNIT=SYSDA
//DSNHPLI PEND
//DSNHPLI EXEC DSNHPLI
```

```
//DB2DBAB JOB (DB2U),DBA,MSGCLASS=X,REGION=3072K,CLASS=A,
//         NOTIFY=DB2DBA
//*
//*      DSNHASMH - ASSEMBLE AND LINKEDIT AN ASM H PROGRAM
//*
//DSNHASMH PROC WSPC=500,MEM=TEMPNAME,USER=USER
//*
//*            PRE-COMPILE THE ASSEMBLER PROGRAM
//*
//PC    EXEC PGM=DSNHPC,PARM='HOST(ASM)'
//DBRMLIB DD DSN=&USER..DBRMLIB.DATA(&MEM),
//        DISP=SHR
//STEPLIB DD DISP=SHR,
//            DSN=DSN.V210.PS.DSNLOAD
//SYSCIN DD DSN=55&DSNHOUT,DISP=(MOD,PASS),UNIT=SYSDA,
//            SPACE=(800,(&WSPC,&WSPC))
//SYSLIB DD DSN=&USER..SRCLIB.DATA,
//        DISP=SHR
//SYSPRINT DD SYSOUT=*
//SYSTERM DD SYSOUT=*
//SYSUDUMP DD SYSOUT=*
//SYSUT1 DD SPACE=(800,(&WSPC,&WSPC),,,ROUND),UNIT=SYSDA
//*
//*            ASSEMBLE IF THE PRECOMPILE RETURN CODE
//*            IS 4 OR LESS
//*
//ASM   EXEC PGM=IEV90,PARM='OBJECT,NODECK',COND=(4,LT,PC)
//SYSIN DD  DSN=55&DSNHOUT,DISP=(OLD,DELETE)
//SYSLIB DD DSN=SYS1.MACLIB,DISP=SHR,DCB=(BLKSIZE=32720)
//SYSLIN DD DSN=55&LOADSET,DISP=(MOD,PASS),UNIT=SYSDA,
//            SPACE=(800,(&WSPC,&WSPC)),DCB=(BLKSIZE=800)
//SYSPRINT DD SYSOUT=*
//SYSUDUMP DD SYSOUT=* 00255000
//SYSUT1 DD SPACE=(800,(&WSPC,&WSPC),,,ROUND),UNIT=SYSDA
//*
//*            LINKEDIT IF THE PRECOMPILER AND ASSEMBLER
//*            RETURN CODES ARE 4 OR LESS
//*
//LKED EXEC PGM=IEWL,PARM='XREF',
//            COND=((4,LT,ASM),(4,LT,PC))
//SYSLIB DD DISP=SHR,
//            DSN=DSN.V210.DSNLOAD
//*       DD  DISP=SHR,DSN=IMSVS.RESLIB
```

```
//*       DD  DISP=SHR,DSN=CICS161.LOADLIB
//SYSLIN DD DSN=55&LOADSET,DISP=(OLD,DELETE)
//        DD  DDNAME=SYSIN
//SYSLMOD DD DSN=&USER..RUNLIB.LOAD(&MEM),
//      DISP=SHR
//SYSPRINT DD SYSOUT=*
//SYSUDUMP DD SYSOUT=*
//SYSUT1 DD SPACE=(1024,(50,50)),UNIT=SYSDA
//DSNHASMH PEND
//DSNHASMH EXEC DSNHASMH
```

```
//DB2DBAB JOB (DB2U),DBA,MSGCLASS=X,REGION=3072K,CLASS=A,
//         NOTIFY=DB2DBA
//*
//*     DSNHFOR - COMPILE AND LINKEDIT A VS FORTRAN PROGRAM
//*
//DSNHFOR PROC WSPC=500,MEM=TEMPNAME,USER=USER
//*
//*           PRECOMPILE THE VS FORTRAN PROGRAM
//*
//PC    EXEC PGM=DSNHPC,PARM='HOST(FORTRAN)'
//DBRMLIB DD DSN=&USER..DBRMLIB.DATA(&MEM),
//        DISP=SHR
//STEPLIB DD DISP=SHR,
//           DSN=DSN.V210.PS.DSNLOAD
//SYSCIN DD DSN=57&DSNHOUT,DISP=(MOD,PASS),UNIT=SYSDA,
//           SPACE=(800,(&WSPC,&WSPC))
//SYSLIB DD DSN=&USER..SRCLIB.DATA,
//        DISP=SHR
//SYSPRINT DD SYSOUT=*
//SYSTERM DD SYSOUT=*
//SYSUDUMP DD SYSOUT=*
//SYSUT1 DD SPACE=(800,(&WSPC,&WSPC),,,ROUND),UNIT=SYSDA
//SYSUT2 DD SPACE=(800,(&WSPC,&WSPC),,,ROUND),UNIT=SYSDA
//*
//*           COMPILE THE VS FORTRAN PROGRAM IF THE PRECOMPILE
//*           RETURN CODE IS 4 OR LESS
//*
//FORT EXEC PGM=FORTVS,REGION=1200K,COND=(4,LT,PC),
//           PARM='NODECK,NOLIST,OPT(0)'
//STEPLIB DD DISP=SHR,DSN=SYS1.FORTVS
//SYSIN DD  DSN=57&DSNHOUT,DISP=(OLD,DELETE)
//SYSPRINT DD SYSOUT=*,DCB=BLKSIZE=3429
//SYSTERM DD SYSOUT=*
//SYSUDUMP DD SYSOUT=*
//SYSUT1 DD SPACE=(3465,(3,3)),DCB=BLKSIZE=3465,UNIT=SYSDA
//SYSUT2 DD SPACE=(5048,(10,10)),UNIT=SYSDA
//SYSLIN DD DSN=57&LOADSET,DISP=(MOD,PASS),UNIT=SYSDA,
//           SPACE=(3200,(25,6)),DCB=BLKSIZE=3200
//*
//*           LINKEDIT IF THE PRECOMPILE AND COMPILE
//*           RETURN CODES ARE 4 OR LESS
//*
//LKED EXEC PGM=IEWL,PARM='XREF',
```

```
//           COND=((4,LT,FORT),(4,LT,PC))
//SYSPRINT DD SYSOUT=*
//SYSUDUMP DD SYSOUT=*
//SYSLIB DD DISP=SHR,DSN=SYS1.VFORTLIB
//       DD  DISP=SHR,
//              DSN=DSN.V210.DSNLOAD
//SYSUT1 DD SPACE=(1024,(50,50)),UNIT=SYSDA
//SYSLIN DD DSN=57&LOADSET,DISP=(OLD,DELETE)
//       DD  DDNAME=SYSIN
//SYSLMOD DD DSN=&USER..RUNLIB.LOAD(&MEM),
//      DISP=SHR
//DSNHFOR PEND
//DSNHFOR EXEC DSNHFOR
```

JCL—DB2 Batch Program Preparation—Using DSNH

```
//DB2DBAB JOB (DB2U),DBA,MSGCLASS=X,REGION=3072K,CLASS=A,
//          NOTIFY=DB2DBA
//*
//*  DSNH EXECUTION - PRECOMPILE, BIND, COMPILE, CICS
//*
//TMP     EXEC PGM=IKJEFT01,DYNAMNBR=20
//SYSTSPRT DD SYSOUT=*,DCB=BLKSIZE=2420
//SYSTSIN DD *
PROFILE     PREFIX(DB2DBA)
ALLOC       DD(SYSPROC) DSN('DB2.V210.DSNCLIST') SHR
%DSNH BIND(YES) ACQUIRE(USE) ACTION(REPLACE)-
 EXPLAIN(NO) -
 CICSXLAT(YES)-
 COMPILE(YES) -
 DBRM('''DB2DBA.DB2.DBRMLIB.DATA(MEMBERNM)''')-
 DECIMAL(PERIOD) DELIMIT(APOST) FLAG(I)-
 HOST(COBOL) -
 INPUT('''DB2DBA.DB2.SOURCE(MEMBERNM)''') -
 ISOLATION(CS) -
 LINECOUNT(60) LINK(YES)-
 LOAD(DB2.RUNLIB.LOAD)-
 MACRO(YES)-
 OUTNAME(TEMP)-
 PLAN(MEMBERNM) PLIB('''DB2DBA.DB2.DCLGEN''') PRECOMP(YES)-
 PRINT(TEMP) RCTERM(8)-
 RELEASE(COMMIT) RETAIN(YES)-
 RUN(TSO) RUNIN(TERM)-
 RUNOUT(TERM) SOURCE(YES)-
 SYSTEM(DB2T) SQLDELIM(APOST)-
 VALIDATE(BIND) -
/* THIS LINE NEEDED TO END THE DSNH INPUT */
```

```
//DB2DBAA JOB (DB2DBA),'UNLOAD',
//       CLASS=T,
//       MSGCLASS=X,
//       NOTIFY=DB2DBA
//*
//* ************************************************************ */
//*                                                              */
//*      UNLOAD PROGRAM DSNTIAUL JCL                             */
//*                                                              */
//* ************************************************************ */
//JOBLIB DD DISP=SHR,
//          DSN=DSN.V210.DSNLOAD
//*
//*      RUN UNLOAD PROGRAM
//*
//UNLOAD1 EXEC PGM=IKJEFT01,DYNAMNBR=20
//SYSTSPRT DD SYSOUT=*
//SYSTSIN DD *
DSN SYSTEM(DSNP)
RUN  PROGRAM(DSNTIAUL) PLAN(DSNTIAU2) -
      LIB('DB2.V210.RUNLIB.LOAD')
//SYSPRINT DD SYSOUT=*
//SYSUDUMP DD SYSOUT=*
//SYSRECOO DD DISP=MOD,
//          DSN=DSN.V210.DSN8UNLD.SYSRECOO
//SYSPUNCH DD DISP=OLD,
//          DSN=DB2DBA.DB2.LOADINPT(TESTTBL)
//SYSIN DD DISP=OLD,
//          DSN=DB2DBA.DB2.UNLDINPT(TESTTBL)
//*
```

```
//DB2DBAA JOB (DB2ACCT),'DB2DBA',
// CLASS=A,
// MSGCLASS=X,
// NOTIFY=DB2DBA
//*
//* EXECUTION JCL FOR DSNTEP2
//*
//DSNTEP22 EXEC PGM=IKJEFT01,DYNAMNBR=20,COND=(4,LT)
//DBRMLIB DD DISP=SHR,
//            DSN=DB2DBA.DB2.DBRMLIB.DATA
//SYSTSPRT DD SYSOUT=*
//SYSPRINT DD SYSOUT=*
//SYSUDUMP DD SYSOUT=*
//SYSTSIN DD *
DSN SYSTEM(DSNP)
BIND PLAN(DSNTEP22) MEMBER(DSNTEP2) ACTION(REP) ISOLATION(CS)
RUN  PROGRAM(DSNTEP2) PLAN(DSNTEP22) -
   LIB('DB2DBA.DB2.RUNLIB.LOAD')
END
//*
//SYSIN DD *
 GRANT EXECUTE, BIND ON PLAN DSNTEP22 TO PUBLIC;
 SELECT * FROM TEMPL;
 SELECT * FROM TDEPT;
 SELECT * FROM TACTYPE;
 SELECT * FROM TEMPRAC;
 SELECT * FROM TPROJ;
 SELECT * FROM TPROJAC;
//*
```

```
//DSQBATCH PROC
//QMF    EXEC PGM=IKJEFT01
//*
//STEPLIB DD DSN=DSN.DB2.DSNLOAD,DISP=SHR
//       DD DSN=DSN.QMF.DSQLOAD,DISP=SHR
//*
//*               PANELS
//*
//ISPPLIB DD DSN=DSN.DB2.ISPPLIB,DISP=SHR,DCB=BLKSIZE=16320
//       DD  DSN=DSN.QMF.DSQPLIBE,DISP=SHR
//       DD  DSN=SYS1.ISRPLIB,DISP=SHR
//       DD  DSN=SYS1.ISPPLIB,DISP=SHR
//*
//*               MESSAGES
//*
//ISPMLIB DD DSN=SYS1.ISRMLIB,DISP=SHR
//       DD  DSN=DSN.QMF.DSQMLIBE,DISP=SHR
//       DD  DSN=DSN.DB2.ISPMLIB,DISP=SHR
//       DD  DSN=SYS1.ISPMLIB,DISP=SHR
//*
//*               SKELETON
//*
//ISPSLIB DD DSN=SYS1.ISRSLIB,DISP=SHR
//       DD  DSN=DSN.QMF.DSQSLIBE,DISP=SHR
//       DD  DSN=SYS1.ISPSLIB,DISP=SHR
//*
//*               TUTORIAL
//*
//ISPTLIB DD DSN=SYS1.ISRTLIB,DISP=SHR
//       DD  DSN=DSN.DB2.DSNHELP,DISP=SHR
//       DD  DSN=SYS1.ISPTLIB,DISP=SHR
//       DD  DSN=SYS1.SDSF.R20.ISFTLIB,DISP=SHR
//*
//*             ***   VIO   ***
//*
//ISPCTL1 DD DISP=NEW,UNIT=VIO,SPACE=(CYL,(1,1)),
//           DCB=(LRECL=80,BLKSIZE=800,RECFM=FB)
//ISPCTL2 DD DISP=NEW,UNIT=VIO,SPACE=(CYL,(1,1)),
//           DCB=(LRECL=80,BLKSIZE=800,RECFM=FB)
//ISPLST1 DD DISP=NEW,UNIT=VIO,SPACE=(CYL,(1,1)),
//           DCB=(LRECL=121,BLKSIZE=1210,RECFM=FB)
//ISPLST2 DD DISP=NEW,UNIT=VIO,SPACE=(CYL,(1,1)),
//           DCB=(LRECL=121,BLKSIZE=1210,RECFM=FB)
```

```
//*
//*        QMF DATA SETS
//*
//ADMGGMAP DD DSN=DSN.QMF.DSQMAPE,DISP=SHR
//DSQPRINT DD SYSOUT=*,DCB=(RECFM=FBA,LRECL=133,BLKSIZE=1330)
//DSQDEBUG DD SYSOUT=*,DCB=(RECFM=FBA,LRECL=121,BLKSIZE=1210)
//DSQUDUMP DD SYSOUT=*,DCB=(RECFM=VBA,LRECL=125,BLKSIZE=1632)
//SYSUDUMP DD SYSOUT=*
//SYSTSPRT DD SYSOUT=*
//ISPPROF DD UNIT=SYSDA,SPACE=(TRK,(9,1,4)),
//         DCB=(LRECL=80,RECFM=FB,BLKSIZE=3120)
//DSQSPILL DD DSN=63&SPILL,DISP=(NEW,DELETE),
//         UNIT=VIO,SPACE=(CYL,(1,1),RLSE),
//         DCB=(RECFM=F,LRECL=4096,BLKSIZE=4096)
//SYSPROC DD DSN=DSN.DB2.DSNCLIST,DISP=SHR
//        DD  DSN=DSN.QMF.DSQCLIST,DISP=SHR
```

Index